LETTERS OF CLARA SCHUMANN AND JOHANNES BRAHMS 1853-1896

LETTERS OF
CLARA SCHUMANN
AND
JOHANNES BRAHMS
1853-1896

EDITED BY
DR. BERTHOLD LITZMANN

IN TWO VOLUMES
VOL. I

VIENNA HOUSE
New York

This Vienna House edition,
first published in 1973,
is an unabridged republication of
the work originally published by
Longmans, Green and Co., New York, in 1927.

International Standard Book Number: 0-8443-0054-3
(Volume I)
International Standard Book Number: 0-8443-0055-1
(Volume II)
International Standard Book Number: 0-8443-0056-X
(Set of Volumes I & II)
Library of Congress Catalog Card Number: 77-163792

Printed in the United States of America

PREFACE

BY MARIE SCHUMANN

Professor Dr. Litzmann, the editor of the letters contained in the present volumes, was not destined to witness the publication of his work. Although he completed it and left it ready for press, it has fallen to me to offer a few words of explanation concerning the various gaps that occur in the correspondence.

The essential facts regarding what happened to the missing letters will be found on pages 488, 489, 491, 493 and 497 of Professor Litzmann's previous work, *Clara Schumann Ein Kunstlerleben.*[1] There it will be seen that in 1886 the friends agreed to return each other's letters, and Brahms gave back my mother's letters to her without reading them again. Soon after this, as she says in her Diary for June, 1887,[2] my mother began destroying them, but fortunately I was able to stop her in the middle of it, and she yielded to my urgent entreaty to preserve them for us her children. Nevertheless a good many had already been done away with, and this explains why there are no letters of hers up to the year 1858.

Brahms also got his letters back, but he told us later on that as he went to Rüdesheim on the very day they arrived, he availed himself of the opportunity to throw them overboard into the Rhine. The fact that, in spite of this, so many of his letters have survived is due to my mother's having

---

[1] The English translation of this work, *Clara Schumann : An Artist's Life,* was published by Macmillan in 1913. As, however, it is an abridged version, it is impossible to give equivalent references to those quoted by Marie Schumann from the German work. But if the reader will turn to Vol. II of the translation (pp. 389, 390 and 393) and refer also to Brahms' letters of May, 1887, and the middle of August, 1887, in Vol. II of the present work, he will find most of the passages to which Marie Schumann alludes.—Tr.

[2] See p. 390, Vol. II, of English *Life.*—Tr.

begged him to allow her to keep back a number of them which were among her particular favourites.

Owing to this circumstance the correspondence is far from complete, but, in spite of this, Professor Litzmann has, I think, through his skilful arrangement and selection succeeded wonderfully in presenting us with a connected picture of the lifelong relationship of these two friends, and in allowing the work to go to press I feel that I am offering the world a gift both rare and precious.

MARIE SCHUMANN.

INTERLAKEN, *December*, 1926.

INTRODUCTION

The present volumes contain the English translation of the correspondence of Clara Schumann and Johannes Brahms, which was published early this year in Germany, under the editorship of Dr. Berthold Litzmann and by arrangement with Marie Schumann, Clara's eldest daughter. The over-abundance of material, and the fact that a good many of the letters have already appeared in the English translation of Dr. Litzmann's *Life of Clara Schumann* made it advisable to reduce pretty considerably the bulk of the original, and the following volumes, therefore, consist only of a selection and abridgment of the German collection.

In his twofold task of abridgment and selection, the translator has proceeded throughout on the following principles—not to omit anything of either human or artistic interest which has not been published in English before; to avoid, as far as possible, the translation of letters which have already appeared in the English version of Clara's *Life*; and not to impair the general picture of the two artists' lives, which is given in Dr. Litzmann's collection. With regard to this last point, however, it should be remembered that, owing to the unfortunate circumstances described in Marie Schumann's Preface, there could not fail to be very serious gaps in the continuous narrative which such a collection of letters might be expected to supply of the lives of the two people concerned, and although it has been the translator's endeavour in his selection and abridgment not to aggravate the effect of the lost letters, it has, of course, been quite impossible to improve in this respect on the shortcomings of the original.

Every effort has been made to produce an accurate and readable translation of the letters ; but when it is remembered that in the corrrespondence of two such intimate friends, who are accustomed in conversation to guess at each other's thoughts and to convey the burden of whole sentences by means of a single word, there must always be certain obscurities of style and expression which no mere knowledge of their native language can overcome, the reader will perhaps understand why here and there it has been found difficult to make certain passages or allusions as clear and comprehensible as might be desired. This is particularly true of many of Brahms' letters. For Brahms was not only a lazy and laconic writer, as he himself repeatedly admits, but he also acquired the vicious Viennese habit of chipping and distorting sentences so that their meaning and syntax frequently become unanalysable. It was not considered advisable to call attention to every example of this, but here and there, where the difficulty has been unusually great, a footnote marks the place.

With regard to the gaps already mentioned, it seemed probable that the reader might feel these blemishes less, and therefore be helped to a greater enjoyment of the letters, if from the outset he were placed in possession of the outstanding facts relating to the lives of the two artists and the principal milestones in their respective careers. For while the reader, acquainted with the history of music, may find such a summary superfluous, except perhaps as a reminder, it was thought that those whose interests have not afforded them the opportunity of obtaining the information, might be glad to have it at hand in the pages of the present work.

Briefly, then, the facts are these : [1]

Clara Josephine Schumann, " one of the greatest pianoforte players the world has ever heard," was born at Leipsic on September 13, 1819, and began the study of the pianoforte under the guidance of her father, Friedrich Wieck, at a very early age. She made her début in public at the age of nine, and when just over eleven gave her first concert at the Gewandhaus, Leipsic. Her next appearance in public occurred about six months later, and in 1831 she published a set of four polonaises. In 1832 she gave a concert in Paris, and everywhere the critics hailed her as a pianist " possessing the brilliant style of the greatest players of the day." From September 20, 1832, Clara Wieck's name is regularly found in the programmes

[1] For the details given in the summary, the writer is indebted chiefly to the articles in Grove's *Dictionary of Music and Musicians.*

of the famous Gewandhaus subscription concerts, as well as
in others in the same hall.   In 1837 she visited Vienna, played
with great success, received the appointment of *Kk. Kammer-
virtuosin*, and thereafter gradually acquired a world-wide
reputation as a pianist, playing in almost every capital and
large town of Europe.

Robert Schumann (1810–1856), author and composer, had
been on intimate terms with the Wiecks for some years, but
it was not until the end of 1835 that his love for Clara was
openly avowed, and it was not until September 12, 1840, after
a series of delays and difficulties, that they were married.   The
difficulties were due chiefly to Wieck's opposition to the match
between Schumann and his daughter, and in the end Schumann
was forced to call in the assistance of the law, and to make
Wieck account for his refusal in court.   Finally, however,
Wieck's objections to the marriage " were found to be trivial
and without foundation."

In 1842 and 1844 Clara toured with her husband, and
" devoted herself not only to his society but to the bringing
out of his music."   In his article on Schumann,[1] Dr. Philip
Spitta writes :   " He [Schumann] created and wrote for his
wife and in accordance with her temperament, while she looked
upon it as her highest privilege to give to the world the most
perfect interpretation of his works . . . and to ward off all
disturbing or injurious impressions from his sensitive soul."

Until 1844 Schumann remained editor of the *Neue Zeitschrift
für Musik*, which he had founded in 1834, and from April 3,
1843, he held a Professor's Chair at the Conservatoire at Leipsic.
But he soon gave this up.   " His nervous affection rendered
change of scene absolutely necessary to divert his thoughts."
And he moved with Clara to Dresden, where he first lived in
the strictest seclusion.   But he became unwell again in 1846,
" he observed that he was unable to remember the melodies
that occurred to him when composing ; the effort of invention
fatiguing his mind to such a degree as to impair his memory."
The moment he improved, he devoted himself entirely to composition.   In the year 1849 alone he produced thirty works,
most of them important, and he remained in Dresden until
1850.   In that year Hiller gave up his post in Düsseldorf and

[1] In Grove's *Dictionary*.

suggested Schumann as his successor, and Schumann accordingly became the musical director of that city. In his new post he had the direction of the vocal union and of an orchestra, and had a number of concerts to conduct during the winter, and he appears to have been very well satisfied with his new sphere of work. But although Schumann's brilliance as a composer caused him to be honoured in Düsseldorf, there is no doubt that, as a conductor, he was inefficient, and it became necessary to find some one to take his place. It was thus that Julius Tausch gradually superseded him, and Schumann began to form plans for leaving Düsseldorf altogether in order to settle in Vienna. But things turned out otherwise. On February 27, 1854, in one of his fits of agony, he left his home unobserved, and flung himself from a bridge into the Rhine. But he was rescued and brought back, and spent the last two years of his life in Dr. Richarz' private asylum at Endenich, where he died on July 29, 1856.

The trials which his faithful Clara underwent during the latter years of her husband's life will be found partly revealed in the letters written to her by Brahms, in the first volume of the present work; for she was the most devoted of wives, and never really recovered her old spirits after the loss of her husband. He left her with seven children (three boys and four girls)—the eldest fifteen and the youngest two at the time of their father's death ; and the youngest, Felix, was actually born during the first year of his father's confinement at Endenich.[1] Clara, however, was brave. Relying upon her great gifts and her growing fame, she shouldered the whole burden with which her husband had left her, and, with the sympathetic encouragement and occasional help of devoted friends, succeeded not only in rearing and educating her seven children, but also in establishing a position for herself, which, although it never secured her either leisure or peace, at least brought her universal honour and some degree of material comfort and happiness. It was but shortly before her husband's death that she paid her first visit to England,

[1] The children in order of their birth were, Marie (1841), Elise (1843), Julie (1845), Ludwig (1848), Ferdinand (1849), Eugenie (1851) and Felix (1854). There was another son, Emil, born 1846, but he died on May 22, 1847.

and " she returned to Bonn just in time to receive her husband's last breath."

Among the many friends who stood by her from this moment until her death in 1896, was Johannes Brahms, and their intimate correspondence begins at the time when Robert Schumann was in confinement at Endenich. In a passage addressed to her children, she refers to what Brahms' friendship meant to her at the time of her bereavement, and she says : " To every man, no matter how unhappy he may be, God sends some comfort, and we are surely meant to enjoy it and to strengthen ourselves by its means. I have you, but you are but children. You hardly knew your dear Father, you were still too young to feel deep grief, and thus in those terrible years you could give me no comfort. Hope, indeed, you could bring me, but it was not enough to support me through such agony. Then came Johannes Brahms. Your Father loved and admired him, as he did no man except Joachim. He came, like a true friend, to share all my sorrow ; he strengthened the heart that threatened to break, he uplifted my mind, he cheered my spirits when- and wherever he could, in short he was my friend in the fullest sense of the word." (See *Life*, Vol. II, pp. 83–84.) For some time, as will be seen from the correspondence, Brahms actually occupied a room in her house at Düsseldorf, and the evidence of his loving care both of her and her children can be gathered from many a letter of his during the early years of her widowhood.

After this, Clara and her family resided for some years in Berlin, with her mother, who had separated from Wieck, and had married a musician named Bargiel ; Wieck also married again, Clementine Fechner. In 1863 she settled in Baden Baden, which became her headquarters till 1874. In 1878 she accepted the post of principal teacher of the pianoforte in the Conservatoire founded by Dr. Hoch in Frankfort, where she lived and worked with great success until the end of her life. She died there on the 20th of May, 1896. Having striven all her life to induce the musical world to recognize her husband's genius, she lived to see her efforts crowned with success, while there can be no doubt that her exertions for her great friend Brahms, which had a similar object, contributed to no small extent to making his work accepted and known among his contem-

poraries. She was undoubtedly far greater as a pianist than as
a composer, but although her compositions are said to reveal
more delicacy than power, they all evince " that earnestness
of purpose which distinguished her work in general."

The many vicissitudes, triumphs and anxieties of her widowed
life, both as a mother and an artist, are sufficiently revealed
in the correspondence that follows, while to all those who may
wish for further information regarding her career, there remains
the voluminous and able work of Dr. Litzmann (*Clara Schumann : An Artist's Life*) to which many references will be
found throughout these pages.[1]

The life of Johannes Brahms was much less eventful ; it is,
in fact, little more than a chronicle of his works. Born on
the 7th of May, 1833, he was his parent's second child, Elise
being the first, and Fritz the third and last. His father,
Johann Jacob, had twice run away from home to devote himself to music, and was a contrabassist in the theatre orchestra
at Hamburg. Brahms studied music first with O. Cossel and
then with Marxsen, and on September 21, 1848, gave his first
concert. After giving a second concert in 1849, he went on
tour through north Germany with Eduard Remenyi, a gipsy
violinist, who, at Hanover, introduced him to Joachim. The
latter, in his turn, introduced him to Schumann, and it was
this introduction that proved the turning-point in Brahms'
career. Schumann was much struck with the genius of the
young musician, and Brahms' first works (Op. 1–6) so much
impressed him that, in addition to recommending him to Härtel,
he also wrote a memorable article " *Neue Bahnen* " in the
Neue Zeitschrift für Musik, in which he hailed Brahms as a
musician of promise, and prophesied the young man's fame
as a creative artist. The writer of the article in Grove's
Dictionary of Music says : " It is impossible to overestimate
this emphatic recognition of the younger by the elder composer,
or to gauge its importance in Brahms' career." A paper war
followed, which naturally aroused the interest of the public in
the young composer, and for some time thereafter the publica-

[1] The reader's attention is called to the fact that in every case when
the *Life* is quoted the reference is to the English translation published
by Macmillan unless otherwise stated. The references to Kalbeck
relate to that author's voluminous life of Brahms in four volumes.

tion of every fresh work of Brahms became the occasion for lively discussion.

For four years (1854–1858) he held the post of director of concerts and of the choral society at the Court of Prince Lippe-Detmold, which gave him plenty of time to devote to composition, and, on resigning this post, he returned for a time to Hamburg. In 1860 Brahms wen; to stay at Winterthur, in order to be near Theodor Kirchner, the composer, who was organist there ; and this remained his headquarters until he took up his residence in Vienna, in 1862, about the time that Kirchner became conductor of the subscription concerts in Zürich. Soon after this Brahms was appointed conductor of the *Singakademie* in Vienna, but within a year after his appointment he gave up the post, and, except for his work as conductor of the *Gesellschaft der Musikfreunde* (1872–1875), held no official appointment for the rest of his life. Henceforth, the history of his career is little more than a record of his creations and his increasing fame, his friendships and his pleasure travels, and about all these matters his own letters and the letters of his greatest friend, Clara Schumann, are sufficiently instructive.

What Clara Schumann's friendship meant to him will probably never be precisely known, for it is often difficult to distinguish between the filial and the lover's attitude in his letters. Be this as it may, however, their friendship was probably the purest that has ever been known in the history of Art, and certainly from the material point of view—that is to say, from the standpoint of publicity and advertisement for his works—it must have been to Brahms of the very utmost value. This may partly account for the fact that, in their quarrels, as will be seen from the correspondence, it is always Brahms who gives in and who acknowledges his error, no matter how justifiable his behaviour or attitude may have been. His noble nature could never forget what he owed both to Clara and to her husband, and the way she turned to him for advice and for help at every moment of her life, shows how deeply she had learned to trust him.

A chill caught at Clara's funeral is said to have aggravated the disease (cancer of the liver) of which Brahms died at Vienna on April 3, 1897 ; but it is curious that he should have survived his lifelong friend hardly eleven months.

The letters cover the whole period of the two artists' friendship, from 1853 to 1896, and form a document of such exceptional interest that they can hardly fail to appeal to every one, whether musical or not, who can be stirred by the spectacle of a friendship so unique and passionate between two such eminent figures in the recent history of Art. Nothing that a biographer is able to tell can possibly equal in accuracy and vividness the information which is to be culled from a collection of letters, because it is only in letters that a character can be directly revealed in all its varying moods and tempers, to a generation deprived of the chance of first-hand knowledge.

Brahms and Clara Schumann both electrified the Age to which they belonged. The former has been called the last of the illustrious line of German composers of the first rank, while the latter has probably never been surpassed as a virtuoso. Behind their public life, which riveted the attention of Europe for over thirty years, there was their private life of love and friendship, of struggle and often of grief, of which no member of the public could have any knowledge, but which, in view of their artistic natures, was kept throughout on the loftiest of emotional and intellectual planes. Now it is this human side of their lives which stands revealed in the present volumes, and every effort has been made in the translation to omit nothing that could assist or complete the picture of these two people both as human beings and as musicians.

THE TRANSLATOR.

LETTERS OF CLARA SCHUMANN AND JOHANNES BRAHMS 1853-1896

VOLUME I

LETTERS OF CLARA SCHUMANN
AND
JOHANNES BRAHMS

1853

ROBERT SCHUMANN *to* JOHANN JACOB BRAHMS *in Hamburg.*

DÜSSELDORF, *Nov.* 5, 1853.

DEAR SIR,

We have got to like your son Johannes very much, and his musical genius has given us some most delightful hours. In order to help him make his début in the musical world I have publicly expressed my opinion of him. I am sending you the papers in which it has been published and feel sure that they cannot fail to bring a little joy to a father's heart.

You may look forward with complete confidence to the future of this darling of the Muses and rest assured of my deepest interest in his success.

Yours very faithfully, R. SCHUMANN.

BRAHMS *to* ROBERT SCHUMANN.

HANOVER, *Nov.* 16, 1853.

REVERED MASTER,

You have made me so extremely happy that I cannot attempt to express my thanks in words. May God grant that my works will soon be able to prove to you how much your love and kindness have uplifted and inspired me. The public praise that you have deigned to bestow upon me will have so greatly increased the expectations of the musical world regarding my work that I do not know how I shall manage to do even approximate justice to it. Above all it will compel me to exercise the greatest caution in my choice of pieces for publication. I am thinking that I shall not publish any of my trios but shall select the sonatas in C and F Sharp minor to be my Op. 1 and 2.   Op. 3 will be the songs, and Op. 4 will be the Scherzo in E Flat minor.   You will readily understand that I am straining every nerve to bring as little disgrace as possible on your name.

I delayed writing to you until I had sent the four works above mentioned to Breitkopf and received their answer, so that I might tell you at once what the result of your recommendation was.   But this we have already found out from your last letter to Joachim.   So all I have to say for the present is that, in accordance with your advice, I shall go to Leipsic within the next few days (probably to-morrow).   Furthermore, I should like to tell you that I have copied my Sonata in F minor and have considerably altered the finale.   I have also improved the violin Sonata.   Thank you a thousand times for the nice portrait of yourself which you were kind enough to send me as also for the letter which you wrote to my father. You have rejoiced the hearts of two or three worthy people by your attention and I am for life, Yours, BRAHMS.

Nov. 29, 1853.

MYNHEER DOMINE !

Forgive this playful form of address on the part of one whom you have made infinitely happy and joyful.   And I have only the best and most delightful news for you.

Thanks to your hearty recommendation, the cordiality of my reception in Leipsic far exceeded my expectations or my deserts.   Härtels have told me that they are ready to print my first attempts, which are : Op. 1, Sonata in C major ; Op. 2, Sonata in F Sharp minor ; Op. 3, Songs ; Op. 4, Scherzo in E Flat minor.   I have also given Herr Senff the following for publication : Op. 5, Sonata in A minor for Violin and Pianoforte ; Op. 6, six Songs.

May I crave permission to put Frau Schumann's name on the front of my second Opus ?   I hardly dare to do so, and yet would be so glad to give you some small token of my reverence and gratitude.

I shall probably get copies of my first works before Christmas.   Imagine what my feelings will be when I see my parents again after barely a year's absence, and when I think of it I cannot describe the tumult in my heart.

May you never have to repent of what you have done for me, and may I always be worthy of you, Your JOH. BRAHMS.

HAMBURG, *Dec.*, 1853.

HONOURED FRIEND,

Herewith I take the liberty of sending you your first foster children (who owe to you their citizenship of the world). And I am very anxious to know whether they may still rejoice in the same indulgent love from you. In their new garb they seem to me too prim and embarrassed—almost philistine. I still cannot accustom myself to seeing these guileless children of nature in their smart new clothes.

I am looking forward with joy to seeing you in Hanover in order to be able to tell you that my parents and I owe to the extreme kindness of Joachim and yourself the most blessed moment of our lives. I was overjoyed to see my parents and my music teacher again, and am spending a most delightful time with them.

With heartiest greetings to Frau Schumann and your children, Your JOHANNES BRAHMS.

1854

HANOVER, *Feb.* 10.

DEAR LADY,

I have just received the enclosed new pieces from Leipsic and I hasten to send them to you. I have ventured to place your name in front of the Sonata. I hope you will not think it as presumptuous as I now do, for I hardly dare to send it to you. At the same time as they arrived I also received the proofs of the F minor Sonata from Senff, which I expect will be ready very soon.

Since you have left, Hanover seems an empty wilderness to us. How I long for the coming of spring which I hope will take us all back to the Rhine again. I trust you will look upon the F Sharp minor Sonata with the same kind and indulgent eye as you looked upon the first, and that in spite of its presumptuous dedication you will continue to think kindly of me. With all good greetings to Herr Schumann and yourself, from Joachim Grimm [1] and myself, Yours very truly, JOH. BRAHMS.

Clara *to* Brahms.

Sunday, June 18.

DEAR AND HONOURED HERR BRAHMS,

Your delicate attention has given me very great pleasure. [2] I cannot tell you what I felt when I read the dedication. [3] But you knew it already when you were writing it. And so please for to-day accept the very hearty thanks in writing, which I hope to give you in person when we meet again very soon. I

---

[1] Julius Otto Grimm, the friend of Brahms and Joachim.

[2] This refers to her receipt of Brahms' Variations for Two Hands on a Theme by Robert Schumann, which afterwards appeared as Op. 9.

[3] " Short Variations on a theme by him. Dedicated to you."

4

have read through the Variations; but reading music affects my head so much that I have not got to know them as well as I should like. I hope, however, to be able to hear it played by yourself in the near future. It is genuine Brahms, and I know you to be both serious and humorous.

I expect to get up on Tuesday,[1] and if you will call on me that afternoon at four, I should be very glad to see you.

The news about my beloved Robert to-day was fair. Apart from a slight disturbance of no very great importance, he has remained quiet. But alas, what small comfort that is for a loving heart that would fain hope !—These are very hard days indeed that I am going through, for when I look at the darling baby at my side, and think of his dear father who, far removed from everything that he loves and, moreover, ill as he is, does not even know of this child's existence, I feel as if my heart must break with grief and pain. But I am distressing you, and that is the last thing I wish to do. So with my kindest greetings, I am, Your CLARA SCHUMANN.

BRAHMS *to* CLARA.

DÜSSELDORF, *July* 20.

HONOURED LADY,

I cannot help writing a few lines to you to say how over-joyed and deeply moved I am about the wonderful news which you received this morning.[2] Does not this show that I have always been right when I said that your dear husband certainly thought of you, although a vague shyness prevented him from pronouncing your name ? It has often been on the tip of my tongue to try to comfort you with some such prophecy, but I have never dared, and lo, now it has been magnificently fulfilled !

The flowers were not intended to bring you a mere greeting, but the promise of a swift reunion. But I must stop lest I excite you too much with predictions of reunion in the very near future. May I beg you to greet Joachim and all our

---

[1] Felix Schumann was born on the 11th of June.

[2] This refers to the fact that she had received that morning from her husband a little bunch of flowers—the first sign of life for a long time. He had given it to a friend who had visited him at the institution at Endenich. See German Edition of *Life*, Vol. II, p. 322.

other friends in Berlin [1] very heartily.   My friendship has to
be great indeed not to make me feel jealous of those who
have the privilege of seeing you just now.

Grimm joins with me in sending the warmest wishes for
your own and your dear husband's happiness.   Yours very
sincerely, JOHANNES BRAHMS.

BRAHMS *to* CLARA.

ESSLINGEN, *Aug.* 15.

HONOURED LADY !

Not once on my whole journey have I been as light-hearted
and cheerful as is necessary on a walking tour, and as I usually
am in any case.   I felt every minute as if I should like to
return, and shall certainly not be tempted to leave Düsseldorf
again this summer.   The exhilarating and uplifting experience
of being with you and having music together, as well as of having news of your beloved husband—alas, how can I do without
these things even for a short time ?   One ought not to travel
when one is as fast anchored to a place as I am at present to
Düsseldorf.   Let me tell you something about my travels—I
reached Heidelberg late on Saturday. [2]   But I would prefer
to have a long talk with you about the magnificent castle
ruins.

I looked for the house in which your husband lived as a
student, but owing to its being the Sabbath the shutters were
up, so I had to be content with conjectures.   I left Heidelberg
at midday so as to be able to get back into the hurly-burly
as soon as possible and to forget my longing.   I went as far
as Heilbronn along the Neckar on foot and saw many beautiful
things on the way ; for instance, the Schwalbennest, Horn-
berg etc.   Until to-day I have had the most beautiful weather
but it is now raining heavily.   In Heilbronn I had a great
struggle with myself ; I wanted to go quickly on to Ulm and
beyond and then to return.   I often have struggles with myself,
that is to say, Kreisler and Brahms struggle together.   But
otherwise everybody has his own definite opinion and carries
his point.   This time, however, they were both quite confused,

---

[1] Clara had gone to Berlin on the 19th.
[2] On the 10th of August Clara had gone to Ostend and Brahms to
the Schwarzwald.

neither knew what he wanted and it was most comical to watch them.   Incidentally tears almost stood in my eyes.

Now I have gone further afield and am already in Esslingen which I reached by rail and am writing to you from there while Eichendorf's poetic spirit is let loose upon me.   All about me there is the darkness of midnight.   The fountains plash sleepily, confused murmurs fill the air, and in my heart is the deepest melancholy.   I often have to lay down my pen because my thoughts overcome me.   I could easily run away from it all and let the woods and castles go hang.   For your own sake, however, I hope that I shall only see you again in three weeks' time.   I have heard many alarming reports about too short a course of sea baths and I sincerely hope that your lady friends will detain you at least three weeks. . . .

I am so much looking forward to a letter from you.   I expect to be in Heidelberg again after the 20th and you might write to me there (*poste restante*) to let me know about when you expect to be back in Düsseldorf.   Perhaps this is presumptuous in me.   But there may be something important to write about, and I may find no letter in Ulm ?   Please greet Frl. Reichmann,[1] Frl. Leser [2] and Frl. Jungé [3] heartily for me, and take good care of yourself.

(On the 12th, 13th and 14th [4] I sent you a thousand greetings.)

Your JOHANNES BRAHMS.

BRAHMS *to* CLARA.

ULM, *Aug.* 16.

HONOURED LADY !

I cannot stand it any longer ; I am coming back to-day. I came here early to-day, and intended to wait until nine o'clock in the evening for a letter from you, then to go on to Tübingen. But it is impossible.   The last post came in at four o'clock

----

[1] Henriette Reichmann, a talented young musician, who had become deeply attached to Clara fifteen years previously.

[2] A well-to-do and cultured blind lady who had been Clara's friend since 1850.

[3] Frl. Leser's lady companion.

[4] These three days are dedicated to Clara, Aurora and Eusebius. It was on the 14th of August, 1837, that Clara and Robert Schumann became engaged.

and I have left my Düsseldorf address here and am coming back. I should not have enjoyed a single moment of the trip. The names Tübingen, Lichtenstein, Schaffhausen, which otherwise would have thrilled me with joy, leave me cold, so dull and colourless does everything seem to me.

I will go home and play music and read to myself until you appear, and I can do so with you. If you wanted to please me very much indeed you would let me find a letter in Düsseldorf. But mind you stay in Ostend at least three weeks. . . . I will explore your friend's native country better another time when I can feel more serene away from you and your dear husband. If the great longing that has possessed me during the last few days has any influence on my playing etc. it ought soon to enable me to cast a spell over people. I suppose Frl. Leser is with you in Ostend ? I feel certain she must be, and I hope that your stay there has been all the more pleasant on that account. Enjoy yourself thoroughly and come back as well and as happy as possible to Düsseldorf. Your JOHANNES BRAHMS.

. . . I am writing in the Waiting Room of the station. I hope this will be sufficient excuse for these confused and hasty lines. A thousand greetings !

BRAHMS *to* CLARA.

DÜSSELDORF, Aug. 21.

HONOURED LADY !

I have received two precious letters from you. Thank you a thousand times for them. You are able by your letters to make me forget for a brief moment that you are far away. Words leave my pen with such great difficulty that it would be surprising if my conversation were not more interesting. I would gladly write to you only by means of music, but I have things to say to you to-day which music could not express. I am diffident about telling you that I too have seen your beloved husband. It seems to me so hard that we, who stand so much further away from him than you do, should see him before you, and I feel that I have no right to this privilege. On the 19th I was in Bonn, and went with Reimers to Endenich. We spoke to the doctor and I was overjoyed when he gave me

hope of being able to see Herr Sch.   It was about four o'clock
in the afternoon.   Herr Sch. had his coffee and then came into
the garden (it was beautiful weather).

Your dear husband has not changed in the least ; he only
seems to have grown a little stronger.   His look is friendly
and bright, his movements are the same as ever, he keeps one
hand constantly to his mouth, and smokes in short puffs as
he always used to.   His gait and his greeting were easier and
more assured.   But this is only natural, for his mind is not
now preoccupied with any great creation, any *Faust*.   The
doctor spoke to him, but unfortunately I could not hear his
replies.   His smile and his appearance, however, after speaking, were the same as ever.   Herr Sch. then turned to look
at the flowers and went further into the garden towards the
lovely view.   I saw him disappear with a glorious halo about
him, formed by the setting sun.

I cannot describe what my feelings were during this visit.
I trembled violently and had to exercise the greatest control
not to call out to him or hasten after him.   I could not wish
that you might have been in my place at that moment, for
you could not have borne it.   I could hardly do so.   And
now let me tell you a little more about what the doctor and
Frl. Reumont said to me.   Your husband showed Frl. R. all
the songs in Scherer's book of songs which he composed years
ago.   Among other things he told her that the song *Du bist
wie eine Blume* was his first, and this is in fact so.   In Frl. R's
room he recognized the fine head by Raphael and remarked
that he had a copy of the same thing in his house in Düsseldorf.   In a collection of portraits of famous men Herr Sch.
picked out all the ones he knew—Schiller, Goethe, Copernicus
etc.   Then he pointed to the poets whom he knew personally
and indicating Goethe, he said with a smile, " Unfortunately,
I did not know him."   That is surely the Schumann we
know !

And now I should straightway like to ask you a favour,
honoured lady, and one which I must implore you not to misunderstand.   Be very cautious in the letters you address to
the doctors at Endenich.   They thought, particularly in regard
to your last letter, that you were hoping too confidently for a
speedy recovery, and they suspected that Herr Grimm must

have written to you in too optimistic a tone. I should like to advise you, however presumptuous it may seem on my part to do so, not to reveal as much hope in your letters as I trust you have, but continue as I do to hope ever more strongly for the complete recovery of the dear one, even if it may not be quite soon. These doctors know neither of you, and even I, before I knew you, imagined that such people as you and such marriages as yours could only exist in the imagination of the rarest people. The doctor does not know what you are suffering. He can only judge you from your letters, and if these appear to be overstrung, he thinks that you must be overstrung. My head was full of what I intended to say to the doctor and to ask him, but when I looked into his cold face, I could not get a word out.

I should much have preferred to tell you this by word of mouth. I should then have been able to put it more tactfully and to have supported my case better. But I hope you will see for yourself that the doctors cannot help judging you to some extent from your letters. If they find them too hopeful they feel constrained to write more coldly. I must not conceal from you either that latterly your husband has been suffering from delusions of hearing. Their periodical recurrence, however, must not alarm you too much. . . . I went to your house and moved Frl. Bertha deeply by my account of Bonn. You have found a treasure in this girl. Such people are rare. . . .

Surely I am a very bad musician. Just fancy, at a concert in Düsseldorf this winter I would only listen to one symphony, and that was by your husband. I fled from a Beethoven Overture and other pieces. What do I want to hear them for ? I said. In Cologne I also declared that there was not much in Mozart and that I could write pianoforte sonatas like his every day ! At least F. H.[1] said as much of me in Mehlem. This gentleman has his own ideas about an artist's career, for he says that the world will only have to wait another five years to hear nothing more about me. There is nothing like such immortality ! But I have gone on chattering so long that I shall bore you and you will forbid me to write to you. . . . I hope we may expect to see you again in a fortnight.

[1] Ferdinand Hiller ?

We are greatly looking forward to it. . . .   Farewell, and come
back much stronger.   With a thousand greetings, Yours very
sincerely, JOHANNES BRAHMS.

Forgive the atrocious writing, but I cannot control my hand
when I am writing.   I write music better. . . .   You ask me
whether I have ever seen the sea.—No !   But I have had
great struggles with myself not to follow you.   The journey
to Ostend and life in a watering place is too expensive, and I
would not dare to undertake it.   When you left for Ostend
my qualms on this score were too strong for me, and if I have
succeeded in overcoming them now it is in any case too late.
I readily believe what you say, and that the people there do
not deserve the magnificent view.   They also do not deserve
that you two, Robert and Clara, should be on earth at all,
and I feel uplifted when I think that I may see the time when
people will idolize you—two such wholly poetical natures.   I
almost wish that the world in general might forget you so
that you could remain all the more sacred to the elect. . . .
Your JOHANNES B.

BRAHMS *to* CLARA.

DÜSSELDORF, *Aug.* 27.

MOST HONOURED LADY !

I cannot help repeating certain passages out of your last
dear letter—" I can well understand that people who do not
know me think I am overstrung. . . .   And I have been wondering whether after all you [that is, I] did not also regard
me as such ? "

Surely, dear Frau Schumann, you did not mean this seriously, did you ?   I was not in the least surprised to hear that
you are now giving a concert in Ostend.   I really expected it,
but I thought with some alarm that it would be a hard day
for you.   I ought to have been able to lend you my attitude
towards the public (that is my cavalier treatment of them)
for the occasion.   I think of you as going to the concert hall
like a priestess to the altar.   This, of course, is just as it should
be.   But I have never had that feeling, as I only know the
public from a distance.   I shun its proximity.   I am very
anxious to know what you played.   I hope you did not over-

tire yourself with certain studies [1] in C Sharp minor.   It won't
be my fault if you have, for I have often enough recommended
you Heller's [2] easy musical wanderings.

I have received a letter from Härtels.   As they heard you
had gone to Ostend they wrote to me.   They have accepted
my Variations, but they point out that they hope I shall not
ask for too large a fee as the success of my works is not yet
assured.   Business people really know no delicacy in money
matters.   One dreads having to write more than three words
about money or fees, and yet people like Härtels can write so
unfeelingly.   But I ought to get ten gold louis [£8].   . . .

I have now completed my library of books.   I have bought
myself Aeschylus's Seven Tragedies and a volume of Plutarch's
Lives.   I shall soon not know what else to buy.   I already
have Shakespeare's and Schumann's Complete Works, Goethe's
Poems, Hoffmann's Fantasies, and many more.   If I get ten
gold louis in the course of the next few days I shall have a
hard struggle to keep away from book shops. . . .   But I
must stop now, otherwise I shall end by copying out the latest
Düsseldorf papers for you merely in order to be able to go on
writing to you.   Surely you will give us the pleasure in your
next letter of telling us when you expect to return.   Will you
be away much longer ?   I have a terrible longing to see you
again, dearest lady.   Don't keep us waiting longer than necessary.   With greetings to Frl. Leser and Frl. Jungé, and with
my most humble respect, Your JOHANNES BRAHMS.

BRAHMS *to* CLARA.

HAMBURG, *Sunday, Oct.* 21.
MOST HONOURED LADY !

Only this once will you have cause to complain of my slow-
ness in writing letters, and you will surely therefore forgive
me all the more readily.   I left Hanover only on Thursday

---

[1] Schumann's *Études Symphoniques*, Op. 13.   Clara had played
these on the 13th of August, 1837.

[2] Stephen Heller the composer'(1814–1888).   He was an accomplished
pianist and wrote a large number of pieces for his instrument.   After
1838 he resided in Paris, where, rarely playing in public, he was much
esteemed as a teacher and composer.   His best-known works are his
Études, the series *Dans le Bois*, and the *Tarantellas.*—TR.

midday.[1] We enjoyed a few more pleasant days there. Joachim and Grimm used to lie on the sofa at twilight while I played to them in the next room.

During my journey to Hamburg I thought more about you than about my parents, particularly just as I was on the point of entering H. because you must just have been playing for the second time at that moment. . . . I found my parents and my sister quite well, and they wished to be remembered very affectionately to you. Quite early on Friday I had the joy of receiving your dear letter. It was my finest welcome in H. I also found my music teacher looking well. When they were asked beforehand who had arrived they both guessed, " Our Johannes " ! I pleased Herr Marxsen [2] very much with the Ballads, and I also had to play him the Variations. I cannot tell you how much I was relieved by your letter. I no longer have any qualms on your account, but how dreadful to have to wait so long for news of your dear one. But the time between now and Christmas will go quickly and then we shall certainly be together again in Düsseldorf ? Or will you be travelling again ? But that we cannot tell yet. Nevertheless I dream a good deal about the winter and how we two will go through it alone together or spend it joyfully with your beloved husband.

I should love to have been present at my apotheosis at your concert.[3] You really did me too much honour ! When I think of you at the piano my pieces seem to me to be consecrated. I was at Herr Avé Lallemand's [4] the other day ; he has the greatest respect for you and your husband. He has the frightful habit of always philosophizing about music and musicians, and Wagner in particular gives him great scope in this respect. You know how I hate to discuss and to analyse musicians and their tendencies. . . . My former acquaintances

[1] On the 17th of October Clara had started from Hanover, whither Brahms and Grimm had accompanied her, on her first concert tour with Frl. Schönerstedt, which was to take her to Leipsic, Weimar and Frankfort.

[2] Herr Marxsen was his music teacher.

[3] On the 23rd of October in Leipsic Clara had concluded the first half of her performance by playing Brahms' *Andante* and *Scherzo* from the Sonata in F minor for the first time.

[4] A music teacher in Hamburg.

here have become very distasteful to me and I cannot understand the life I used to lead. After having spent that magnificent summer with you it would be impossible for me to
stay here. Forgive the expression " magnificent " ; it was
after all a magnificent summer in spite of the terrible cloud
that overshadowed it, and I shall never forget it. Perhaps
the winter will be infinitely more beautiful. It cannot help
being at least as good. Farewell, most honoured lady, and
think kindly of Your JOHANNES BRAHMS.

BRAHMS *to* CLARA.

HAMBURG, *End of October.*

MOST HONOURED LADY !

What can I say in return for such a sign of deepest friendship ? How can I thank you ? What can I do to deserve
it ? I know so well how unwillingly you let such a precious
letter [1] leave your hands even for a moment, and yet you send
it to me ! But you must surely know the joy you have given
me. I was deeply moved to see how affectionately your husband thinks of you. This letter again contains nothing but
love and beautiful feeling. Every qualm and every anxiety
must vanish on reading it. I am ever more convinced that
his mind only wants strengthening and that he will soon be
back. I return you the letter with a thousand thanks. Will
the next one be addressed to me ? . . . My imagination has
pictured a number of hateful scenes. I thought of you constantly among Liszt's Apostles or with the Princess. How
distasteful much (all, most ?) of it must have been to you !
You are probably now surrounded by nothing but Philistines ?

In Erfurt, Frankfort, Darmstadt and even Mannheim, I
cannot imagine that there can be any other sort of people.
Heine, it is true, writes that Goethe and F. Hiller were born
in Frankfort, but only that, they were only born there. . . .
Incidentally, you imagine my life here as being more wretched
than it is. It is so delightful to be with my parents, and I
should always like to take my mother away with me. If you
could only see how I kill time apart from music and books
you would laugh. . . . If only you could telegraph to me
" Good morning ! " every day, I would be electrified, and

[1] From Robert Schumann.

would be so happy that the whole of the twenty-four hours would be like play to me. . . . I played your beautiful Variations [1] to my teacher and I am to tell you all sorts of nice things about them. He likes them as much as I do (not so much).

I also played him the F Sharp minor [2] and the F minor Sonatas. He said he had heard you play the former (as Cl. Wieck). He is extremely pleased with the improvement in my playing. That too I have to thank you for. Only since I have heard you and have been able to entertain and please you with my playing, have I succeeded in conveying to other people what I feel. Indeed, if anything passably good is in me, or ever likely to come out of me, have I not to thank you two and your great love ? But I have talked to you too long already, and will stop so that this letter may be sent off to-day. Farewell then, and let me soon have the pleasure of a letter even if it is only two lines from you. I shall wait from to-morrow onwards with the greatest longing. Your JOHANNES BRAHMS.

ROBERT SCHUMANN *to* BRAHMS.

ENDENICH, *Nov.* 27.

DEAR FRIEND,

If only I could come to you myself and see you again and hear your magnificent Variations,[3] or my dear Clara's, about the wonderful performance of which Joachim has written to me ! How splendidly the whole is rounded off, and how one recognizes you in the richest brilliance of your imagination and again in your profound artistry in a way that I had not yet learnt to know you—the theme surging up here and there, now so secret, anon so passionate and profound. The theme then disappears again, but how magnificent is the end after the fourteenth, so full of artistic skill as it leads in a canon to the second. The fifteenth in G Flat major with the genial second and last part. And then, dear Johannes, I have to thank you for all your kindness and goodness to my Clara. She is always writing to me about it.

---

[1] Variations on a theme by Rob. Schumann, dedicated to Brahms, Op. 20.

[2] Schumann, Op. 11.

[3] In F Sharp minor on a theme by Schumann.

As you probably know she sent me yesterday, to my great joy, two volumes of my compositions and the Boyhood of Jean Paul. And now although I treasure your handwriting I hope soon to be able to see it in another form. The winter i͟s comparatively mild. You know the district of Bonn. I always enjoy looking at Beethoven's statue and the magnificent view towards the Siebengebirge. The last time we saw each other was in Hanover. Write soon to your respectful and affectionate R. SCHUMANN.

BRAHMS *to* CLARA.

HAMBURG, *Nov.* 30, 11 *o'clock.*

. . . The conditions which you impose for the use of " thou " [1] I had long promised in spirit to grant you. I have no secrets from you. In thought I confide everything to you. Is that not the same as if I did so in words ? . . . You ask whether I should like to accompany you to Bonn. You surely did not write this as a question ? I should prefer to do so to-morrow rather than the day after to-morrow. I did not associate the two names Mendelssohn and Kullack. I use such names as Kullak etc. to annoy people when I am angry. I do not use M.'s name before people who are unworthy of it, but only when I am particularly proud of a certain piece.

You ought not to suspect me of having so little judgment and so little love for innately deep music (and not only for this). Who knows whether it is you or I who love *his* music best ? In Lübeck you were less pleased with the A major Symphony than I was. I readily acknowledge that you have heard M.'s works far more often than I have and it is not my fate to be so spoilt in these matters as my dear mother. Since you have gone I have not been in a single pub, so you can set your mind at rest on that score. My passion is not nearly so great as you imagine. . . . Farewell for to-day. There is so

---

[1] On parting from Brahms in Hanover on the 23rd of November she had comforted him by promising to call him " thou " in her letters for the future. Those readers who are aware of what this means to French and German people will not need to be told that the use of the second person singular denotes the height of friendship, See *Life*, Vol. II, p. 94.

much noise all round me that writing is difficult. A thousand thanks once more for your last letter. Your JOHANNES.

BRAHMS *to* CLARA.

HAMBURG, *Dec.* 2.

DEAREST FRIEND,

I was deeply distressed by your last letter. What can I say to you ? How can I comfort you,—I who also require comforting ? How dearly you are having to pay for your husband's precious letter. What a terrible enclosure ! [1] I could feel no real joy at my good fortune ; I could think only of you and your sorrow—not that the doctor's letter has deprived me of all hope, because I cannot believe that the spring will not make you the happiest of women. But how terribly hard it is that our hopes for the immediate future should be snatched from us ! My poor friend, how you must be suffering ! But your fears also are only for the winter, are they not ? You too hope that the worst will then be over ? Your husband is not suffering as much as you are. What a comfort this must be for a woman like you. I cannot stir from my conviction that your dear one's illness is cured but that his mind, unlike his body, is not yet fully restored. A letter from you makes him forget his loneliness for whole days and what a wonderfully soothing effect music must have upon him !

You remember how the doctors commented on your husband's first letter which you thought " unexpectedly sensible." You don't know what trouble I had to prevent the doctors from announcing to you, when in Ostend, that your husband's correspondence would be reduced. Remember, too, how much of his behaviour strikes the doctors as unnatural. When I saw him he put his hand to his mouth as usual, and the doctor said portentously to me, " Look, he often does that ! " I replied, " He has always done that." " Yes," he said, very gravely, " many people have told me that already." There is much even in your husband's letter which the doctors will not be able to explain. But oh, how childish I must appear to you with my inadequate attempts at comfort. All we can do is

---

[1] With the letter addressed to her and Brahms in Breslau by Robert she had received a note from the doctor saying that she must not expect to see her husband again for months.

to have hope and faith.   It is no good thinking about it, for that neither brings hope nor fosters or strengthens it.   But you may derive comfort from the dear letters, they are so beautiful, so full of love.   Was not the last to you the most beautiful of all ?   But I ought not really to say that.   For see how he thinks of me—with what fond affection !

But forgive my letters and believe me when I say that I am graver at heart when I think of you than you can possibly gather from my letters.   When I write to you I feel as though I were speaking to you.   You bear your grief so proudly that one easily forgets all the pain of it and becomes cheerful; I am still young and often boyish, you must forgive me.   You must surely believe and know that I really feel things deeply, and that although my youthful spirits or levity make me appear different, they can never allow me to forget.   I have sent the letter direct to Joachim.   How great your friendship for us must be to have allowed you to make this great sacrifice on our account.   One cannot speak one's gratitude, one can only prove it.   With deepest love and reverence, Your JOHANNES.

BRAHMS *to* ROBERT SCHUMANN.

HAMBURG, *Dec.* 2.

DEAREST FRIEND,

How can I tell you the pleasure your dear letter gave me ? You have so often made me happy already by referring to me affectionately in your letters to your wife, and now at last I possess a letter !   It is the first I have had from you, and it is infinitely precious.   Unfortunately I received it in Hamburg whither I had gone to visit my parents.   I should much have preferred to receive it from the hands of your wife.

I expect to be back in Düsseldorf in a few days.   I long for it.   The all too generous praise which you have thought fit to bestow on my Variations has filled me with joy and hope. Ever since the spring I have been diligently studying your works.   How glad I should be to hear your praise about this too.   During the whole of that time I have been in Düsseldorf, and it will be an unforgettable experience for me.   For, it has taught me to honour and to love you and your magnificent wife ever more and more.   Never yet have I looked so confidently and cheerfully into the future, or believed so firmly in a magnificent time to come. How I wish that you could be near us and long for the time when you will be restored to us. Then I shall never be able to leave your side but shall always be striving to be ever more worthy of your friendship. Farewell and think kindly of me. Yours most respectfully, JOHANNES BRAHMS.

ROBERT SCHUMANN *to* BRAHMS.

ENDENICH, *Dec.* 15.

DEAR FRIEND,

If only I could come to you for Christmas ! Meanwhile my splendid wife has sent me your portrait, your familiar features, and I know its place in my room very well, very well —under the looking-glass. I still continue to feel uplifted by your Variations. I should like to hear many of them performed by you and Clara. I have not mastered them perfectly yet, particularly the second, the fourth, as regards the tempo, and also the fifth ; but the eighth (the slowest) and the ninth. —Clara wrote to me that on page fourteen the music recalls something. What is it ? Out of a song ?—And the twelfth —oh, if I could only hear it performed by you both ! Clara has also sent me Rückert's poem to us, the original. I am sorry about it, although it has pleased me, for she has taken it out of the Album. She also wrote to me about some Ballads by you. What have you published since we parted ? Not the Scherzo ? [1] Surely. How pleased I should be to know something of your new work. Write to me soon again, dear Johannes, and tell me something also about our friends. I was glad to hear that they remembered me in Hamburg. If only I could see that town again which I saw very shortly after the fire there. You will probably be in Düsseldorf again by now. We have not seen each other since Hanover. They were happy times.

I am so glad to hear about the marked talent of my little girls, Marie, Elise and Julie. Do you often hear them play ? Farewell, my trusty friend. Speak of me and write again. Your devoted ROBERT SCHUMANN.

---

[1] The E Flat minor, Op. 4.

BRAHMS *to* CLARA.

HAMBURG, *Dec.* 15.

DEAREST FRIEND,

. . . In my last letter I forgot to tell you something that is causing me great anxiety. Your husband reads the newspapers a good deal. Is not that very risky ? I wish you would write to the doctor and ask him to glance through them beforehand very carefully, to see that there is nothing about you in them. There is something about your travels in almost every number of the *Illustrirte Zeitung.*

. . . I should like the doctor to install me as attendant and nurse for Christmas. If that were possible I am sure the worst would then be over. I would write to you every day about him and the whole day long I would speak to him of you. What do you think ? Are you going to give him more than the portrait, as I suggested, and some beautiful flowers as well ? For if you are thinking of sending him the Ballads (or anything else) you ought certainly to inquire of the doctor first whether Herr Sch. will be able to play the piano on Christmas Eve. Otherwise it would be better to send him the music later. Then Joachim, Bargiel and Brahms would have to send all their new things together. What do you think of that ? . . . I shall not go to Düsseldorf another time if you desert me. How glad I should have been to write you a very fine sonata rather than all this drivel. You must often have thought—" What has Johannes done for me ? " . . .

I have written you a dreadful letter. I can see that. So I shall write you a second one from out the Thousand and One Nights. It describes my condition exactly although its writer was a prince and I am a composer.[1] . . . [The letter ends] " Would to God that I were allowed this day instead of writing this letter to you to repeat to you with my own lips that I am dying of love for you. Tears prevent me from saying more. Farewell !

CAMARALZAMAN EBN. BRAH."

When Ebn Brah had finished the letter which he had written

---

[1] Here follows a page of quotations from the *Arabian Nights*, taken from the love story of Prince Camaralzaman and the Princess Badoura, which is described in the tales told on the two hundred and twenty-second to the two hundred and thirty-eighth nights.

with so much sighing and weeping he took it to the Prussian
Post Office, dropped it into the letter-box and said, " Take
this letter, I entreat thee, to my beloved lady, and greet her
for me."

J. B.

BRAHMS *to* ROBERT SCHUMANN.

DÜSSELDORF, *Dec.* 30.

MOST HONOURED FRIEND,

There is much I should like to write to you about concerning Christmas Eve, how it was enlivened for us thanks to
Joachim's news, and how he talked to us the whole evening
about you, and your wife wept silently.   We were all filled
with the joyful hope of seeing you again soon.

Thus all those days which might be days of twofold woe,
you change into days of rejoicing for us.   It was on your
birthday that your wife was allowed to write you her first
letter.   On Christmas Eve the friend to whom we would most
readily grant this privilege, was allowed to speak to you first,
whilst in our hearts we hoped we might soon be able to follow
him.   On the first day of the holidays your wife conducted
the festivities.   She will already have written to you about
it and have described how beautifully Marie and Joachim
played your A minor Sonata and Elise acted in the children's
play.   She will also have told you how she rejoiced my heart
with the complete works of Jean Paul.   I did not expect to
call these my own for many years to come.   Joachim got the
scores of your symphonies which your wife had already presented to me some time ago.

I returned here on the evening of the 23rd.   How long the
separation from your wife seemed to me !   I had grown so
used to her uplifting presence and had spent such a magnificent summer with her.   I had grown to admire and love
her so much that everything else seemed empty to me and I
could only long to see her again.   I brought a lot of beautiful
things back with me from Hamburg, from Herr Avé the score
of Gluck's *Alceste* (the Italian edition 1779), also your first
dear letter to me and many from your beloved wife.   I have
to thank you above all for a beautiful word in your last letter
—for the affectionate " thou."   Your kind wife has also glad-
dened my heart now by using this beautiful and intimate

word to me.   It is the greatest proof I have of your attachment and I will strive to deserve it ever more and more.   There is much more I should like to have written to you, dearest friend, but it would only be a repetition of what your wife is telling you, so let me close with the heartiest of handshakes and greetings, Your JOHANNES.

1855

DÜSSELDORF, *Jan.* 25.

MY BELOVED FRIEND,

Night has come on again and it is already late, but I can do nothing but think of you and am constantly looking at your dear letter and portrait.[1] What have you done to me ? Can't you remove the spell you have cast over me ? For instance, at the present moment I really ought to be writing important letters to other people, but I cannot do it. . . .

To-day I gave my first lesson to little Miss Weil, to-morrow Frl. Wittgenfels [2] comes. Cramer's Studies Nos. 1 and 2, and one or two pieces out of Sch.'s Album. How the Studies and the scales reminded me of Hamburg ! It is really no fun to have to teach children such things. Oh, if only I could teach the important works of Bach, Beethoven, Schumann, Schubert, how pleased I should be. I wish I could become famous.

How are you ? I did not want to ask you to write, but do so long for letters from you. Besides I know only too well how you are—you are holding your head up. So just write me a word or two occasionally and I shall be happy—just a friendly greeting to say that you are keeping well and that you will be back in 14, 13, 12, 11, 10, 9, 8, 7, 6, 5, 4, 3, 2 days !

Last night Frl. Bertha insisted on giving me something hot to eat. It tasted so good that I should like to have told you what it was, but when I asked Bertha about it, she thought I was chaffing her. This evening I bought myself a bottle of

---

[1] Clara had started on her concert tour in Holland on the 15th. Brahms had accompanied her and Frl. Schönerstedt as far as Emmerich, where he left her, but rejoined her two days later at Rotterdam, where he stayed till the 23rd. On the 24th he had already written her a letter from Düsseldorf, where he had a room in her house, giving her news of the children and the maid Bertha.

[2] A mistake for Wittgenstein.

23

punch-essence, so that I can drink to your health every night
at supper.

Have you received a letter from Endenich yet ? If not we
can only suppose that one must have gone astray, and, if the
doctor has not written, it simply means that there is no change
in his condition and that nothing alarming has occurred.   And
this is what I think is really the case.

Morning of the 26*th.*

. . . Eugenie has got a bad cold, she has no appetite, her
head is very hot and she is constantly falling asleep.   The
boys are very well, including Felix.   No headway is being
made with the alphabet yet in spite of any amount of loaf
sugar. . . .   Do cheer me up with a few lines soon.   I want
them so badly, but above all I want you.   Your JOHANNES.

BRAHMS *to* CLARA.

DÜSSELDORF, *Jan.* 29.

MY DEAR FRIEND,

How alarmed I was by your letter of yesterday and stirred
to the heart, it so clearly bears the brand of deep suffering.
What you must have gone through and are still going through !
Alas, at the moment I should certainly have felt unable to
comfort you, for anybody who in such circumstances is able
to use smug words of solace cannot feel the pain himself.   But
now I really would like to be at your side in order to be able
to remind you of many things.   I am not sending the letter
to Joachim but back to you direct.   Owing to the nature of
the last lines,[1] you have forgotten the first pages and overlooked the whole of the doctor's comforting letter.   At the
first shock I felt the same as you did, but now I am able to
take pleasure in the whole of the dear letter, and I want you
to do likewise.   I cannot help remembering how often Herr
Sch. had premonitions of death and how often he used to alarm
you with them.   At the time of the *Requiem* he thought that,
like Mozart, he had written it for himself, and during his illness
he used to tell me how often he had similar fears.   All this
you will now be able to think over more quietly and then it

---

[1] On the 26th Clara had a letter from Robert which ended as follows :
" My Clara, I feel as if I were facing some terrible calamity.   How
dreadful if I should not see you and the children again."

is only the words themselves that will seem sad. If I did not
return the letter to you, this sad sentence would allow you no
peace. You can send it to Joachim later on. There is no
need for me to tell you the pleasure your husband gave me by
dedicating precisely this piece to me. This and the Violin
Phantasy in A minor are my favourites among his concertos.
I have a right to be proud of this first dedication to me. If
only the second in print could be the Heinrich Overture.[1]

And now let me tell you how deeply moved I was by your
letter to Robert. Few people are capable of such warmth
and understanding and you pass so calmly and beautifully
over precisely that part of his letter which upset you, that
what you have written cannot fail to comfort and encourage
him. I do not believe that the " attack of nerves " (it
is only your husband who calls it " convulsions ") was really
serious. We might have expected that such attacks would
recur (although in a milder form) for a long time to come. . . .
To-morrow (Tuesday) I shall go to Bonn. But I must tell
you frankly that I have no hope of being able to see him. The
only thing I shall do, mistakenly perhaps, is to hide from the
doctors how often Herr Sch. has alarmed you before with
premonitions of death. I should be so glad to be able to give
him your portrait. But you might certainly write to the doctors (later on) and tell them that he has often said such things
before (as, for instance, when he wrote the *Requiem*). Early
on Wednesday, therefore, I hope to be able to send you news.
This is my only reason for going to Bonn. But do not expect
more. Don't even reckon too soon on the promised letter from
your husband. You know how often this leads to disappointment. . . . I send you the most hearty greetings and God
grant that I may be able to give you good news on Wednesday,
Yours, JOHANNES.

BRAHMS *to* CLARA.

DÜSSELDORF, *Feb.* 3.

FAIR AND HAUGHTY DAME !

What crime can I have committed to deserve so distressing a
letter as your last. As far as I can remember all I did was to
write curtly, but my intention was not disrespectful. If only,

[1] By Joachim.

my dear Frau Clara, you would never be angry with me about my writing ! Have I not often told you how seldom I succeed in getting my thoughts out of my heart and on to paper ? It is exactly the same with my composing. You know how seldom I write. For a long time I can go on thinking and feeling without being able to strike the right note, no matter how warm my sentiments may be. It simply won't flow out of my heart. Thus I often sit before a blank sheet of paper and long to be able to write comfortingly and even beautifully to you—but I have never yet succeeded, for I am not such a good hand at words as I am at music. . . .

There are a number of important things I want to say to you. I wrote nothing to your dear husband about your journey etc. You surely must have known that I should never have done this without your permission or without having sent the letter to you—but you ask me about it as if you did not know this. I only wrote to the dear man about his dedication, about my visit and Bargiel's Opus 9. In any case I feel sorry now that I did not go to Bonn after all. And yet I gathered from your letters that you had felt the same about it as I had—that we should try to avoid worrying the doctors, besides which I also felt that your Robert's remark was not as serious as I had at first thought. All I wanted to go to Endenich for was to be able the sooner to send you news that he was already better. I did not hope to do anything more for the present. . . .

As to England, I think you have done rightly in accepting, sad as it will be for me to have to think of you so far away. You have no idea of how indispensable your presence is to me, you have not the remotest conception. But I shall remain in Düsseldorf. This will surely allow you to go on your travels with less anxiety as you will know that a true friend remains near your husband. The camelias are blooming magnificently.[1] We have pressed one of them for you. The pot has now been returned to Robert's room. . . . A thousand thanks for the many dear letters which I have received from you. They give me untold joy. With heartiest greetings, Your JOHANNES.

[1] In a previous letter written on the 24th of January Brahms told Clara that he was sitting in his room with her medallion before him and a pot of camelias from Robert's room.

I can make canons in all possible artistic forms.   I am wondering how I shall be able to get on with fugues.

BRAHMS *to* CLARA.

DÜSSELDORF, *Feb.* 7.

HIGHLY HONOURED LADY !

This evening I wished to copy the whole of the Adagio from the Quartet, but I cannot finish it ; I must stop in order to write you a few words.   Above all let me thank you most heartily for your letter to-day.   My face has been beaming so ever since it arrived that Bertha cannot make it out.   Only this morning I wrote to you to tell you what a different one I expected.   How kind and affectionate you are !   . . . By now I hope you are in bed and that Frl. Agnese has again got her night cap on with the enormously long flap which hangs outside the bed.   I wonder whether you got my letter to-day and feel kindly disposed to me for having tried so hard to write as I should.   I feel so happy, so peaceful and quiet, everything is so still, your portrait is looking kindly down upon me and I should like to stay the night here, lost in thoughts of you ; possibly you are thinking of me too.   I feel as if you were.

Oh, if only the time could go by quickly.   I long for peace —for you.   If only you could be quite happy again !   You have suffered long and severely enough.   How rarely do I have moments of such perfect peace as the present, and yet I believe that when this period is over they will come more often.   I certainly used to have them in the past, in spite of many great sorrows, because in those days I did not want the time to pass to make way for better times to come.   At the present moment I am thinking too much of you, and I get no peace.   But one thing I have resolved to do, and that is to get some fine music paper for my letters to England and occasionally send you a song or a melody instead of words.   It is in any case more eloquent than my words, but I can send it to you without music paper !

This afternoon I told the boys that you had sent me kisses for them, and they fled from me in such haste that I was quite alarmed !   But they soon returned to fetch their kisses away, though I had to make them up, as yours were too intangible !

I don't know what more to write except to send you

a thousand, thousand hearty greetings, and no one can send
you heartier ones than Your JOHANNES.

BRAHMS *to* CLARA.

DÜSSELDORF, *23rd and 24th Feb.*

MY MOST BELOVED FRIEND!

I feel that I have so many beautiful things to tell you this
evening that I really don't know where to begin.   From two
o'clock till six I was with your beloved husband, and if you
could see my blissful expression you would know more than
any letter could tell you.   He received me as warmly and
cheerfully as he did the first time, but did not show the same
subsequent excitement.   Then he handed me your last letter
and told me what a delightful surprise it had been to him.
We spoke about your travels.   I told him that I had seen you
in Hamburg, Hanover, Lübeck, and even in Rotterdam.   He
then asked particularly whether you had occupied the same
room in Holland as you had the previous winter.   I told him
your chief reason for avoiding it, which he quite understood.
He was very much pleased with the Bach, Beethoven, Schumann programme.

Then I showed him your portrait.   Oh, if only you could
have seen how deeply moved he was, how the tears almost
stood in his eyes as he looked ever more closely at it.   " Oh,
how long have I wished for this ! " he said at last, and as he

―――――――――

[1] Adagio from the septet in G major, Op. 36.

laid it down his hands trembled. He continued to look at it and often stood up to get a closer view of it. He was delighted with the inkstand and also with the cigars. He said he had not had any since Joachim's. This is probably true and he may have left some of those lying about. But he told me that he does not like to ask the doctors for anything (he also said to me most emphatically, " Clara must certainly have sent me some often, but I do not get them ").

He then invited me to go into the garden with him, but as to what we talked about, I cannot possibly remember it all, but I don't think you could mention anything we did not discuss. I asked him quite calmly whether he was composing anything. He then told me that he had written some fugues, but that I was not to hear them because they were not properly arranged yet. He spoke much and often about you—how wonderfully, how magnificently you play, for instance the canons, particularly those in A Flat and B, the Sketches, " It would be impossible to hear ' *Abend* ' and ' *Traumeswirren* ' played more beautifully than by her ! " He inquired after all the children and laughed heartily over Felix's first tooth. He also asked after Frl. Bertha, Frl. Leser, Frl. Jungé, and Frl. Schönerstedt, Joachim (and how earnestly !), Hasenclever,[1] etc. etc. Later on he also asked after Bürgermeister Hammers, Nielo,[2] Massenbach,[3] etc., inquiring whether they were still in Düsseldorf. He told me a lot about your travels, the Siebenge-birge, Switzerland and Heidelberg, and also spoke of Gräfin Abegg.[4] He looked through my C major Sonata [5] with me and pointed out many things. I begged him to send you a greeting (in writing) and asked him whether he did not wish to write to you more often. :" I should love to," he replied, " always and always, if only I had paper." And he really hadn't any. For he does not like to ask the doctors for any-thing and they think of nothing unless he asks for it.

Whereupon I had paper brought. He disliked its large size

---

[1] Dr. H., Schumann's doctor and a member of the Committee of the *Gesangverein*.

[2] Member of the Committee of the *Gesangverein*.

[3] *Regierungs Präsident* (Governor of the District).

[4] Meta Abegg, to whom, as Countess Pauline d'Abegg, the Variations Op. 1 were dedicated.   [5] Op. 1.

very much, nor was he at all pleased with my way of reducing
its dimensions. Again and again he sat down and with a
most friendly expression on his face seemed as if he wished to
write. But he declared that he was too much excited and
would write the next day. I can only hope that the next day
will not keep us waiting as long as usual. He wrote in my
notebook with a pencil the things I was to get for him—a
scarf ; his everyday one is worn out and the one he was wearing was too " grand " for his taste ! As for the copies of the
Signal, I will look through this year's numbers and send them
to him (when I have made my selection), then I will write to
Senff to tell him that Herr Sch. wishes to read this paper. We
also spoke about the new *Zeitschrift für Musik* and what a lot
of nonsense and gossip it contained. . . . He spoke very
enthusiastically of Joachim, as enthusiastically as he usually
speaks only of you. He talked a good deal about the musical
festival,[1] and of how beautifully J. had already played at the
rehearsal. Surely such sounds had never been heard on the
violin before ! We then played a duet. He asked me to play
the *Cäsar Overture* [2] with him, but he would not take the lead.
" I am the bass," he said. We did not keep strictly together
but how long it must be since he played a duet ! He said
that with you he used to play it much faster or else that you
used to play it so. He thought highly of the arrangement.
. . . The piano was badly out of tune ; I have arranged for
it to be tuned.

When I wished him good-bye he insisted on accompanying
me to the station. On the plea of going to fetch my coat I
went downstairs and asked the doctor whether this could be
allowed, and to my great joy he said it could. (I did not say
any more to the doctor and had not even seen him before
this.) An attendant followed us or walked beside us all the
time (a few steps away). It was very fine to see the heavy
doors, which are usually bolted, opened for us to go out. . . .
He was very pleased with my Hungarian hat just as he used
to be in the old days with the cap etc. You can imagine my
joy when I found myself walking cheerfully along with my
friend for quite a long time. I never once looked at my watch
and in reply to his questions always said that there was no

[1] Of 1853.   [2] Op. 128.

hurry.   So we went to the cathedral, and to the Beethoven monument, after which I brought him back to the road.

He often made use of my glasses because he had forgotten his own and incidentally found no difficulty in keeping up with the well-known Brahms pace which is often too much for you.   On the way he asked me whether his Clara also took a walk every day.   I told him (though not quite truthfully) that whenever you were in Düsseldorf or any other place with me I took you for a walk every day, as you did not like going out alone.   " That I readily believe," said your Robert, very sadly, " in the old days we always went out for walks together." We talked a good deal about his books and his music and he was as happy as a king when he saw how well I knew them all and their proper places.   We chaffed each other a good deal over this, for in the case of some of the books he had to stop to think and I had to do the same in the case of others.

I left him on the Endenich Road.   He hugged and kissed me tenderly, and on parting sent greetings to you alone. . . . On the way there were moments when I felt almost intoxicated with happiness, and you can well imagine how much I longed for you to be in Düsseldorf.   Your letter was a real joy.   It made me feel as if I were holding your hand.

I cannot write you anything sad about him except that occasionally he expressed an emphatic wish to be out of the place.   At such moments he always spoke in low and indistinct tones, because he is frightened of the doctors ; but he said nothing that was not lucid or showed any signs of confusion.   He mentioned the fact that in March he would have been in Endenich a year, and it seemed to him as if he had first known the place when everything was beautifully green, the weather perfect and the skies blue overhead.   But alas ! I can only tell you in simple and dry language all that we had to say to each other.   The beautiful side of it all I cannot describe—his fine, calm demeanour, his warmth in speaking of you and his joy over the portrait.   Just picture all this as perfectly as you can.

Surely you will have no questions to ask after such an exhaustive letter ?   But how I wish I could write more briefly and more beautifully. . . .   And so with heartiest greetings from your Robert and myself ; and be content at least with my good intentions, for you know how gladly I would give you more joy if I could, with heart-felt love and respect, Your JOHANNES.

Heartiest greetings to dear Joachim.

BRAHMS *to* CLARA.

DÜSSELDORF, *March* 3.

BELOVED FRAU CLARA,

Seldom have I been made so happy by a letter as by yours of to-day. From the very earliest moment you were vividly in my thoughts, and at breakfast I had to lay my book aside because I so distinctly felt you sitting by me. How happy you have made me ! I wrote to your husband yesterday and sent him the scarf and the copies of the *Signal*. . . . I have only good news to send you about the boys. They seem to me to grow merrier and stronger every day. I have put away a large bag of sweets from Frl. Hartmann, and they have to earn every one of them by hard work. They even have to wrestle with each other for them. The one who throws the other for the third time gets something. And so they often have to have thirty fights before they succeed. Next Sunday the two little girls have invited themselves to a meal with us chiefly because we are going to have potato salad which we have not had for a long time.

Another letter has come from England. Oh, if only that fatal journey were not to be ! When I think of all you have to put up with already I cannot imagine how you will survive it. I cannot give you any word of encouragement or good cheer, I can only advise you not to do it. But you really must consider whether you would like to take Frl. Bertha with you. If I were to remain here, everything would be all right. We must talk it over. Is Joachim at last going to play his Variations in public at a small soirée ? If so do send me the programme. I have nothing more to say. I had not really anything to write about except to send you and Joachim a thousand greetings and to thank you for every letter you send me. I also have to send you hearty greetings from Frl. Bertha—and, as for myself, I make so bold as to breathe the gentlest of kisses on to your lovely hand. And so with heartiest greetings, Your JOHANNES.

BRAHMS *to* CLARA.

DÜSSELDORF, *Wednesday morning, March* 14.

I was just about to write to you, my dearest Frau Clara, when the enclosed beautiful letter [1] arrived. All that I need really do is just to add my greetings and you will be satisfied. As a matter of fact I never expected to get it, for I had not much faith in his " to-morrow," and was all the more pleasantly surprised. Don't you think that the last three letters from your dear one have been much more cheerful, more full of life, and almost mischievous ? . . . I shall send your dear Robert some music paper and Paganini to-day. I could not find the piano edition of the Rhine Overture for two hands. I cannot resist sending him the Sonata in F Sharp minor. . . . I feel very sad at having to write to you so far away to-day.[2] If I did not know that these were the last few days I could not write to you at all. Writing gets more and more difficult each time. Oh, if only I knew whether to expect you on Sunday or not ! Last Sunday I went with Bertha, Marie and Elise to Grafenberg, and stayed there from midday till eight o'clock in the evening. We were a very lively party and were running about the whole time, tearing through the thickest bushes. The others complained of the cold, but I was so hot that I had to go about the whole time without a hat and often had to fling myself on to the grass and could not get up again. It was beautiful weather, the sun was quite warm and set magnificently. I was thinking the whole time of you. I started thorough Bass with Frl. Agnes on Monday. I hope it will stimulate her to be a little more alive. It would be a pity if with her fine talent she went on vegetating. I cannot believe that talent is merely the apish quality of imitation, or that it can confine itself merely to playing, although one may not have any proof of anything else and must be prepared only for virtuosity.

[1] This was a letter from Schumann thanking Brahms for the scarf, the copies of the *Signal*, etc., and discussing business concerns with Härtels. Apparently he had written at the same time to Joachim, Clara and Simrock and expressed the same wishes to her as in his letter to Brahms. Although the date of the latter was the 11th of March it was probably only written on the 12th or 13th as it reached Brahms on the 14th.—TR.

[2] Clara was on a concert tour in Pomerania.

Another thing, have you thought of writing to your husband to tell him that you will undertake to write to the publishers for him, if he will only look through the works and put them in order ? I have many reasons for wishing you to do this. Your husband might one day write in a hurry and say something which you would not like to send on. Also any doubts or refusals on the part of the publisher might agitate him etc. etc. You might perhaps have to add something that had escaped his memory. It is surely not advisable to reveal one's private concerns to everybody ! I wish you would think this over. When you are back, instead of reading aloud to you in the evening, I shall occasionally tell you about the household in Hamburg to which I once took you. With the spring coming on as it is, I cannot help thinking of those other spring days. I would like to tell my dearest of friends many things about the lovely time I had there.

As you have not yet written to say that you are coming back from Stralsund at once I suppose you are staying on longer. But as soon as you can decide please make sure and write to your Johannes who is aching to see you again. Will you please send my letter from the dear master to Joachim and ask him to return it to me here.

BRAHMS *to* CLARA.

DÜSSELDORF, *Wednesday, March* 21.

MY DEARLY BELOVED CLARA,[1]

There was no letter by the first post this morning from you. You have no idea how longingly I wait for every post. Every day now seems to me an eternity and I cannot settle down to anything or get myself to work. I cannot even play or think. You must certainly be staying on longer, and I have ceased to hope that Monday will be your last concert. Be calm and confident and hope as I do that when once you are here you will be able to recover from all your exertions and bear many things more easily. You may be sure that I will do all I can to help you in this. I cannot help being painfully stirred when I look through all the letters you have written me on this tour. The first have such a courageous tone about them, and the

---

[1] He addressed her by her Christian name for the first time in a letter of the 17th of March.—TR.

last are so gloomy and sad. But I cannot write calmly or
cheerfully, it is as much as I can do to bear the parting. I
really ought not to write to you any more. I only make you
sadder. If only I could have heard the *Manfred* music with
you ! This and the *Faust* are probably the most magnificent
things that your husband has ever written. But I should like
to hear it as a whole with the text. What a staggering impression it must make ! I often marvel at the melodramatic passages such, for instance, as Astarte's appearance and spoken
words. That is really the highest form of musical expression.
It stirs one to the core. What I am particularly looking forward to is that, besides taking walks, we shall also kill time
with counterpoint.

We ought to set each other exercises, the same for each,
and then make a collection of them. If Joachim should come
he must join us in this. We have often talked of doing such
studies together. It seems to me it would be wonderfully
interesting and amusing, and I shall see if I cannot find some
fairly good exercises. We must also go for walks often. It
is impossible to remain shut up in a room for long in the spring.
. . . Forgive my writing, but I cannot help it. My thoughts
are not at home because you are not there. I send you the
best of all spring greetings. When we walk to Eller we see
the snowdrops growing in the open. Your JOHANNES.

SCHUMANN *to* BRAHMS.

[*20th*] *March.*

Your second Sonata, dear friend, has once again brought me
nearer to you. It was quite strange to me ; I live in your
music, one movement after the other of which I can play more
or less at sight. Then I offer up thanksgiving. I liked it
from the first, the pp., the whole movement—there has never
been anything like it before. The andante, these variations,
and then to crown all the scherzo, it is all so different from
other things. And the finale, that *sostenuto*, the music at the
beginning of the second part, the *animato*, and the conclusion
—in short, without further ado, a crown of laurels to this
Johannes who hails from regions so strange ! And how I liked
your songs.[1] The very first delighted me. I seemed to know

[1] Op. 3. Six songs.

the second, but oh, the third—that has (in the beginning) a melody that our dear girls will rave about.   And how magnificently it ends.   The fourth is quite original.   In the fifth the music is as beautiful as the text.[1]   The sixth is quite different from the rest, the melody—the harmony on the words *Rauschen* and *Wipfeln* pleases me.

And now let me thank you for all you have sent me, for Paganini's *Capricci* and the music paper.   I have harmonized a few (five) already, but the work seems to me harder than my free arrangements of old.   The reason is that in the violin he often has such a peculiar bass.   In any case my former piano solo arrangements would greatly assist my present work.

Do you know Joachim's Variations for Pianoforte and Viola very well, my dear Johannes ?   Have you perhaps heard them played by Clara and Joachim himself ?   This is a work which by the power of its imagination and variety rises far superior to his overtures and his *Phantasiestücken* for violin and pianoforte.   He draws unsuspected secrets out of the viola and the piano.   How I should love to hear the first variation played by Joachim—what melody !   How different is the second with the deeper chords of the viola.   The fourth is like a dream. In the fifth it is just the opposite—very serious (and at the end the excellent organ-point).   The sixth is remarkable owing to its theme in the bass.   The other voices join in with the beginning of the same theme.   The ninth and the tenth (with their gipsy and Hungarian character) are as national as possible in their feeling, and the concluding variation completes the work and makes it one of the greatest of masterpieces.

I read in a copy of the *Signal* that the municipal authorities of Düsseldorf have offered the post of Musical Director for open competition.   I wonder who it will be ?   Not you ? Perhaps Verhulst [2] might be willing if he were offered it.

Now let me ask you one or two favours.   Will you send me the poems of Elizabeth Kulmann [3] and an atlas.[4]   If I am not mistaken, about two years ago Herr Schubert of Hamburg

---

[1] Eichendorff's " *Aus der Heimat hinter den blitzen Rot.*"
[2] Musical Director at the Hague and Schumann's old friend.
[3] Schumann was passionately interested in her poetry.
[4] Regarding his morbid use of atlases, see *Life*, Vol. II, p. 137.

sent two atlases with a large number of other books as a present.
. . . Hoping to see you again soon, ROBERT.

BRAHMS *and* CLARA *to* SCHUMANN.

DÜSSELDORF, *March* 27.

BELOVED FRIEND,

A thousand thanks for your dear letter to me to-day. How
much I enjoyed it all ! And further special thanks for having
been the means of enabling me to give your wife the most
delightful of all greetings when she arrived. Your letter to
her came an hour or two before she herself appeared. I am
delighted that you have got to know Joachim's Variations.
I knew beforehand that you would love them. I also regard
Joachim's works as surprisingly beautiful and new, and I look
forward to each fresh one as an event.

We shall soon send you his Heinrich-Overture, but I should
like always to bring the most beautiful things, including this
Overture, to you myself. I should hate to have this pleasure
taken from me ; you will enjoy it immensely. How often we
think alike ! We had already thought the same as you about
Verhulst. You ask for an atlas. As a matter of fact I had
already thought of sending you the fine one that goes with
Humboldt's works. For the present I am sending the Schubert
one. If you want the other just let me know. We forgot to
send the arrangements of the Paganini Studies yesterday, so
here they are now. Your wife's absence has seemed very
long to me. It is really hard enough when we two are obliged
to yearn for the other two (you and Joachim) ! What a pity
it is we all have to be separated. I greet the spring right
cheerfully and am full of the most beautiful plans and hopes
for it and the summer.

Once more heartiest thanks for all the kind things you feel
about my F Sharp minor Sonata. But fortunately you yourself have written that certain men (particularly yourself) often
discover stars where others see only mist—and where perhaps
there really is only mist. With heartiest love and respect.
Your JOHANNES.

A hearty [1] kiss, my dear Robert, from one who loves you

---

[1] This paragraph by Clara was written on the last empty page of
Brahm's letter.

passionately. You must now have my letter of Sunday. Will you write to me again soon ? If only you knew what your letters were to us—what a blessing, and how overjoyed I am again and again by our deep sympathy in everything musical. There is not a feeling you have on this question that I do not share, and you always voice this sympathy so lovingly. Oh, if only I could press you to my heart again ! Think of me as I think of you, Your CLARA.

BRAHMS *to* SCHUMANN.

DÜSSELDORF, *May.*

BELOVED AND RESPECTED FRIEND !

Let me thank you most heartily for having so kindly thought of me on the 7th of May.[1] How surprised and delighted I was with the beautiful present and the kind words in the book ! Altogether it is not often one can expect to have so happy a day. Your dear wife understands so well the art of celebrating such a festivity—but you know that better than anybody. I had a pleasant surprise in a photograph of my mother, my sister and of you, and in the afternoon Joachim arrived, we hope in order to stay some time.

A little while ago, as you know, I heard the *Bride of Messina Overture* in Hamburg, and I cannot tell you how much I was moved by that deeply serious work, and after the *Manfred* too. I wished the whole time that you were there to hear it with me so that you might see what joy you give through your magnificent works. For a long time I had been particularly longing to hear *Manfred* or *Faust*. I hope we shall yet hear the last of your works—the greatest of all—together. It was only your long silence, which caused us some anxiety, that prevented me from sending you my thanks sooner. So let me thank you again most heartily for having so kindly remembered me on the 7th of May 1855. With deep love and respect, Your JOHANNES.

[1] On Brahm's birthday " Robert sent him the original score of the *Bride of Messina Overture* and some very kind words came with it. I gave him Dante and Ariosto, as well as photographs of Robert and his mother and sister." This is a quotation from Clara's Diary, *Life*, Vol. II, p. 109.

BRAHMS *to* CLARA.

DÜSSELDORF, *Wednesday, June* 20.

MY CLARA,

I cannot look idly on while Bertha packs all sorts of things and sends them to you. I feel I must close everything snugly and warmly up with the tenderest of greetings. The parcel must have my seals too. If only I could send you something really beautiful, which could plainly express my love for you and show you how much I long to have you back !

We are having the most unpleasant weather here, probably as bad as it is with you, and early this morning I was quite depressed by the bitter cold. To-morrow (Thursday) we shall have a meal here and shall have a place laid for you, and I shall think of you the whole time. I am playing the Haydn Trios with Joachim ; one can get on easily without the 'cello because the piano bass suffices practically all the way through. Joachim has bought all Beethoven's Sonatas (pianoforte solo arrangements). And now farewell and think often of your faithful JOHANNES.

BRAHMS *to* CLARA.

Saturday, June 23, *Morning.*

MY BELOVED CLARA,

This morning when I came down I was welcomed by your two last letters, one of them containing the little nosegay, the stalks of which look like silk. . . . This time you are quite right to be indignant about the abominable weather. I am also to quite an exceptional extent. I am so sick of the icy damp air that I have already got up a dozen times to make sure that all the windows were closed. I don't do that often. But, my beloved, you see, as soon as you are here again the sun will come out, and summer will return in all its glory. All that has happened is that it has lost sight of you in the little principality, that is why it is mourning. . . . Early this morning Ferdinand showed me the name Bertha which he had scratched on a piece of paper. To-day and yesterday the boys regaled themselves with Brunswick cake. I always kiss them from you, but I would very much like to give you the kisses back again. I am not yet sure whether I am going to

Mehlem, so will you go on writing here ?   With loving greetings, Your JOHANNES.

BRAHMS *to* CLARA.
DÜSSELDORF, Monday morning, June 25.

This morning again I had no letter from my dearest of all friends and yet I am hoping most confidently that ere another half hour has gone I shall be able to write happily below that one has come, for it is now almost eleven o'clock.   Meanwhile, my dear one, let me tell you about yesterday.   In the afternoon Joachim, Allgeyer and I went to the Grafenberg.   The weather was tolerable, not exactly promising but overcast. It is also gloomy to-day.   The principal point is that I have once more acquired a passion for jumping.   You would be surprised, I can jump very well and for a long time, at least twice as far as my height, and very high.   Instead of going to the well-known " beautiful view " we went to the Geresheim hills, where I think it is really more beautiful.   We must certainly go there together often.   In the evening we had music at Joachim's. . . .   When at last you return I am looking forward to reading Herder's Collected Folk Songs with you. We must do that before anything else.   I cannot tell you how I long for your return.   I can no longer exist without you. I want so much to be able to hold your hand again and to sit beside you.   Everything and everybody seems to me so cold. Yesterday Frl. Leser sent me a large cake for St. John's Day. This has never happened to me before on my name day. . . .

I am always very sorry when I can send you nothing from Endenich, but the usual news from the doctor ought to come to-day or to-morrow.   If I could have had the slightest hope of seeing or speaking to the dear man I should in any case have gone there.   But I cannot hope for this.   I am firmly convinced that on your return the sympathy that binds you two together will manifest itself and Robert will send a letter to greet you on your return.   But we must not stake too much on that.   And now farewell.   Please go on loving me as I shall go on loving you [1] always and for ever.   Wholly yours, JOHANNES.

---

[1] Although apparently Clara must have been addressing Brahms in the second person singular for some time, this is the first appearance of Brahms' use of *thou* in his letters.—TR.

BRAHMS *to* CLARA.

Tuesday, 11 *o'clock*, *June* 26.

All I shall do to-day is to send you the most loving greetings —this is what I thought an hour ago when I sat hopelessly waiting for a letter and could not for the life of me write a line. Then you had not gone to Pyrmont and had written to me, and what an affectionate, beautiful letter ! The little sprig of flowers also looked at me lovingly. Then a letter came from the doctor as well. It is true that it contained nothing very cheering, but on the other hand nothing disquieting. I should hardly feel inclined to send it to you with this if you did not know that one was due to-day. His exhaustion seems to be lasting an extraordinarily long while,[1] much longer than I expected, but it must take a turn now. You and I must hope for that. As far as I can see there is nothing in the letter to give rise to doubts or misgivings. . . . I will think of you this evening. Are you sending me the programme ?[2] . . . With a thousand hearty greetings, Your JOHANNES.

BRAHMS *to* CLARA.

Wednesday, June 27.

BELOVED FRAU CLARA,

At last the longed for Sunday is drawing ever nearer ! If only it brings you ! I am really quivering with expectation. Each time I am parted from you it becomes more difficult to grow accustomed to it. May I reckon on receiving a nice long letter to-morrow to compensate me for my waiting to-day ? Yesterday evening Joachim played in a quartet at von Dietz's, five of Haydn's. I really felt it was almost too much. I can enjoy three at the most, after which I can listen no longer, and cannot get away from the last one. These quartets are really wonderfully beautiful and masterly, and contain, particularly in their magnificent adagios, an amazing wealth of fine and original ideas. They played one in E Flat major, which, people say, was connected with Haydn's complaint that ladies were incapable of sitting through a quartet. He wrote it as the result of a wager. At the end of the exquisite finale

---

[1] Ever since May, to use the expression of the doctors, " the process of recovery had been arrested."

[2] Of her concert at the Detmold theatre.

he dupes the ladies in a priceless way by pretending several times to come to an end, and then always beginning again. We roared with laughter over it.   To-day Joachim and I went to the Grafenberg for lunch.

How did things go yesterday at the Theatre ?   I thought of you the whole evening.   While the last two quartets were being played I leant out of the window and thought more of you than of the music.   Joachim will probably arrive to-morrow at the same time as my letter, or before.   Are you coming back on Sunday for certain ? [1]   Has it occurred to you to have a sort of farewell festival ?   And now hearty greetings. Write to me from Pyrmont, and above all write quickly.   With fond love, Your JOHANNES.

BRAHMS *to* CLARA.

Sunday, Aug. 12.

MY BELOVED FRIEND ! [2]

I have been diligently playing and reading the whole day and thinking of you the whole time, and now I will quietly tell you all about it.   I am always thinking of you.   For a long while I have not thought of anyone so tenderly and incessantly as I have of you, and to-day I began to hope quite early for a letter from you in the evening, which would give me all news of the dear ones in Hamburg. [3]

My swollen mouth has got worse.   This morning I kept a fig in my mouth and bound it round with wool.   But as it only got more inflamed towards midday, I tore it all off in a pet. It is too much of a bore to have to go about all muffled up.

Frl. von Meysenbug has written me a letter smothered in sugar.   I am now her highly respected and genial master. What funny ideas people get into their heads when a young man writes something out of the way.   Many a young man probably wishes he had the wings of an eagle, and may even

---

[1] On the 2nd of July Clara returned to Düsseldorf and on the 12th they made their joint excursion to Ems.

[2] Having returned to Düsseldorf on the 30th of July Clara remained until the 9th of August, when she went to Düsternbrock near Kiel to recuperate, and there met Frau Livia Frege.—TR.

[3] On her way to Düsternbrock Clara stayed with Brahms' parents in Hamburg.

imagine that he has them. Then he falls among books and
music and soon sticks fast in the mire and forgets how to fly.
Fortunately I do not often fear that such a fate will overtake
me. But I frequently feel sad that I no longer seem to know
how to compose or how to create. I wish this time would
soon be over and I could become freer and more full of courage.
I could fall sick with longing for a new fresh strain. Just
fancy, I sometimes feel convinced that I shall fall quite ill and
then become twice as healthy as before. At other times I
imagine that I have been sick and that I am now recovering.
How unhappy I should be perhaps if I had not got you. You
teach me every day afresh that one does not derive vitality
(= vital creative power) from books, but only out of one's
own soul. One must not absorb, one must express. You must
always remain at my side as my guardian angel, and then I
shall certainly become what I should and can become. I am
not reading all this rigmarole through again. Forgive me, and
allow yourself to be heartily embraced by Your JOHANNES.

The children are all well. Bertha is very melancholy and
my new pupil has up to the present proved a dolt.

BRAHMS *to* CLARA.

Tuesday, Aug. 14.

MY DEAR FRIEND !

Now what am I to do with the Plutarch ? I cannot prevail
upon myself to send it back, as I had heroically resolved to
do. Hitherto I have only been able to read isolated Lives
from Plutarch, I have never yet been able to get him complete.
Even the edition of which I spoke to you belongs to a " cheap
classical library," and it would certainly not be as complete
as this one, nor would it in any case have so many notes and
commentaries.

How delighted I shall be if you bring it to me. Plutarch's
Lives exercise a remarkable power over me, and in that case
I shall have him complete and by the same translator. I was
not at all surprised by what you wrote to me about Coriolanus.
On reading the Life for the first time one often wishes that he
might have been different, softer, more human. If you read
it more often this impression goes and you are able to endure
the excessive roughness and hardness of this colossal hero, if

he shows his hardness at the right moment, as for instance
at the time of the elections. But the drama does not end
with his treachery. I always forget it when I come to the
scene with his mother and his death. That wipes out every
other impression. Incidentally I ought to tell you that Shakespeare made a close study of Plutarch. In Coriolanus, Julius
Caesar etc., whole speeches are taken bodily out of Pl., and
in Coriolanus particularly the action is based entirely upon
him (the sequence of scenes). Beethoven also loved to read
Plutarch, and when listening to his music one often imagines
that one can see the outline of one of Plutarch's heroes. Many
thanks for all the nice things you say to me in your letter.
This morning I received the letter from Kiel. . . . Frl. von
Meysenbug is having lessons from me, probably two piano
and one theory at one thaler apiece, which makes three thalers
[9/-] a week. Little Jung has two lessons at twenty *silbergroschen*, which makes forty *silbergroschen* [3/6 or 4/-] a week.
N. [?] and Wollenhaupt at one thaler each = 2 thalers. The
Arnold girl = one thaler a week.[1] I shall be a rich man ! I
shall be in a position to pay all my debts soon and in addition
to give one friend the complete works of Schiller and another
the complete works of Goethe. And then there is also the
money I shall get from the Ballads, about which I shall write
shortly, and from Whistling. . . . Bertha is a bit too much
of a good thing with her love-sickness. The children are very
well and good. This love business is a funny thing. I am
again confirming my old observations. It alters people so,
often for the worse. When they begin by being so happy in
their love and regard it as the most important thing of all,
for which alone the world exists, I can't stand it at any price.
. . . (Besides it's likely to grow ; and I don't trust these
officers.)

My swelling has now entirely gone. Yesterday I was so
furious that in spite of the cold weather I went out. This de-
fiance gave it such a shock that it lost patience and disappeared.

And now let me give you just one tender little kiss for my
sister. But for yourself a right hearty one such as you are
used to receiving from Your JOHANNES.

[1] This means that at this time Brahms was earning from 21*s*. 6*d*.
to 22*s*. a week with his lessons.—TR.

BRAHMS *to* CLARA.

[*August* 15], *Wednesday.*

BELOVED FRIEND !

I feel I must talk to you a little, it is so pleasant and does me so much good. I certainly do not know what about, but you must be satisfied with the most ordinary things and listen to how I spend my day and the important people I meet ! Joachim is not here yet, neither has he written. I like your new home [1] much better than I usually do when you are away. I am quite delighted with the place and for Düsseldorf it is a regular Paradise. I spend most of my time in your room, and am now in your little sitting-room. I am reading a lot of Arnim [2] now and like him immensely. I cannot understand why Arnim is not more read (by intelligent people). He is one of the authors I like and respect most, and the more deeply I learn to understand and grasp him the more I like him.

You must have *Waldemar* [3] with you. Read it. You will be particularly surprised by the first part and the calm way in which it progresses and grows more and more interesting as episode succeeds episode. Did I not give you a number of his plays to take away with you ?

I was at Frl. v. Meysenbug's to-day. She plays quite well and I like her. She is quite a stranger to Bach and plays him without any understanding whatsoever. . . . I am now going to write to my father about Plutarch. I am certainly looking forward with great joy to possessing it but I have long hesitated to write about it. Please do not give me any more presents except just a very small book as a souvenir at Christmas or on my birthday. I have had so many, so very many precious things from you ; I always feel happy when I look round me and think that all my things are from you. Other

---

[1] On the 6th of August Clara had left Bilkerstrasse and had moved to a new house at 135 Poststrasse, in which " a delightfully pleasant room " had been found for Brahms.

[2] This must be the poet and novelist Achim von Arnim (1781–1831), who wrote novels full of poetry and originality, in which the fantastic element, however, played too prominent a pa.. . With Brentano he also compiled a collection of the popular songs of Germany.—TR.

[3] *Der falsche und der echte Waldemar*, Complete Works, Vol. 18.

things I do not even notice, neither do I wish for them.[1]   With a thousand greetings, Your JOHANNES.

BRAHMS *to* CLARA.

Sunday, Aug. 19.

Clara, dear Clara, at last I have a letter from you to-day. I had long hoped for it but I shall wait for the one to-morrow before I answer. . . .   I feel ever more happy and peaceful in my love for you.   Every time I miss you more but I long for you almost with joy.   That is how it is.   And I knew the feeling already but never quite so warm as it is now.   Joachim [2] is very jolly.   We go for a lot of walks together and have plenty of music.   He is now with Herr Allgeyer.   I have left him over there in order to be alone with you.   We have just played, sung and discussed the *Manfred*, as is only right.   We greatly enjoyed it, particularly the part where Astarte appears, which we played again and again ; it moved us deeply, as did also the last part.   The proofs of the Variations and of the Hebrew Songs [3] have arrived.   The Variations are really magnificent.   To-day we were at Frl. Leser's and to my horror she complained that I had forgotten her ever since Tuesday. This is what comes of having so many lessons. . . .   You tell me nothing about how you live and I should be so glad to know whether you are not too sad and lonely.   Until you come back I am taking my meals with Joachim in the taverns in Düsseldorf.   Now write to me soon that I love you ? and more, much more than two years or even two months ago ? [4]   With deepest friendship, Your JOHANNES.

BRAHMS *to* CLARA.

Monday, Aug. 20.

What a lovely long letter I received this morning.   A thousand thanks !   I was also delighted with the exquisite flowers. Those from Hamburg were, by the bye, just as beautiful.   Did I not write and tell you that ?   Your letter found me still in

---

[1] See footnote on p. 72.

[2] In a previous letter (August 17th) Brahms had announced Joachim's arrival.—TR.

[3] Joachim, Op. 10 and 9.   [4] See footnote, p. 72.

bed (7.30 a.m.) and from this you can see that I do not get
up early but really very late.   I cannot get to bed at night,
although I have formed the firm resolution to have more regular
hours of sleep.   After supping with Joachim, and sometimes
Allgeyer, out in the town, I only reach home at about 10 o'clock.
Then I start reading with your portrait before me, and I am
glad to be alone and glance from time to time towards you and
talk to you, or read.   Thus the time goes by quickly, and as a
pastime I play with the handle of the bell-pull, and find to my
joy that the rope is still intact.   It is difficult to tell you what
I do the rest of the time, because it is all so irregular.   I play,
I read, I write or talk to you either in your room or in mine.
Then there are the lessons and Joachim or Allgeyer between
whiles.   To-day I begin theory with Frl. v. Meysenbug.   As
I have written myself dry, aye and am already getting on in
years, I find I can do no composing, but I have written something for your birthday or for your return all the same.   Meanwhile I leave you to guess what it is.   We go daily to the
Stockkämpchen or across the water.   On the way to the *Stockkämpchen* yesterday we (we three) bought a lot of plums and
pears, and then we had some sour milk and smoked.   Joachim
had a whole cigar and then he was very ill, very !   After that
we had to have some soup !

N.B. In Bach's *Allemande* in B Flat I think it right to play
the A Flat *legato* :

The A Flat in the bass is correct :

because that particular voice continues on the single notes
A Flat, B Flat, C, D.

The E flat is also right

because E Natural would be impossible.

I think the first-mentioned A Flat particularly beautiful. I am always very punctilious about ornamentations, although slovenly editions of the works often force one to follow one's own taste in these matters, and therefore I play the following passages so :

I often regard prolonged mordents ($\mathcal{W}$) as trilled notes, and I do not take the small notes before the principal note, as I do with the simple mordents ($\mathcal{W}$).

Altogether I do not treat mordents, trills, and small runs in Bach as ornamentations, not *leggiero* (that is, except where it is specially called for), but I think one ought to accentuate the trilled note in such cases, as was probably necessary with the old weak pianos. Yesterday, after writing to you, I had to play my C major Sonata ; it was such a long time since I had done so.

Now I will look for all the things that you want and pack them and send them to you this afternoon together with my warmest greetings. I cannot tell you how much I enjoyed your letter to-day. It tells me so much about your life and tells it so beautifully. The children are all well and good. Bertha wrote to you yesterday. Everybody sends you greetings and most of all, Your devoted JOHANNES.

BRAHMS *to* CLARA.

DÜSSELDORF, *Friday, Aug.* 24.

I can tell you all about last night, as I shall never forget it as long as I live. Let me begin by telling you that everything ended happily.   At about eleven o'clock we came home from Frl. Leser's.   It was very sultry, as it had been the whole day.   The moon was shining and the weather was magnificent. Only yesterday I had had my bed changed so that I might lie with my head towards the window.   I read for a long while, but about two o'clock I woke up in a great fright to find that the most appalling storm was raging.

It looked as if the whole town were on fire, while in addition there were the most terrifying claps of thunder.   A shower of hail smashed my window and the wind howled through the whole house.   I crept terrified into the darkest corner of my bed and believed that it was an earthquake or the end of the world.   Then there was a clap of thunder as if the world were splitting in half.   Bertha came shrieking into the room and begged me to go to them as they were half dead with fear. By chance Gretchen had been put to sleep downstairs.   They were both crawling about on their knees and screaming, believing the Day of Judgment had come.   The two boys were also crawling about in the room.   I then took them on my lap and let them fall asleep.   Felix was fast asleep and Eugenie was quiet.

I cannot tell you how overwhelming the storm was.   At the end of an hour it calmed down a bit and I struck a light. We looked at the windows and closed the shutters.   The panes of a number of them were lying on the ground.   I returned to bed, but of course I could not sleep.   Through the two windows I watched the two storms ; the sky was full of burning clouds from which the forked lightning shot from all sides. The storm continued to rumble, and before long there was a fresh shower of hail as heavy as the last, and more lightning. I jumped out of bed and bolted all the doors, which constantly rattled with every gust of wind.   Then I lit the light again and went back to the children's room.   The hailstones fell as if the windows were being struck with a knout.   The panes continued to drop into the room and there was water everywhere.

The colossal turmoil continued for another hour.   Never in one's wildest dreams could one have imagined such weather. Other storms are mere child's play beside this one.   It gradually died away towards morning.   Thirty-five window-panes

have been smashed. Those facing the *Schwanenmarkt* were
more protected. In my room all those facing the Poststrasse
are smashed and bits of glass had reached as far as the bed.
What I felt like I cannot tell you. I shall never forget it.
The whole night I thought of you and was full of fear that
you might be getting the same thing away from home. If
ever such a storm should occur again I would go with all the
rest downstairs into the kitchen. You may rely implicitly on
my keeping my head. I am all the calmer when I see people
behaving like Bertha. I shall be very careful ; the whole
time my one thought was of the children and I kept them
constantly under my eye. One simply could not open the
door of the room to go out, at least I found it impossible.
Towards morning heavy clouds still continued to form overhead, and to-day it is even more sultry than yesterday. Still
things grew more peaceful towards morning, and then came
your dear, dear letter and everything smiled again.

In the whole town there is hardly a pane of glass on the wind
side of the houses that has remained whole. In the barracks
on the Rhine there is not one. Altogether in various houses
seven hundred windows [?] have been blown in. The heat is
frightfully tiring and what with having had no sleep and having been more agitated than ever before in my life, I cannot
write to you as much as I should like. I shall write more
to-morrow.[1] At present it is impossible. Do not be angry
with me for my letter of yesterday. Let my love for you be
the excuse, just as yours is for you. Do you agree to this ?
Go on thinking kindly of me. I shall improve in time and
deserve it more. With heartiest greetings, Your JOHANNES.

BRAHMS *to* CLARA.

Nov. 1.

Yesterday your letter from Hanover arrived. To-day (while
we were at breakfast) the one from Berlin. It is full of pleasant news, that the concert was so successful and that the
rehearsal was so good. I thought a good deal of you while
listening to *Joseph in Aegypten*, and I still have the beautiful
simple music ringing in my ears. Fancy your having played

[1] On the 25th of August Clara came back unexpectedly to Düsseldorf.

my Gavotte ! [1]   I was surprised.   But I believe it was a good
thing to have the *Sarabande* just before it, for it enabled the
Gavotte to make a more vivid impression.   It is the same
thing with the movements of a sonata which do not make the
same impression singly as they do as a whole—the andante,
following the first serious movement, having a soothing effect
etc. and the scherzo again striking a more cheerful note after
the andante.   But in the spirit I heard with real joy how
beautifully you played it as usual. . . .

Now here is a curious thing—on Monday evening I had an
animated discussion with Otten about your husband's Overture
to Faust and he was delighted to hear that it existed, for he
did not know about it.   And then early on Wednesday I read
in the papers that " Herr Dr. Otten will certainly produce the
Overture to Faust by Richard Wagner, which has just appeared,
at one of his concerts."   I can't help wondering why on the
day before he had inquired so earnestly about another Faust
Overture when he already had one up his sleeve.   He surely
can't announce at random a work entirely unknown to him
and risk producing it ?

I am so glad you are so pleased with Julie. [2]   Write to me
about it and tell me how she looks and whether she is still as
jolly as ever.   My people greet you heartily.   I am putting
into this letter a few flowers which were standing by the coffee.
I thought that you would be certain to have some also in front
of you.   Let me embrace you most warmly, Your JOHANNES.

The money from Härtels [3] came yesterday.   Greet Julchen
for me, my beloved Clara !

BRAHMS *to* CLARA.

HAMBURG, *Nov.* 3.

MY MOST BELOVED CLARA,

I really did not want to write to-day, in the first place owing
to the ridiculous cost of postage and secondly owing to the

---

[1] She played this in Göttingen.   She had started on her concert tour
this year from Hanover, where she parted from Brahms on the 27th
of October.   Her first concert was in Göttingen.

[2] Julie Sch., Clara's third daughter, who was then ten years old,
had been living since the summer of 1854 with her grandmother
Bargiel in Berlin.   [3] For the Ballads.

fact that there is no news. But since I have received no letter, and the day seemed so empty, and I hoped that it would seem the same to you to-morrow in like circumstances, and you would perhaps receive no letter on Sunday, and I did not know whether your concert was to-morrow, and finally, have important things to report, I am writing ! ! Ever since I have been here I have been going past a shop in which I have discovered the most beautiful soldiers. Yesterday I went in with the object of buying an acrobat for Felix and at the same time to have a look at the soldiers. I found a delightful creature who will amuse you too, and left the place with a heart full of longing. I continued to consider the matter and came to the conclusion that all I was doing was beating about the bush, and that I must go in and buy in the end. And now I have the most delightful battle piece I ever saw, with a little tower as well. I am delighted with it. At Christmas at Düsseldorf I will parade all my troops and you will have pleasure out of them too.

At home here everything is going well. I am practising diligently at Hein's. I am not held up much as Avé's step-father is dead, Otten has a frightful cold, and Grädener has a concert coming off. . . . I don't know whether your concert is to-morrow or Monday. Write to me all about yourself—how you are, how you spend your time, practise, read etc. My parents were overjoyed with Joachim's portrait. Tell him about it, will you ? He is sure to be pleased that his picture is hanging there. What is Bargiel doing ? Has he written anything ? I suppose we shall all be together in Düsseldorf at Christmas ? I long for it as much as if I had not seen you for months. I wish we could scour the town together some time for toys for the boys. At any rate I shall wait a bit before buying my presents. My parents, Fritz and Elise wish to be remembered to you. With fond love, Your JOHANNES.

BRAHMS *to* CLARA.

Tuesday, Nov. 6.

MY BELOVED CLARA,

What lovely things you are hearing and making others hear. I almost envy you ! Idomeneo, the Eighth Symphony and how much more ! I knew perfectly well that Berlioz' Flight into Egypt would make exactly the impression upon you which you say it has. One is, however, too prone to stigmatize as affected and coquettish this sort of simplicity in a man like Berlioz, who is inclined to be hard on one's ears. I have often heard it, and it has always enchanted me. I really like it best of all Berlioz' works. Now Jussef [1] writes about plans which you communicate to me, and I sit here and wait and quietly enjoy your dear words and my Shakespeare, and then these plans [2] come into the bargain and I have to think over them too. . . . I dined with the Ottens on Sunday. When I am invited on Sundays to well-to-do people I always behave rather funnily. I don't eat much at lunch, and the whole of the afternoon I keep thinking about what we are going to have in the evening. And then, when there is as little as there was at the Ottens, I do not feel satisfied, although I did not go there feeling hungry at all. . . . Yesterday I played to Herr Marxsen and was very glad to find him so thoroughly satisfied with me. I played a great many things to him, including Bach's Variations. How I should have loved to be at your concert ! How beautiful it must have been ! I am sure I shall not get as much success as a performer. You will see, I shall come a cropper ! . . . I will write more to you soon, and yet I will have no more to say to-morrow than I have had to-day. I can only repeat how much I love you and how I long for you more and more every day. Your portrait was the first thing I saw in the new mirror. Farewell ! With most loving greetings, Your JOHANNES.

BRAHMS *to* CLARA.

BREMEN,[3] *Nov.* 20.

MY DEAREST FRIEND,

I must send you a few lines and many many greetings before I go to my concert. Early to-day at the rehearsal everything

---

[1] I.e. Joseph (Joachim).

[2] This refers to a proposed concert tour to Danzig which Clara, Brahms and Joachim actually made between the 14th and 19th of November.

[3] Between the 8th and 19th of November Brahms had met Clara in Berlin and had given concerts with her and Joachim in Danzig, after which, returning to Berlin, he left there to give a concert of his own at Bremen.

went very well, that is to say, better than I dared to hope. The musicians had already practised for three hours, I could therefore only play the concerto [1] through once, so that any subtleties in accompaniment could not be thought of. And yet I played so strictly to time that they were all surprised, and we all kept together the whole time. The piano has a dreadful touch and not a trace of strength or richness of tone in the middle. I followed your advice and practised last night in the hall itself. It was exceptionally good.

So I trust everything will go off successfully, and even more successfully in Hamburg. And how are you ? I hope I may find a letter awaiting me in Hamburg. How I look forward to it ! I shall not leave until to-morrow evening by omnibus for Hamburg. With heartiest greetings and hoping that you are rejoicing with me that Christmas is not too far away and that we shall all see each other before then, with remembrances to all, particularly to Joachim, Your JOHANNES.

BRAHMS *to* CLARA.
BREMEN, *Wednesday, Early Wednesday, Nov.* 21.

I will now write you a longer and more exhaustive letter than that of yesterday when, owing to some one being with me, I could only write hurriedly. Everything went off very well yesterday, I mean, of course, only to the extent that I can now entertain genuine hopes of some day being able to play well and with confidence in public. I did not write to you yesterday that I was feeling very unwell. Owing to a severe cold, which had gone to my head, it was only with the greatest effort that I was able to concentrate my thoughts.

I shan't say anything about the journey. At Bremen I woke up with a most dreadful headache in the morning. They had lighted a fire in my room and it was black with smoke. Then the window and door had to be opened and I had to lie in the middle of it. After which, of course, it was very cold etc.

The concert went off very well and I was loudly applauded after the first and last movements. The accompaniment was also much better than in the morning. I played very calmly, and heard every note from the orchestra, and we kept together

[1] By Schumann, Op. 54.

the whole time. I don't find it so very difficult to play with an orchestra, and it certainly is a real joy. After the Phantasy [1] (in which, however, I came a cropper over the first run in the bass) I was given an enthusiastic call. They insisted on my playing again but I could not bring myself to do so. The soprano managed better when her turn came. After a tedious song by Grell there was a mere flutter of a few hands and she kindly consented to sing again. Then followed a Symphony by Haydn which went very well and is wonderfully full of life. The Genoveva Overture came next and I was delighted with it. It went much better, in fact quite well. The Euryanthe Overture brought the performance to a close with a swing, but the adagio was played much too quickly and without spirit. . . .

I am confidently hoping that I shall play well at the concert in Hamburg. Every failure and every sign of mediocre playing, as in this case, I regard quite calmly as an experience, and I continue undisturbed on my way. It must come right in the end. Mertel had hardly gone before Hahn arrived, so I must close, and with a thousand greetings and kisses, Your JOHANNES.

My love to Joachim, Bargiel, etc., and also to little Julchen who bade me good-bye with eyes so heavy with sleep.

BRAHMS *to* CLARA.

Sunday, Nov. 25.

Your letter of yesterday reached me too late for me to be able to write to Berlin, but you must have received a letter from me on Saturday in any case. How much I love your beautiful letter ! It is lying before me now and I feel as if I cannot answer it. I should prefer to copy it out. . . . Let me tell you first of all that everything went well yesterday, even at the second rehearsal as well. I was loudly applauded, for Hamburg it was quite enthusiastic. I really did play with both fire and restraint. It was decidedly better than at Bremen. Let me give you the programme : 1. Mendelssohn's Symphony in A minor, the scherzo of which delighted me, though I was bored with the andante. The first movement pleased me very much, the last less. [2]

---

[1] Schumann's C major *Phantasy*, Op. 17.

[2] The words, " the scherzo . . . less " in this paragraph were crossed through by Brahms.

2. Aria by Mozart, sung by Frau Guhrau with orchestra. To my great joy she was accompanied by two basset-horns, which had been procured with great difficulty. I don't believe any instrument blends so perfectly with the human voice as the basset-horn, the tone of which seems to come half-way between the cello (bassoon) and the clarinet.

Otten is always rather inclined to go too slowly which was not to the advantage of this Aria. But it was wonderfully beautiful. Then followed a Bach suite for orchestra (three trumpets) of which the overture, an aria, a gavotte and gigue were played. This was the most beautiful of all. What a marvellous effect, yet how much better it could and ought to have been. I can't write to you about it. I should like to play the score through with you. Then came the E Flat major Concerto which went with a good swing.

Frau Guhrau sang *Das Veilchen* and a song by Marschner ; I accompanied her and led her along so that some day I may be able to do the same with Chiarina. After this I played the Canon in B minor by Robert, and then, at Otten's and Avé's urgent request, I played Schubert's March. They were both equally and quite enthusiastically applauded. The *Euryanthe* Overture brought the concert to a close. The Carnaval would have been too long. That is why I had to leave it out. But I should like to play it some day.

I was much more pleased with Frau Guhrau than I have been before. She is in many respects very different from what she used to be. And then there is also the fact that one sympathizes with her for her really sad plight. She told me with some emotion about her time with you, then about her brief marriage, on which she now looks back as on a desert. She sang beautifully at the concert, particularly *Das Veilchen*. I was delighted about the concert in Berlin and about the Heinrich Overture etc. At the first rehearsal Otten also played Wagner's Faust Overture, which I disliked exceedingly. I advised him very strongly to consider whether he ought to have the honour of being produced in Hamburg for the first time.

You know that we once discussed whether one ought to make complementary notes after trills in Bach. I said that my taste was strongly opposed to it. Now let me copy out for you a chapter out of my Ph. Em. Bach who, you must acknowledge, was the best of teachers, particularly of his father's works.

2nd Section, 3rd Part, § 13

" Trills above a note which is somewhat long, whether it goes down or up, always mean that there must be a complementary note. When a jump follows the note with a trill the complementary note also follows. The same also applies in regard to emphasized notes. When a trill is not followed by any note, at the end for instance, or when it comes over a sustained note etc. there is always a complementary note.

§ 14. Dotted notes followed by a short note going up may also have trills with complementary notes."

Later on he says " The complementary note must be played as quickly as the tr."

But we ought in any case to read Bach carefully together. . . . A thousand greetings from everybody and above all from me, Your JOHANNES.

I have bought a sonata for two pianos by W. Friedmann Bach (MS.) which is certainly very rare, and other things ! !

BRAHMS *to* CLARA.

Tuesday, Dec. 4.

What a long time it always seems to me now, dear Clara, before I get a letter from you. Every day I wait with longing and feel so certain that one will come that I am quite miserable if I am disappointed. Perhaps, after all, I will tell you something about my library. I have a MS. of Beethoven's ! !— a copy of the last A Flat major Sonata (110) with corrections and title written in by his own hand ! Avé gave it to me. He has a number of such MSS. and he was not even aware of the existence of some which I found upstairs. . . . And I also have B.'s Eighth Symphony, copied most beautifully, and many things by J. S. Bach and Ph. E. Bach etc. I also have a large number of books. I shall have them all sent by a bookseller to Düsseldorf. . . . I always write to you of a thousand things which really seem so irrelevant when I am thinking of you. I should like to talk to you only of agreeable things and always be sending you the fairest of wishes. But

I can never find the words to express these things, so you must content yourself with looking at my letters and then imagining all the beautiful things that might be in them. I regret every word I write to you which does not speak of love. You have taught me and are every day teaching me evermore to recognize and to marvel at what love, attachment and self-denial are. I am but rarely capable of sentiment, and then only when I am alone with my thoughts. The moment I write it all vanishes quickly away. I wish I could always write to you from my heart to tell you how deeply I love you, and can only beg you to believe it without further proof.

Please write to me at once and tell me when you have decided to come to Düsseldorf or Hamburg and whether and when I ought to go to Detmold!! With greetings from all, heartiest of all from me, Your JOHANNES.

BRAHMS *to* CLARA.

Saturday, Dec. 8.

I wanted to write to Detmold again, but I must first send you my greetings and my best thanks for the dear letter received this morning. You have told me nothing about your playing, particularly of Op. 106! Did you play it and how did it go? Beautifully? [1] How I should have loved to have heard the C major Symphony! [2] Out of the five it is my favourite, and of its four movements I prefer most decidedly the adagio. Only a German could have composed such an adagio. His deeply earnest eye alone could look so full of love when in the greatest suffering. A reminiscence of this beautiful adagio would interest you in Bach's *Musikalisches Opfer*, if you do not know it.

I have to play the C Sharp minor Studies here almost every evening and they are all enthusiastic about them. I also play Carnaval, Davidsbündler and Kreisleriana a good deal. Yesterday Jaëll [3] arrived here. We spent the evening together at Avé's. He raves about everything under the sun, not least of all about my things, and he played the F Sharp minor

[1] The sign of interrogation is struck out by Brahms himself.
[2] Schumann, Op. 61.
[3] Alfred Jaëll, pianist. Writing about him in May, 1858, Joachim says, " Jaëll is here, the same shallow, mercurial fellow as ever."

Sonata publicly in Frankfort.   He looks exceedingly comical,
so very well fed.   Wagner is his God, evidently a kind one,
for he can blaspheme him with impunity with the most atrocious
transcriptions.   He played some of his stuff to us yesterday,
also some arrangements of songs by Schumann and Franz.
It would be difficult to produce more wretched and more
shallow rubbish, and yet Hoffmeister gives him a year's salary
for producing such inferior work.   The first contract is to
last another eighteen months, so even if he wished to do so
he could not spare the world ; for a certain number of his
pieces must be printed.

I shall probably have to play your husband's Third Trio
at Otten's.   We only lack one cellist.   I am very much
looking forward to it.   To-day the Lobgesang will be played,
then Beethoven's Phantasy with chorus, and the chorus from
the Idomeneo, the andante and finale from Chopin's E major
Concerto (which I don't enjoy very much) and the Tannhäuser-
Lohengrin Phantasy.

[The end of this letter is missing.]

BRAHMS *to* CLARA.

HAMBURG, *Monday, Dec.* 10.

BELOVED CLARA,

This letter is to wish you a very good morning.   I should
have liked it better if it could have wished you good-night
after the very bad journey.   You will not be out of my mind
for a moment to-day.   You are always before my eyes ; I
can still see you sitting at the window of the railway-carriage
looking sadly out at us.   I hope you will not cry too much
to-day.   You ought to have seen me yesterday.   I was so
angry and ultimately so desperate.   We played trios at Otten's,
first Jaëll played Rubenstein's G minor, which is no better or
worse than his other things—now insignificant, then atrocious,
and anon having a touch of profundity.   Then I played your
husband's number 3, which aroused the wildest enthusiasm
such as was certainly not vouchsafed to Rubenstein, in spite
of Jaëll's brilliant playing and pyrotechnic skill.   Then J.
played Chopin's C minor Scherzo, and I the F by Bach.   J.
and I thereupon had dinner at Grädener's and I got more and
more to dislike this wine merchant's traveller.   Then on Gr.'s

small piano he tinkled out some of his own and Liszt's pieces until our hair stood on end. It appears that artists and members of the public have already told him many unpleasant things about Rubenstein, but for the moment he let fly about L. My head was absolutely swimming and I sat quite solemnly at the piano and played away in B and B Flat at the same time. We were all quite dizzy, Jaëll alone excepted. The whole day I longed just for one hour at home. How wearing it was, but how blissful I felt when a little before ten o'clock I was sitting at home and abandoned myself to silent bliss ! I have told them all that I am leaving to-morrow. But don't you believe it. I must be quiet for one whole day and leave Jaëll to go to Hanover. At the concert on Saturday he played very well. He plays with skill and *bravura*, but such trash. During his solo piece and the Tannhäuser I left the hall, but came back again just as he was playing again by request some execrable variations on an Italian melody. I may be wrong to talk to you about such rubbish, but I do it with the blessed feeling of having survived it. Please write here. With a thousand hearty greetings, my Clara, Your JOHANNES.

1856

HAMBURG, *Early Tuesday, Jan.* 15.

BELOVED CLARA,

I am now in Hamburg and my first morning shall be given up to you. I will first tell you about Leipsic and my journey, and then I shall pack up the books—a substantial greeting. In your last letter to Leipsic you were very anxious to have *Paul et Virginie* and I ought to have sent it from there and yet I always hesitated. Now I am sending it to you with a novel which I got from Joachim on the journey. He always has a lot of such things with him, which for the greater part he never reads. Charlotte Ackermann [1] was a beautiful fellow citizen of mine and her life is so arresting that it must interest you. But it is sad, it will make you cry a good deal, and if this frightens you you had better wait for Düsseldorf to read it. It may be a little bit long-winded, and I did not like the way the author first makes his characters act and think and then proceeds to give his own views and explanations. I have read *Gyges und sein Ring*.[2] I always enjoy Hebbel's beautiful language. Everything in him seems to me so different from Hermann Grimm, in whose whole style and everything I always think I see the blasé Berliner. I am never conscious of any warmth in his work ; almost everything in it is distasteful to me.

Paul et Virginie is a most enjoyable book. Read that on your journey. In every one of the scenes one can imagine oneself to be either P. or V. and one always feels delighted. That is the real thing, to be capable of happiness at the mere

---

[1] The title of a novel by Otto Müller which was widely read at the time. It is a tale connected with the Hamburg Theatre of the last century (1854).

[2] Which had just been published.

thought (or dream) of experiencing the joy and the pain of it all.

I was very much interested, as you may well imagine, in what you told me about M. Seebach,[1] particularly about the wreath. I should like to hear the *Haideknaben*.[2] I like it very much, best of the three. I think the general effect must be beautiful. I have just received the *Don Juan* from David and am greatly delighted with it. Somebody else has sent me forty variations by Archduke Rudolf (R.E.H.) on a theme by Beethoven (on account of their curiosity). Hanslick is also a writer on music. His book *Vom Musikalisch Schönen* [Concerning the Beautiful in Music] which Sahr thinks such a lot of, I tried to read ; but I found such a number of stupid things on first glancing through it, that I gave it up. . . . The evening at the Frege's was certainly a subtle revenge for so many boring hours in L. I played Bargiel's Trio first, the finale and particularly the theme of which met with violent disapproval, especially on the part of Frau Frege. To me they are the most characteristic and most sympathetic parts of the whole Trio. Then I played the Hebrew Songs with David, and Joachim's Variations, which gradually provoked not only indignation etc. in all the listeners without exception, but also bored them to tears. Frau Frege had already sung both my songs and yours. I am only very moderately interested in singing. The one thing that pleased me was the way she sang your folk song in A. She did not sing my best (the first) particularly well, and as for the others they interested me only remotely. David was the only person with whom I had a long talk about J. Joachim. If J. develops as I think and hope he will, his brooding and self-castigation will cease owing to the fact that others will castigate him, and then all these same people will in ten years' time show more enthusiasm over his present works than I do now or ever shall. There is more in J. than in all of us young people put together. Something must come of it all.

I did not write to you about Genchen's [3] wound on the head, because I thought that Bertha would be certain to make enough of it in her letters. It was not at all serious, if only

---

[1] Marie Seebach, at that time member of the Burg Theatre.
[2] Schumann, Op. 122.   [3] Eugenie.

no scar remains on her pretty little face ! If it does then I obviously cannot marry her, and I am no longer bound by anything ! A thousand greetings, my dearest Clara, and let me implore you to go on thinking as kindly of me as I do of you. Have the goodness to write as fully as possible about all that concerns your health and activities, Your faithful JOHANNES.

BRAHMS *to* CLARA.

HAMBURG, *Tuesday evening, Feb. 5.*

MY DEAR CLARA,

I should like to write to you about something very important. I have often wished to do so before and once I tore up what I wrote because I thought it would agitate you unnecessarily. I hope it will do so as little as possible. Just think it all over as quietly as you can.

The offer from Leipsic [1] really concerns you less than your husband. Your Leipsic friends refuse any longer to allow you to go on toiling and moiling to earn the money required by the dear man during his illness. David, Härtel, Voigt, Preusser, etc., insist upon paying a sum of seven to eight hundred thalers [£105–£120]—that is, the expenses entailed by the illness, in the first place for the past year, and to continue it annually. This is not a gift that they wish to make you but an offering of love and gratitude to a respected artist. When I was in L. the whole thing was settled one Sunday morning. They had been discussing it most eagerly for a whole year, as well as the various means by which it might be nicely and tactfully done. It is not improbable that they are still disputing about ways and means in true German fashion. Now if you had seven to eight hundred thalers annually from this source (because you cannot refuse it) would you need to undertake the dangerous journey to England ?

I have thought a good deal about writing all this to you, for you know how disinclined I am to suspect people of such nobility and generosity. But, if by means of this your journey were to become a matter of doubt, perhaps I might write to David (in my own name) so that you might hear something definite, and possibly everything there is to know about it.

[1] See *Life*, Vol. II, p. 131.

For fine resolutions don't bring one a farthing, and unfortunately this would not be the first time that they had ended in smoke. Write and tell me whether, even if all turned out as I expect, you would still require so much money, or could earn what is necessary on the return journey. Do not think that everything would then be in order, or that the money would be there or even on its way. Possibly all these fine words will remain fine words, for when once they are in black and white people find them moving enough as words alone. If, therefore, I write to David about it, just regard it as another concert tour. Incidentally I may tell you that only six or seven people are concerned in the matter and no one else knows anything about it.

You know your Leipsic friends and their circumstances better than I do. Just write and tell me what you think of the whole affair. But please don't allow yourself to be too much agitated by it. It is very questionable whether it is worth while. Just regard it as an experiment which, like the success of your English tour, is still doubtful. I would simply write to David that you had made arrangements for an extensive tour, that you did not feel disposed to abandon it lightly, and that I should be glad if he would write at once about the matter either to me or to yourself.

Now to something more cheerful, dear Clara; for one becomes so depressed by these matters. This evening young Otten presented me with a copy of *Paul et Virginie* (the library edition) beautifully bound. Owing to the fine binding I should like if possible to exchange my copy for yours. Would it be all right ? (I mean in view of the respective inscriptions !) Both in Hamburg and in Leipsic I have often tried to bargain for it, because I wanted it badly.

On Otten's birthday (Friday) I will play him Em. Phil. Bach's violon Son. with Böie.[1] I have a few myself, and in Düsseldorf I think you will be delighted with them, particularly with one in B Flat minor. I don't know whether they will ever be printed. . . .

I am enclosing the letter from the doctor. Surely it sounds more comforting, if only the progress continues. I am constantly turning over in my mind the possibility of a hydro-

---

[1] A violinist of Altona.

pathic establishment. We really must talk seriously about this matter and make inquiries. I have great faith in the healing power of water and—of life in the open. In any case I implore you most solemnly, if I should ever fall ill and you are close at hand, to send me at once to a homeopath. . . . And now, dear Clara, write to me to tell me what you think about the Leipsic project, whether I ought to do anything in the matter, and above all, whether it will make any difference to your touring plans. But do not let it weigh too heavily on your head (your beautiful head).

I suppose the Variations[1] did not please you. I now notice how long the post takes and what a time my sentence is in coming. Let me kiss you. I always think of you with the same love, which grows stronger and heartier every day. Continue to think kindly of Your faithful JOHANNES.

BRAHMS *to* CLARA.

HANOVER,[2] *Monday, Feb.* 17[18].

. . . Yesterday and to-day I played Joachim's magnificent Variations, and once again I have enjoyed them immensely, particularly the first one and the Hungarian. I do not forgive the people of Leipsic for having so little love and respect for J. that they cannot even listen quietly to something by him. We get on so well together that you would be delighted. Artists must have peculiar natures and must be particularly sensitive, for even those who agree most find it so difficult to stick together (in life). The faith and the opinions of genuine artists are probably all so definite that they are separated by them. I have made the most wonderful resolutions for my return, how industrious I shall be ! I believe that it is Goethe who says that he who would be a poet must command poetry.[3] I see every day how little I am still able to do this. I treat my Muse so shyly and tamely that it looks as if I doubted very much whether she would accept me. But I must learn to do it well. . . . To-day I bought a small pipe which

---

[1] This must refer to Pianoforte Variations on an Original Theme (Op. 21), which were composed about this time.

[2] Brahms had gone to Hanover towards the middle of February and not, as Kalbeck says, at the end of January.

[3] *Faust*, Part I, the Prelude in the theatre.

Joachim and I smoked during the evening. It made us both very ill, J. particularly. I have been admiring J. extremely in his practising of the Ninth. If only he were not often too profound for the musicians. But the ladies cannot of course help being delighted, and they are ! Altogether he is a fine fellow. There is more in J. than in all the young composers put together, and how much more ! I have the greatest respect for him. I cannot help thinking a good deal about what will come of it all. Who can tell ? One is so readily inclined to exalt to the skies. What sort of influence will life have on J. ?

. . . I wish you would deal with me as I do with the children. I never bring anything back for them. The more eagerly they expect it the better, for then they learn by experience and don't expect it a second time. I remind you that if I find that the scar still shows on Genchen's forehead the contract is cancelled !

If you see Volkmann, do write to me about him. He is surely very talented. Do you know his B Flat minor Trio and his A minor Quartet ? Get him to play his Trio to you. And now good-night, dear Clara. Sleep well. . . . Think of me and dream of a magnificent JOHANNES.

Of one better than this one.[1]

BRAHMS *to* CLARA.

[DÜSSELDORF] *Friday, Feb.* 22.

Here I am again sitting alone in my little room, drinking my afternoon coffee. I first had a look at everything so as

[1] One of Brahms' letters, dated February 12th, 1856, is missing from this series, but it is quoted in the German Edition of the *Life*, Vol. II, p. 404, and is as follows :—" It always saddens me to think that after all I am not yet a proper musician ; but I have more aptitude for the calling than probably many of the younger generation have as a rule. It gets knocked out of one. Boys should be allowed to indulge in jolly music ; the serious kind comes of its own accord, although the lovesick does not. How lucky is the man who, like Mozart, and others, goes to the tavern of an evening and writes some fresh music. For he lives while he is creating, though he does what he likes." This letter, in which Brahms concludes with the half comical and half desperate cry of admiration—" Such a Man ! ", and then crushes his pen peevishly down on the paper, can unfortunately no longer be found among Brahms' correspondence.

to be able to report fully to you.   Bertha only got my letter from Göttingen to-day, when I had already arrived.   I saw the two boys first, and they ran cheering towards me.   Bertha came up from downstairs.   She almost fainted with fright. The children are all looking splendid, healthy and happy and they can read and count now.   They can also sing songs by the dozen.   Bertha sees to that very nicely.   I then had a glance at my library and had to arrange it differently because of the substantial additions.   As for money I have about 200 thalers [£30].   I was forced to keep the whole of the 96 from Göttingen, because J. refused to take any. . . .   If the girls pass through here I will give them the History of the World, which I wished to present to them at Christmas.   I had a meal with the children to-day and enjoyed their company very much.   I am very glad now that I brought them nothing, for their good behaviour is all the more gratifying.   In my opinion children cannot help their joy in seeing one again being swamped by their joy over the presents one brings.   It must be so.

On my last evening in Hanover I got a letter from you, dear Clara, also one from J. which pleased me very much.   I have after all told J. about your earnings.   I cannot help thinking how beautiful it will be if both of us can march forward vigorously and become great musicians of the first rank. Each of us sets the other above himself, so what could be more natural than that we should be obliged to quarrel, so long as we quarrel with ourselves ? . . .

In my opinion there is no other really born musician among the younger men.   In this respect I cannot consider isolated works.   The whole man ought to be musical, ought to breathe music.   I am often at a loss to imagine what Joachim will become when he is fully developed.   I cannot understand why he thinks exactly the same of me, and yet, on the other hand, it often seems to me comprehensible. . . .   Do you not know Ferdinand Schubert in Vienna ?   You never write to me about him.   Have you ever looked at the whole of Schubert's works including the posthumous ones ?   His brother is said to have got them all arranged together in one room.   I was so glad to hear that you had played something of Schubert's.   If only for the dear name's sake one ought to do it, even if one could find nothing suitable (from the point of view of the public). If I were in any way a respected and respectable pianist I should have given a public performance of one sonata long ago (the one in G, for instance). Properly played, this could not fail to delight an audience.

Up to the present I have forgotten to enclose the letter from the doctor. What I think about hydropathic establishments remains the same. Whether Herr Schumann feels inclined to go or not ought not really to weigh with us. Men who have once tried hydropathic treatment and exercise in the open air generally continue these habits in private life. They become a second nature to them. I wonder what guarantee for the future there is in the sort of cure to be got in such establishments, or for instance, through magnetism. It is just this kind of cure that offers such a guarantee, and nothing is more necessary for our invalid.

It is very very lonely here without you and I look for you everywhere and constantly think of you. If only you could come soon, but just now I don't wish to worry you with my suggestions ; the journey is as bearable as any could be for you, and I comfort myself with that thought. But now I must close so that the letter may go off to-day. With thousands of greetings, Your JOHANNES.

BRAHMS *to* CLARA.

DÜSSELDORF, *Tuesday Evening, Feb. 26.*

I am a good child, am I not, beloved (or beloved friend) ? I have now bought some nice note-paper and envelopes [1] because my dear Clara wished me to. But by way of compensation I now have two pipes, and have just this moment lighted up the long Turkish one. Must I throw it away too ? As often as I fill my pipe I think how nice it would be if I had a beautiful tobacco-pouch (which would hold a good lot of tobacco) from the fair and noble lady. I cannot be bothered to buy one, for any cigar case answers my purpose just as

---

[1] The letter is written on yellow note-paper with a spray of roses stamped in the left-hand corner. Beneath the spray in Brahms' hand is written " For Clara." On the second sheet appear the words " Again simply for Clara," and underneath drawn with the pen are two roses.

well.   Yesterday I wrote a short *Benedictus* (canonical) for
four voices, which sounds very fine to me.   I am playing a
good deal, Bach and Beethoven, and always think of you
while I do so.   Very often I turn to one side in order to smile
at you over a beautiful passage.   This evening I have had
your room made comfortable for me and am writing there
now.

Yesterday I was at the theatre, and saw Kätchen von
Heilbronn acted.   But it was frightfully cut about.   Now
I love Kleist as I love few others.   I always read his
plays and his stories with the same delight and prefer them
to anything new. . . .   To-morrow I shall have to get up
early to receive the girls.[1]   What they will have to do!   I
shall give them three pages of pictures to cut out, and a book
in two parts to take with them.   I don't know how I am
going to do the sharing, but without it things will not go
straight.   I shall give it to them very cunningly, so that
neither feels that she has a special right to it.   Then they
can settle it between themselves.

Ferdinand is too lazy, Ludwig is too self-willed, and Felix
is even more so.   Genchen is for the moment just a little bit
too passionate.   But they are all very good and charming.
Yesterday Ferdinand received a number of smacks because
he would not read.   There was a tremendous confabulation
as to what each should give to the girls to-morrow.   Frl. Leser
is giving oranges and chocolates, Fr. Agnes apples, Bertha
sandwiches, and I, without saying a word, books.

Frl. Wittgenstein too expects lessons to begin again on
Saturday.   She shall be made to play Bach's Inventions and
Symphonies so that she may become confused in her raptures
and learn to recognize that one cannot and need not be always
" ohing " and " ahing " in dealing with music.   I wonder
what it will make her feel like.

I was delighted with your letter to-day, especially on learning
that you had heard the gipsies playing.   I have long wished
to do so.   I should like to study them, to remember and make
a note of their melodies.   In any case I am very much looking
forward to what you will have to tell me about the Hun-
garians and the gipsies.   They are a curious people.   I could

---

[1] Clara's eldest daughters, who were travelling *via* Hanover to Leipsic.

not get the truth about them out of Reményi,[1] he told too
many lies about them.

. . . Bertha sends hearty greetings. . . . I long for you
to be back, every day more and more. Good-night, with a
thousand hearty greetings, Your JOHANNES.

BRAHMS *to* CLARA.

DÜSSELDORF, *May* [2] 16.

MOST BELOVED CLARA,

What a lovely letter I had to-day and it was so very long
that it was just as if we were sitting together and having
the most delightful of talks. . . . I am overjoyed with the
Shakespeare and when you return I shall look forward to your
always reading it aloud to me while I listen attentively.
Reading it alone does not give me the proper amount of
pleasure. I no longer know enough about the pronunciation
etc. I don't think you are altogether right about Ries and
Wegler.[3] My memory is not sufficiently good to be able to
say for certain, but what would become of all historical research
and biographies if undertaken with an eye to the susceptibilities
of the subject ? The sort of biography which you might
write about your Robert would certainly make very beautiful reading, but would it as certainly have any value for
history ?

I know little about the Overture to *König Stephan*, and
have never heard it. But its Opus number is over 100 ! I
take it that it will be A 1. You must not take Beethoven's
letters to Ries about *Missa*, Op. 106, and money matters, too
seriously. He was never so badly in need of money as that.
It must have been merely worry or anxiety (unnecessary). . . .
I have had a letter from Hamburg saying that everything
is all right there, although it is still very cold ; but I suppose
it is even colder where you are. Here the chestnut trees
are in blossom, the spring here is like our whole summer ;
really almost over ? I shall take no notice at present of the

---

[1] Eduard Reményi, a Hungarian violinist.

[2] Clara had returned to Düsseldorf on the 16th of March, and on
the 8th of April she had started on her much discussed visit to England.
See *Life*, Vol. II, pp. 130–134.

[3] *Biographical Essays on Beethoven*, by Wegeler and Ries (1838).

recent unexpected attack on me.[1] But one thing I should
like to beg of you—do not ever throw away a pretty ribbon
from your hat, or anything of that sort, but give it to me so
that I may tie it round your letters or something equally
precious, or I might use it as a book-marker. Don't laugh
at me ! With a thousand greetings, and loving messages,
Your JOHANNES.

BRAHMS *to* CLARA.

May 24, Evening.

BELOVED CLARA,

I had written you a letter this afternoon, but now I have
received such a nice long one from you that the smallest
token of gratitude I can give is to regard what I have already
written as too bad and begin again. I am just as much persuaded as I ever was, in fact more so after your letter of to-day,
that you ought to come back if you can't carry on any longer.
Even if you don't fulfil your present engagements you will
get just as many offers next year, or another year. Because
everybody is well aware that it is only on account of your
health. I have often thought—how often I cannot say—of
joining you. But I was afraid it might be regarded as improper,
for everything gets into the papers. And as it was impossible
for me to regard the consequences of your premature return
from England as seriously as you do I was all the less able to
make up my mind to come. I am convinced that owing
to your poor state of health you can quite calmly cancel
everything, and they will receive you just as kindly next year.
I should love to come. But would it be right ? If Bargiel
went too then nobody could say anything. But surely it
would cause too much comment if I, who have no business
over there, were to come ? I have already thought that
by next year I might be a fairly good organ virtuoso, and
then we could travel about together, and I would let my piano
playing go hang in order to be able always to go on tour with
you. It is a remarkable thing, I am surely not a sensitive
man, I should have thought I was quite free from nerves or
prepossessions, and yet something has been telling me all
day that I ought to write to you about our wills, a subject

---

[1] Compare the next letter.

which has occupied my mind for some time. I am always wanting to make mine, but my divine indolence prevents me, however serious my mood may be. As far as you are concerned it is a very good thing that you should have provided for every contingency, but for heaven's sake dispatch this kind of business with as little excitement as possible. By all means think of all conceivable eventualities, but don't dwell on the most distressing, and don't get over-anxious about it, just as one leans on the banisters in order to go safely without necessarily thinking of falling.

I wish you would put a note on all my letters that after you they belong to me alone. This is what I intend to do with yours and will do in the future. But I continue to hope you will realize that you can come back sooner. You must do so. In any case it is advisable. You must hope to gain further recognition another year. In your present state you may perhaps be unable to turn the consideration of the English public to account, because you are ill.[1] " I shall take no notice at present of the recent unexpected attack on me." I mean the one about " thou." My idea was that I could not avail myself immediately of your kindness and love as you might regret it later on. That is why I always continued to write to you in the second person plural. I take it then that all these tactics of siege and assault had some connection with the unanswered question ? Or is that not so ? . . . The organs in the concert halls of which you speak may be very practical for us next year, but in any case they are very beautiful. I am so sorry to hear that you occasionally tear up one of your letters, because I should be glad to receive ever more and more of them, no matter how sad they were. I don't expect jolly ones. In the chest devoted to Stockhausen's things I am putting a precious volume of music, from which you must often play of an evening and pick out my favourites. I wish you could bind up your letters for me as nicely and I wish it would always be necessary to do so. . . . With a thousand greetings, dear Clara, and hoping you will continue to think kindly of me, Your JOHANNES.

[1] The original of this sentence is so obscure, owing to the writer's extremely loose German, that this can be regarded only as an approximate rendering of his meaning.—Tr.

BRAHMS *to* CLARA.

DÜSSELDORF, *May* 31, *Evening*, 8 *o'clock*.

MY BELOVED CLARA,

I wish I could write to you as tenderly as I love you and tell you all the good things that I wish you. You are so infinitely dear to me, dearer than I can say. I should like to spend the whole day calling you endearing names and paying you compliments without ever being satisfied. If things go on much longer as they are at present I shall have some time to put you under glass or to have you set in gold. If only I could live in the same town with you and my parents. How often have I wished that this could be!

I quite forgot to enclose the programme [1] the other day, so do so now. Yesterday at midday only fifteen tickets had been sold in Cologne, and on the night itself it was not very full. So much for Cologne. But he sang the Müller songs magnificently. I don't think I have ever enjoyed singing as much as I did yesterday evening. The only annoying feature was the eternal noise. It is extraordinary how absorbed one becomes in the songs and what experiences they give one.

Get some one to sing them to you consecutively. Don't be satisfied with one, but do not forget to read the verses first carefully, so as to get a complete appreciation of the whole. I have a golden rule—always to be as rowdy as possible in the evening at bedtime, and to be boisterously jolly. It is a habit I have kept from my childhood days. I don't mind sleeping in company a bit. Yesterday with Stockhausen, Jahn [2] and Dietrich we played the fool in every possible way, and I enjoyed it thoroughly and did not get tired.

Yesterday Stockhausen gave me a sort of match-box like the one I gave you to take away, and when I opened it I saw that there was gold inside. I gave it to him back and ran away because I did not want any money at all. But after he had left to-day I found it in my cigar case. Five Frederichs d'or.[3] I must confess that I really am fond of money and gladly pocket large sums; but it worries me all the same.

---

[1] Of a concert Brahms gave with Stockhausen in Cologne on the 29th of May.

[2] Professor Otto Jahn, Mozart's biographer.

[3] About 4 guineas.

Will you try to find out whether he had anything left over, otherwise I prefer not to keep it. Don't trouble about sending a writing-case here for the 8th of June if it is impossible. Early to-day in Cologne I bought your Robert the largest atlas I could find, eighty-three gigantic maps beautifully bound and new. To my astonishment I never bought a book for myself at the secondhand bookseller's. I shall take the Kosmos-Atlas to him myself. If your writing-case should come then please allow me to make him a present of the atlas. But only if you do not mind and you are not anxious to make him a lot of presents. But I really think that two atlases ought to be enough. Too many things might excite him. I say this to comfort you in case your present should not arrive. The large atlas is magnificent. . . .

N.B. The doctors [1] told me nothing new about Robert except that for a long time he had been asking for a very large atlas. Now for your letter. I am coming to Ostend [2] and we shall have a look at the sea together. I would not like to remain too long in Antwerp. I prefer to spend the time on the Rhine.

I took a Klems [3] with me to Cologne and Bonn. The *Kölnerzeitung* gives me unstinted praise. And now another joke. Yesterday evening we were some time together (in Cologne). Hiller, Rheinthaler, and Bischof arrived rather late. Before I was introduced to him he dashed towards me, shook my hand vigorously and congratulated me warmly. I had not expected this in the least, for I have never visited him and my position as a *Zukunftmusiker* [a musician of the future] makes me really his natural foe. . . . Polyphony means many voices, and nowadays one must distinguish carefully between polyphony and a mere mass of chords. A volume of sounds from Bach should not be compared with the latter. . . . I am delighted over the increase in your library. But do write me a nice letter soon. Your letters are like

[1] Ever since April the doctors had pronounced Schumann's condition as incurable. See *Life*, Vol. II, p. 236.

[2] Brahms met Clara in Antwerp on July 4. On the following day they made their joint excursion to Ostend to show Brahms the sea. On the 6th they returned to Düsseldorf. On the 29th Schumann died at Endenich.

[3] Brahms means probably a Klems grand piano, i.e. an instrument made by the firm of Klems.—Tr.

kisses. My parents' birthdays will be in a few days. I have
sent them fifty thalers [£7.10.0], with the pressing request
that they should spend them and devote one thaler to punch
and cakes. I wish I could be there. And also there. And
have my Clara with me here too. Affectionate greetings,
Your JOHANNES.

BRAHMS *to* CLARA.

Friday midday, Dec. 4 [*5th*] [1]

MY CLARA,

. . . Your remarks about the value which I attach to your
own and J.'s applause are amateurish. You know perfectly
well how pleased I am if my things please my friends, and
you also know whose praise I value most. But if I think of
the actual value of the thing itself, the matter is of course
different. Then I should like to have some one who, after
approaching it in an unfriendly spirit, was compelled to approve
of it subsequently.

Joachim philosophizes and thinks a good deal about music
and everything that may help it to prosper, and it is because
I think some of his ideas so splendid that I am always encour-
aged if my things come up to his standard. It is just like the
various grades of the law. The highest tribunal of all, however,
is your loving nature and its yea.

I am not over-fond of Scarlatti owing to the similarity of
his pieces (in form and character). But I like to play individual
pieces well enough and I happen to have a good volume of
them. . . . Your remarks about young people remind me
of Otten's sons. He complains bitterly that not one of them
will work ; but I blame him for this, as he has gratified their
every whim. They have all the toys and all the books they
ask for. They have looked at all the large illustrated books
in their own home, and the consequence is that the other
day, when I was trying to think of a Christmas present for
the younger one, I was at an absolute loss. I even ascribe his

---

[1] After Schumann's death Brahms and Clara had gone to Gersau
with Brahms' sister and had stayed there from the 14th of August till
the 13th of September. Brahms had then remained in Düsseldorf
until the 21st of October, when he went to Hamburg. The memorial
celebrations for Schumann had taken place on the 22nd of November.

pale cheeks (in spite of the fact that he gets lots of exercise) to his being surfeited in mind and body. It would certainly be splendid if you were to come on Tuesday, but I will not try to persuade you to do so. I know that if you can you will get away quickly enough. I shall be on tenter-hooks now every day. Yesterday we had some music at Avé's. Everybody likes my A Flat minor Fugue [1] very much indeed. On Sunday I shall try it again on the organ. With heartiest wishes for your welfare, and begging you to kiss me, Your JOHANNES. [2]

[1] A Fugue in A Flat minor for Organ without any Opus number.
[2] Clara celebrated Christmas with Brahms and her four youngest children in Düsseldorf.

1857

Brahms *to* Clara.

DETMOLD, *Sunday, early, Oct.* 11.

MY CLARA,[1]

What a pleasant surprise you gave me yesterday evening. I returned home an hour before my *Singverein* [2] and I found your parcel awaiting me—first the beautiful letter so nice and long, and then the magnificent present. I cannot reconcile myself to your spending so much money, but apart from that I acknowledge that the gift has given me the greatest pleasure. It is so exquisitely tasteful and practical and provokes such pleasant expectations of letters such as the one which I found enclosed. A thousand thanks, and more thanks still for your letter. I can see you looking out of your letter and smiling at me. My dear Clara, you really must try hard to keep your melancholy within bounds and see that it does not last too long. Life is precious and such moods as the one you are in consume us body and soul. Do not imagine that life has little more in store for you. It is not true. It is true only of a very few people. If you abandon yourself entirely to your present depression you will not enjoy happy intervals as much as you might. The more you endeavour to go through times of sorrow calmly and accustom yourself to do so, the more you will enjoy the happier times that are sure to follow. Why do you suppose that man was given the divine gift of hope ? And you do not even need to be anxious in your hope, for you know perfectly well that pleasant months will follow the present unpleasant ones, just as they do every period of unhappiness. Do not make light of what I say, because I mean it. Body and soul are ruined by persisting in melancholy,

---

[1] In the last days of September Clara had moved from Düsseldorf to Berlin. The change caused her much distress, and she was unable to shake off the depression which she ultimately felt.

[2] A choral society.

and one must at all costs overcome it or not let it come into being. It is just as if one fed one's body on the unhealthiest food and comforted oneself with the reflection that in the summer one would try the milk cure. For a while the latter might do good, but the body would be debilitated and would quickly perish. . . .

You must seriously try to alter, my dearest Clara. Every morning make the determined resolution to spend the day more equably and happily. Passions are not natural to mankind, they are always exceptions or excrescences. The man in whom they overstep the limits should regard himself as an invalid and seek a medicine for his life and for his health. The ideal and the genuine man is calm both in his joy and in his sorrow. Passions must quickly pass or else they must be hunted out. Consider yourself for the moment, my dear Clara, as a serious invalid and without necessarily being anxious, but on the contrary, with calm and perseverance, try to look after yourself. Forgive all this chatter, but I have never learnt to arrange my thoughts and to express them clearly. Just think all this over and act accordingly, and then everything will be better and you will feel happier every day, and all those who belong to you will be made happier through you.

Yesterday I had the *Singverein*. While practising I felt as if I had already been at the work for twenty-five years. My voice is of no little use to me on these occasions, because I have to shout so loud, and it is an advantage which like every other I exploit to the full. My voice sounds quite majestic. While the choir is singing I exercise it and yell above the din, really only on my own account in order to get practice. We intend to do the *Zigeunerleben* [1] and I am sure it will soon go splendidly. How childishly easy such things are compared with old church music, and my *Salve Regina* [2] is easy as such things go. This piece would please you very much. I can't tell you very much about Rovetta, except that he lived about 1640. Both pieces please the singers very much, and they are taking great pains with them. The *Zigeunerleben* is exquisite and sounds wonderful. Yesterday with Bargheer [3]

[1] By Schumann, probably in Grädener's arrangement.
[2] By Rovetta.
[3] Conductor at Detmold at that time.

I had to accompany the Prince in his songs.   I hope it won't often happen. . . .   I cannot agree with you about Debrois' [1] essay.   What he writes about me (as the charming principal figure) I found sensible beyond expectation, with the exception of one or two obvious absurdities, as, for instance, when he says that my B minor Var.[2] was not intentionally based upon the corresponding piece by your husband.   Surely it is as plain as a pike-staff !   N.B. the piece in question follows upon the theme in F Sharp minor, so the whole thing is quite simple. About Joachim he only talks nonsense.   The unfortunate part about Debrois is that here and there he makes such amateurish blunders that the people of Leipsic could cut him up frightfully.   But whoever wishes to write against this Liszt clique must talk nonsense.   For these people hold their own thanks only to the lowest and most confused personalities and gossip, and one must expose all this if one wishes to destroy their lair.   The most stupid part of it is that this little fellow Debrois insists on regarding himself as the apex of the musical world.   Who to-day can ever be in a position to say that anything has reached its limit when it can never have any limit at all.   Little people have always wanted to put full stops after geniuses, even after Mozart, if we go back to an earlier generation. . . .   Only a creative genius can be convincing in art. . . .   Send me a description of your new abode soon.   I am still capable of being surprised.   Every day I think of the joy I shall have in going to Hamburg at the New Year.   Now I shall exult inwardly.   With hearty greetings, my beloved Clara . . . and remembrances to Woldemar, Your JOHANNES.

Go for walks and look through Woldemar's things carefully and sympathetically.

BRAHMS *to* CLARA.

[DETMOLD] *Monday, early, Nov.* 9.
DEAR CLARA,

You will now be on the way to Munich, possibly already there.   If so you will be sending to the post to see whether there is a letter from me.   I send you the heartiest greetings

[1] Debrois van Bruyk of Vienna.
[2] One of the Variations in Brahms' Op. 9.

from here, and hope that everything will go well with you in Munich and that the time will pass by quickly. Do not miss going to see the galleries and museums if possible, and if you have done so already you will probably find time to do so again. You should also visit the Walhalla and the Bavaria on your first Sunday. You can certainly find time for that and should not miss it on any account. If only there were a Walhalla here that I could visit, for my holidays continue indefinitely.[1] I hope the family won't expect me to make up for this lost time at the end. I could not very well do that. I am practising Mendelssohn's G minor Concerto so that one day I may really be quite lovable. I visited Kanzleirat von Rosen[2] yesterday. He told me a lot about your husband and also asked me many questions about you both.

I don't find the *Niebelungenlied* at all difficult to understand, and whenever I get a chance of reading it, it gives me great pleasure. I am now studying a little Latin, that is to say I have begun by writing out the declensions, and I hope that I shall be able to persevere in it. I am much too lazy. I might feel very miserable about this if for this also I had not too little capacity. . . . How is Nettchen[3] getting on ? I am sure you like having her with you. Greet her for me. . . . Farewell, dear Clara. With heartiest greetings, your JOHANNES.

[1] The noble family were away.

[2] Gisbert Rosen, a friend and fellow student of Schumann's at Heidelberg, afterwards Senior Judge at Detmold.

[3] Nettchen Jungé, sister of Elise Jungé, Frl. Leser's companion. She was accompanying Clara on her concert tour.

1858

Hamburg, *Wednesday, Jan.* 27.

Beloved Clara,

I have at last received your dear letter which was a long time coming. What a pest about your toothache ! To think that this trouble should have come to you now ! There was a meeting of the *Verein* [1] yesterday and it was very full. Avé, Grädener, Hafner, etc. were there. The quintet went very well, but the first violin was bad, and we only have an upright piano. Afterwards Mozart's musical joke [2] was most excellently performed. I had never heard it before and could not help laughing loudly over this priceless bit of fun. Have you ever heard it, or do you know anything about it ? . . . I have just received Erlach's Folk Songs (four thick volumes) from Avé. My library can never dwindle. I hear nothing of Joachim (I wrote to ask him for my Concerto movement) and I begin to fear that after all he is really ill.

You ought to bear the idea of Stuttgart [3] in mind. It would not be at all a bad thing if you found it at all profitable. It probably depends a good deal upon the Crown Prince, for the King is old and could only pay you your salary for a year or two. It is surely an unhappy state of affairs to have to support yourself and your family in Berlin by means of lessons. In the summer we shall then be able to explore the country in Swabia and heaven knows where else. Are you aware that your husband gave me my first lessons in chess ? I ought at least to return this kindness, and I hope awaken your interest in the game.

[1] This refers to the newly founded Hamburg Musical Society of which Otten was the founder.

[2] Probably the Terzetto for Soprano, Tenor and Bass, " *Das Bandel.*"

[3] Clara had been offered a post at the Conservatoire at Stuttgart with a fixed salary.

I have got rid of the Wasielewski [1] biography. I shall not buy it after all. It is impossible to derive the smallest pleasure from it and I believe that the most impartial readers will come to the same conclusion. In my opinion only a good friend or an admirer can write a biography. Impartiality is a good thing (it is also very difficult), but it must not degenerate into coldness. One can have no possible use for narrow-mindedness, and where it is found, as almost everywhere in this case, it is really unnecessary to quarrel about loftier matters. But to write and read a biography of your Robert ought to be a joy. . . . I and all mine greet you heartily. Spare yourself as much as you can, and keep as cheerful as possible. Wholly yours, JOHANNES.

BRAHMS *to* CLARA.

HAMBURG, *Wednesday, Feb.* 24.

BELOVED CLARA,

I ought not to wait till there is something to answer. Your bad arm and your renewed concert activities must teach me patience. To cheer you up let me tell you of a little musical episode that has happened here. The Schubert Duet is already back at my place and will not be performed. [2] Grund told me that on the piano he did not like the work at all, but that the instrumentation was beautiful—the work itself tedious and unmelodious. They tried it once the other day and after the rehearsal the conductor Lindenau and the rest confirmed this verdict and the work was laid aside.

There are no melodies in it !

It is boring !

Otten's concert was not very good. They hurried the Schubert Symphony to death and the Overture to the *Bride of Messina* fared even worse. . . . A boring Concerto by Spohr

[1] This refers to Wasielewski's Biography of Schumann. In reply to these remarks of Brahms Clara appears to have suggested that Joachim and Brahms might write one, and in a subsequent letter Brahms replied that skill as well as a good heart was necessary for the work, and therefore that neither he nor Joachim could ever undertake it.— TR.

[2] Joachim's arrangement of the piece for orchestra.

and an even more boring one by Bott [1] himself were also
not edifying.   The lady singer was fairly good and the *Robes-*
pierre Overture [2] concluded the entertainment.   The score lay
open on the desk.   Otten looked into it, caught hold of it,
held it up in the air, shut the book up and handed it to Böie,
who stared at him with astonishment.   Then Otten extended
his two wings and—started off with all the wondrous beauties,
which his magic wand was to conjure out of the orchestra,
in his own head.

I did not see Otten again, but I really must decide to go
out to him one of these days.   On the other hand he might
also have contrived to give me a word of thanks for playing
at his old penny popular. . . .

Do not be surprised, dear Clara, if I do not speak about
my own works.   I do not like to and I cannot do so.   All of
you, particularly you, think me different from what I am.
I am never, or very seldom, in the least bit pleased with myself.
I never feel quite happy, but fluctuate between contentment
and depression.   But I am so little given to complaining to
others about my lack of genius and skill, and dislike doing
it so much, that I naturally look different from what I feel.
In addition I feel so happy when at times I am able to please
other people and particularly yourself, for instance, that people
notice my mood and think that I am self-satisfied and confident of victory.   Oh, if one could only look inside oneself
and find out how much of the divine one has in one's constitu-
tion ! . . .

Write and let me know how your arm is getting on, and
let me tell you that I have been suffering for some weeks with
a bad finger,[3] which looks as though it were going to last for
some time, as I am constantly forgetting to dress it and make
no attempt to restrict my playing on account of it.   It is a
sort of fissure which has been aggravated by the cold and the
heat.   Farewell, beloved being.   Write to me at length about
yourself.   Your JOHANNES.

Everybody sends you greetings.

[1] Jean Joseph Bott, a pupil of Spohr's.
[2] By Litolff.
[3] This trouble appears to have recurred all through his life.

BRAHMS *to* CLARA.

HAMBURG, Sunday afternoon, Feb. 28.

BELOVED CLARA,

All yesterday evening and to-day I had to copy out the adagio and rondo (the piano part and the score) and correct the parts in a great hurry, that they might be duplicated; both copyists were waiting for them. Please, therefore, forgive this belated and perhaps short letter, as I have written enough. So my concerto [1] will not be played here either! The whole thing is typically Hamburgian. Crantz will not give me his Erard, but with the utmost amiability offers me all kinds of old tin kettles. . . . There is no piano to be had anywhere else and I don't want to appeal to [Frau?] Apel because I don't want to be under any obligation to her. I shall probably go to Hanover at the end of this week, or shall I wait for you? But if you come you would probably prefer to remain quietly in Berlin, and quietly or not quietly I should be with you. I got your dear letter from Geneva. From the bad music in which you have had to take part and particularly from that to which you have had to listen, you will soon recover. You must play to me a good deal. I can do so ever less and less. Quite seriously.

Allgeyer, Allgeyer! I should have written to him long ago but I did not know his address. You can readily believe that, all the time I was reading the Wasielewski biography, I was thinking of the possibility of a rejoinder etc. But in skimming it I could find nothing which made such a step either necessary or seemly. I also thought that I might find among his letters to Schumann one signed " your very humble servant," with the rest in a similar style, which I might have printed as a supplement to his book. But before opening up such a scandal one should think it well over. In order to refute his criticisms one would have to write fresh ones. But is this our particular function, our *forte*? Should we censure him for passing over the most magnificent songs and arias in silence and dwelling on something that just happens to suit his taste? Such blunders bring their own punishment upon them, for whoever reads even the most superficial notice of the

---

[1] *Concerto in D minor*, Op. 15.

Myrthen, the Eichendorff, and the Heine songs [1] etc., will hear the heavenly music ringing in his ears, and will be bound to slam the book to for a while when such discords as Wasielewski's break upon his ear. But we must look at the book more carefully together and think it over.

This evening I am playing my concerto to Avé and Grädener (who do not know it at all). I have practised the first movement terribly hard. I don't think that you will be able to endure it, or does my fear of the performance with all the other instruments exaggerate my qualms ? But I wish that some day I could hear the adagio and the rondo played in public by you. Perhaps you might play it next week at Detmold and I would conduct. [2]

Farewell, dearest Clara. Write to me often and send me a definite date, and tell me what I should do about Hanover. Heartily yours, JOHANNES.

Greeting to Rieter [3] and Kirchner, [4] although I do not know them.

BRAHMS *to* CLARA.

                                        HAMBURG, *June* 25.
BELOVED CLARA,

. . . Do exactly as you please with my things, and if you are sure it will not be misused have anything that is lucky enough to be liked copied out. All I would beg of you is not to allow your own enthusiasm to fire others to a pitch which they will afterwards misunderstand. You expect much too prompt and warm a recognition of any talent which you happen to appreciate. Art is a republic. You should accept this principle much more whole-heartedly than you do. You are much too aristocratic. I cannot deal with this fully now, but some time when we are together I shall do so. This struck me very forcibly in the matter of Henkel, and in another way with regard to Grimm. Do not confer a higher rank upon

[1] Brahms is here referring to Robert Schumann's Op. 25 (26 songs), Op. 39 (12 songs) and Op. 24 (9 songs).—TR.

[2] She played it for the first time on the 3rd of December, 1861, at a Philharmonic Concert in Hamburg.

[3] Rieter-Biedermann, the well-known music publisher.

[4] Theodor Kirchner, who was then at Winterthur.

any artist, and do not expect the minor ones to look up to him as something higher, as consul. His ability will make him a beloved and respected citizen of the said republic, but no consul or emperor. But more of this when we meet. Write to me again soon, and do not often keep me waiting as long as you have this time. Do not regard my folk songs as anything more than the most sketchy studies, otherwise you would be most dissatisfied with them. But possibly in one or two of them you will find a promise of better things. You might improve the accompaniment and try to make it freer. With love, Yours, JOHANNES.

CLARA *to* BRAHMS.

WIESBADEN,[1] *July* 1.

I cannot tell you, my dear Johannes, how much I have enjoyed your folk songs. If only I could express all that my heart feels about them! But I become ever more and more convinced that I must learn to hold it in check. It pains me terribly to have to do so towards you in musical matters, for you should and must know that I am not influenced in what I say by blind enthusiasm for you. Has it not happened often enough that I was quite unable to enjoy something or other of yours, and that I assumed a definite stand against you in the matter? Does blind enthusiasm behave in this way? And when you suspect me of wishing to press my views upon others you seriously misunderstand me. I express myself warmly when I think I have found a sympathetic listener —a thing a woman's heart is quick to discern. But you stand much too high and are much too precious in my opinion for me even to allow your name to pass my lips in the presence of people who are unfriendly or cold towards you. With men like Grimm, Joachim, Woldemar, Kirchner, etc., I express my feelings hot from my heart, but from such people I expect a prompt appreciation of the creations of your genius.

I wish you would interpret my feelings a little more generously than you often do. Anybody reading what you have written me about my enthusiasm would think me an extremely hysterical person who worships her friend like a god. And, after all, what does it all amount to? All I did was to show Herr

[1] Clara spent June and July in Wiesbaden to drink the waters.

Bogler your choral prelude, and play it with him, and then
when I saw his delight, to give him, not without great joy
—this I readily confess—the name of the composer. You
are not, there, dear Johannes, either to see or hear when I
speak about you to others. Honestly I do not get excited
about it. But that I am often mightily captivated by the
wealth of your genius, that you always seem to be one on
whom heaven has showered its fairest gifts and that I love you
and honour you for so many magnificent qualities—all this
is true, dearest Johannes, and has taken deep root in my heart.
So do not try to kill it all in me by your cold philosophizing
—it is impossible.

It might make me more cautious in what I say to you,
but why should you wish, by your coldness, to destroy the
beautiful confidence which enables me to tell you everything ?
You have already done this, for in the matter of your folk
songs I feel that I have not the courage to tell you the joy
most of them have given me. Perhaps next time it will be
easier to unburden my heart without restraint. I am now
seriously studying the concerto and cannot disguise my joy
over it, although your reproaches still haunt me. They have
pained me more than anything has done for a long time,
because they were so unjust. I should probably have done
better to be silent about it all. But my heart was too full.
I have always considered myself so fortunate to be able to
be to you a friend who understands you, and who is in a position
to recognize your value as a musician and as a man. And now
come these reproofs. . . . I am very much upset by what
you write about Göttingen.[1] That you so much dislike the
idea of going there is hateful to me. If Frl. Werner [2] were
not going to the Tyrol for six or eight weeks I would have
changed all my plans. But this is impossible owing to the
children and their bathing, which I must be there to super-
intend if Frl. W. is away. But let me make the following
proposal to you, painful though it is to me. If you have
such a great desire for work why not remain quietly at

[1] The letter is missing. See *Life*, Vol. II, pp. 164–165, for details
about Clara's stay in Göttingen with the children.

[2] Elizabeth Werner had become Clara's housekeeper in May and had
undertaken the education of the girls who were at home.

Hamburg, where I could pay you a visit later on if you wish to see me ? I should prefer the pain of being separated from you than to see you unhappy on my account in Göttingen because you were forced to be idle, although I cannot for the life of me see why you could not also work there if, for instance, you were to lock yourself up every morning and insisted upon doing so. I am waiting for another letter, my Johannes. If only I could find longing as sweet as you do. It only gives me pain and fills my heart with unspeakable woe. Farewell ! Think kindly of Your CLARA.

Write to me as often as you can. One requires to be cheerful during a cure and whence would good cheer come to me if not from you ?

CLARA *to* BRAHMS.

WIESBADEN, *July* 8.

A thousand thanks for your dear letter which made me very happy. It is a long time since you have written me such a nice one. . . . I cannot tell you how glad I am about your new appointment.[1] They were such a long time writing that I began to be anxious. It will enable you to earn money in the most pleasant manner, much more pleasant than giving lessons in Hamburg, for you would have to give such a lot to make up that sum. Have you accepted it for another three months ? From the 1st of October to when ? Have you not hinted that you would also like to work with the orchestra ? And thus a very pleasant time awaits you, and what a reception they will all give you ! But I must beg you, dear friend, not to ascribe all I say about the folk songs to the songs themselves. One has only to consider how different the songs are with and without your accompaniment. You yourself must know only too well that such accompaniments, such interpretation, such a grasp of the character of each song, and such a profound combination of melody and harmony, often so delicately blended that one cannot think of the one apart from the other, could only be the work of a genius, of a nature full of poetry and music, such as you are and such as you know you are. This conviction stands imbedded in my soul like an immovable rock. Once more you will smile at my enthu-

[1] In Detmold.

siasm. But who, except you and your music, is responsible for this ? The other day I was reading something *à propos* of enthusiasm in a letter from Goethe to Schiller, in which, referring to a criticism of German literature by Herder in which he metes out praise and blame with a sparing hand and turns and twists about with every sign of reserve and caution, etc. Goethe says, " It seems to me that if writings like actions are not criticized with loving sympathy and with a certain enthusiastic partiality, there is little in it and it is not worth troubling about. [I think this is going rather far.] The only reality, and that which begets further realities, is the pleasure, joy and sympathy we find in things." [1]

If Goethe could say this, ought I not to feel myself above your censure ? I would gladly tell you more about certain details in your songs, for instance, about an A in the *Reiter* and how beautiful it is, and about a wonderfully touching C in *Der Tote* [*Gast*]. . . .

[The end of the letter is missing.]

CLARA *to* BRAHMS.

BERLIN, *Monday, Nov.* 8.

. . . Now you say that I would have given you some pleasure by doing so, I am sorry that I did not write to you about the Hungarian Dances,[2] for you know how I like to please you. I only refrained because I feared that you might say something unkind to me, as you have so often done in similar cases before. You know, without my telling you, how hard it must have been for me, because it would have given me the greatest joy to write to you about them. I am also thinking of playing them in Vienna and Pesth. I am only doubtful whether I should play them all, or only the one in C minor. . . . Think of me and write to me soon, Your CLARA.

[1] This refers to the third volume of Herder's *Humanitätsbriefen*. Goethe's letter to Schiller is dated the 14th of June, 1796, and the passage above quoted ends with the following words : " Everything else is vain and merely destructive."

[2] On the 14th of October, Clara had for the first time played Brahms' *Tänze in Ungarische Weise*, from the MS.

CLARA *to* BRAHMS.

VIENNA, *Dec.* 9.

I would have written to you again sooner, but was so worn out by my concert last Sunday that I could not. . . . After my concert, which by-the-by was packed, I found awaiting me at home a letter from Joachim telling me of Bach's [1] and Dirichlet's [2] death. Both pieces of news upset me so much that I was unable to sleep all night. Such events as these remind us of the vanity and evanescence of all things. . . . After all we are only human and cling to life—but memory alone supplies no adequate substitute for what has been lost. If only heaven would do as well by me and quickly snatch me away, the sooner the better. . . .

You are wrong about the Hungarian Dances, for they are exceedingly rhythmic. I knew that at once from the title " Hungarian," and if they did not make the expected impression, the fault certainly lay with the public, because they had hoped to hear familiar Hungarian melodies. I am going to play them at my third concert here, that is if I give another, and this will only be decided after I see the kind of audience I have at the second (next Sunday). I have had some pleasant evenings at the *Burg-theater* again and also at the *Kärntenertortheater*. For the first time since my childhood I saw the *Räuber*, with a young actor of twenty-two in the part of Franz, which he played extremely well. Then I also had the great joy of hearing *Iphigenie auf Tauris*. It would be impossible to describe the pleasure it gave me. You know what it is. To hear such music for the first time is a pleasure fit for gods. . . . I live in a house, [3] or rather on a spot, where Mozart's house formerly stood and where he died. The present owner has had a very fine memorial placed at the entrance of the house. Whenever I pass it I always feel a thrill of reverence. If only on each occasion I could receive a breath of music from him I should have enough to last my whole life ! . . . I am enclosing the programme of my next concert. It contains nothing extraordinary, but is nevertheless fine. Farewell, dear Johannes. Write soon and remember Your CLARA.

[1] A pupil of Joachim's.   [2] Rebecca Dirichlet, née Mendelssohn.
[3] Mozarthof in the Rauensteingasse.

CLARA *to* BRAHMS.

VIENNA, *Dec.* 20.

I should have been glad to send back your things sooner but I was unable to do so because I wanted to get more than a superficial knowledge of them. You know that the reading of a score is not an easy matter for me, and it takes me some time. Yesterday and to-day I have at last succeeded in having a few hours alone, and now to my joy I know everything thoroughly. But I cannot summon up the courage to write to you in detail about them. All the same I will try to imagine that things are still as they were before, and that I can tell you all that my heart feels with complete confidence. You know that I can say little that does not come from my heart. It is there that the music makes its first appeal, and when once it has captivated me I can begin to think about it. What charms me most is the Serenade.[1] I liked it from the opening bars and think it sounds exquisite. The second motif forms a beautiful contrast to the first and when once I get beyond the progressions in the third, fourth, fifth and sixth bars I feel perfectly happy. When the bassoons and the clarinets come in I begin to warm up and continue to do so more and more until the D Flat major is reached, when on pages 14, 15 and 16 the piece proceeds with wonderful subtlety and depth. From there onwards to the A major and the last pp. is heavenly, but I cannot get accustomed to the return to the first motif by means of the organ point in A. According to natural law ought not the organ point to have been on E ? I say " natural law," because no other can be considered when natural feelings are so peremptory—to me it sounds insipid. The end with its return to the second motif and its wonderfully sweet conclusion on A major is again very beautiful. How delightful the oboes are, and then the basses with the second motif. What strikes me as so ingenious is the triplet movement with the four quavers which pervades the whole—how powerful the effect must be in the fortissimo passage in the middle ! In short I can only compare the effect of the whole with that of the most beautiful, which is the D major Serenade. But I find the development in this one much more successful. Is this Serenade to be given any more movements ?

[1] Op. 16.

I like certain parts of the *Brautgesang* [1] very much, some—
e.g. page 14 from C major onwards, and then later where the
four voices come together—I like extremely. The last bar on
page 15 is wonderful. But it has struck me that here and there
the motifs are a little bit commonplace, for instance, on hearing
the melody

I should have thought of Hiller or some other musician and
not of you, and even the opening

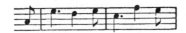

makes the same impression on me.

Forgive me. I dare say what I have said is silly, but every
time I played the piece through I felt this more and more.
I cannot imagine the piece pleasing through its melodies but
rather through its harmonies.

I was deeply struck by the *Grabgesang*. It is magnificent
for the altos to sing alone first and then for the sopranos to
enter with " *Gottes Posaune wird angehn.*" How impressive
the big drum must be just before. I think the music between
the parts on pages 4 and 5 is wonderful, as is also the crescendo
in the accompaniment when the bassoons and clarinets play
in unison. But the most magnificent of all is the passage
which begins *die Seel', die lebt*. I had to play it over again
and again because I was so loath to leave it. The only thing
I don't quite like is the second bar in A major. The music
seems to halt there a bit, whereas both before and after it
surges along so beautifully. The end with the altos again
must be most impressive. Have you heard it ? If only one
could hear it ! I have had it in my mind for days. I should
like to have it sung at my grave some day—I believe that in
writing it you must have thought of me !—

The song I like best is *Scheiden und Meiden*. I constantly
had to look at the title because I could not help thinking

---

[1] Chorus of women's voices with soprano solo on Uhland's text,
Das Haus beneide ich und preis es laut.

it must be a folk song, I mean a popular melody. *In der Ferne* stands out from the rest as being particularly thoughtful. I think the verses too are charming—oh, but I like all the songs !

Thank you, dear Johannes, for having sent me these things. Leave me my joy in them and do not spoil it by your customary remarks. It won't make me feel any different. But whatever criticism I have made I shall be glad to defend. I am much more ready to err on the side of fault-finding than on that of praise. I am sending the music with this letter and I hope you will receive it early enough to be able to get it in order in Detmold before the New Year. I have been thinking all along that this time you would stay longer there. Has the Prince not asked you ? Aren't you giving any concert in the theatre ? Why don't you write to me about the Marshal's wife ? [1] Don't you ever come across her ? Has the Prince asked you to come next winter ? . . .

I am sending you a programme of my last concert. Your dances were much more appreciated here than in Pesth. The applause was never ending and I had to play again. . . . Bach's Gavotte in D minor has become a great favourite with the people of Pesth and Vienna—some ass in Pesth has had them printed with the heading " Played by Cl. Sch. at her concerts." People here have been clamouring the whole time for me to play the *Kreisleriana*. But they seem to me so unsuitable for a concert. However, I must give way, for Spina [2] says that I shall attract bigger crowds if I play them. But I shall have to make a selection. It would be impossible to give them all. Unfortunately, one can hardly ever play with an orchestra here, it costs too much. . . .

For various reasons I am sorry that you should speak so contemptuously about your concerto. So just lock it up in the cupboard—you cannot take it from me even if you can deny me the pleasure of playing it. . . . Yesterday in the large *Redoutensaale* they produced the *Peri*. The choir and orchestra were good, but the soloists were feeble, devoid of all poetry (the *Peri* excepted). But it pleased tremendously.

---

[1] Clara probably means the wife of the Marshal of the Court, von Meysenbug, the mother of Karl and Hermann von Meysenbug.

[2] The head of the firm of Diabelli, the music publishers, who made Clara's business arrangements.

I revelled in the magnificent music. Surely the instrumentation is often quite wonderful, but at times I was conscious of a little monotony, particularly in the wind instruments. You will hardly believe, however, what a large following Robert has won here and how the understanding of him has increased. The other day, for instance, the Second Trio aroused the greatest enthusiasm, as did also the Quartet in F major, the adagio and scherzo of which the audience encored, as they also did in the trio. Indifferent as I am to the verdict of the public, this nevertheless gave me much pleasure. They are wearing their pens out writing about him here. Some of the asses are doing so at the expense of Mendelssohn, but others, like Hanslick, Bagge, and Debrois, are writing very well. A day or two ago I received a letter from the latter in which he said that he had not called upon me because he had heard both directly and indirectly that he had no place in my heart, and that he could not bear to be one of the things which I regarded with indifference. Of course I did not answer. As if it were so easy to win a place in my heart ! For that a man must have the highest credentials. Good God, in this my pride really does count for something ! Please greet the Princess for me. I really will write to her soon.

I have had a very nice letter from Joachim. He wrote to me about his Hungarian adagio [1] which you have praised so kindly. Please tell me something about it. Is it clearer than his things are as a rule ? I should be so glad if one day he would write something really pleasing. I am so dreadfully annoyed by the almost complete misunderstanding of his productive powers on the part of musicians.

You too ought to publish something again soon, I mean a collection of pieces. It is not good to have too long intervals. I don't pretend to understand it, but this is what I feel. Write to me soon if you can, and let it be a long letter. . . . Farewell and don't forget me, Your CLARA.

---

[1] *Konzert in ungarischer Weise*, Op. 11.

1859

Hamburg, *Wednesday, Feb. 2.*

At last, dear Clara, I have had a sign of life from you. Sahr sent your letter on to me. Now I have got plenty of news for you. Up to the very day of the concert [1] in Leipsic I felt sure you would come, and I was very much disappointed after I had waited up to the last moment in vain. I found Leipsic as boring as usual and knew nothing and nobody that could have afforded me any particular pleasure. My concerto went very well. I had two rehearsals. You have probably already heard that it was a complete frost; at the rehearsals it met with total silence, and at the performance (where hardly three people raised their hands to clap) it was regularly hissed. But all this made no impression on me. I quite enjoyed the other music and did not think of my concerto. Nobody said anything to me, except David, who was of course full of compliments. Rietz [2] and Sahr, whom I asked, told me it had not pleased them. . . . The *Faust* [3] went very well, but it was very tiring to have to accompany at the piano for three hours without being able to stir or pass a word of criticism. To perform the whole thing (even with an orchestra) on one evening seems to me unwise. If I were you I should try to prevent rather than encourage it. The third alone has a better effect than when it follows the first two. Besides which the pieces rarely have even the faintest connection with each other, but we must discuss this together one day. . . . Here I have found everything all right. They have made my room look splendid with chairs and a sofa-bedstead. . . . Farewell. I shall remain quietly here for

---

[1] January 27.

[2] Julius Rietz, at that time Conductor at the *Gewandhaus*.

[3] This refers to a performance of Schumann's *Faust* at the Freges' house. See *Life*, Vol. II, pp. 169–170.

the moment. I shall write again soon. Hearty greetings to all, Your JOHANNES.

CLARA *to* BRAHMS.

VIENNA, *Feb.* 16.

DEAR JOHANNES,

Once more I have waited longer than I ought to have done before writing to you ; but this is what happened. When I first got the news of the unfortunate reception of your concerto I straightway sat down to write to you. I felt that a kind word would be some solace to you. But then I was afraid that you would answer me shortly and that I should feel offended. It has taken me a long time to get over it,—not that a bad reception can in the least diminish your great worth as an artist, but it pained me very much to think that such an icy breath could reach your warm artist's heart, for no one is so far above everything as not to prefer a friendly reception to the reverse. Livia Frege wrote and told me how decidedly hostile everybody was, particularly Rietz, and I was afraid that this might have cooled your enthusiasm even at the rehearsal, so that you did not play your concerto as well as you can play it. Otherwise it is impossible to explain the remark that you were not technically competent to play your own work, for no one dreams of such a thing, when a composer is playing his own compositions.

But you tell me that it went very well with the orchestra. So all one can think is that if even the musicians were not stirred it was due to the hostile atmosphere having been too overpowering. Did you not try the Serenade at all ? If you had played this first, your victory would have been certain, because it is a much clearer work. I could not be annoyed by what you sent me, for it is such vile rubbish, so low, that it only deserves contempt. I can well understand that the first movement of the concerto is still giving you trouble— how strange that it should be so wonderful in detail and yet as a whole so difficult to enjoy, inspiring though it is. Why is it ? I cannot make it out. Livia wrote to say that the first movement was clearer to her than the adagio and the finale. But I can't understand that either. I am so sorry that I cannot manage to hear it. It is most unlikely that I

shall come to Hamburg. As things are at present I shall
probably be in Prague at that time, that is to say, far enough
away—I must seize every means of making money.

But although you may not have to contend with hostility
in Hamburg you may have to meet stupidity. . . . I am
very busy here and do not stop working from morning to
night. I hardly ever go to the theatre because it is impossible.
The whole of the morning I give lessons, and in the afternoon
and evening I deal with my correspondence, practise, and see
visitors. I do all this in a state of the utmost exhaustion,
for my lessons take it out of me terribly and I have to give
at least three a day, one after the other. But I am rewarded
by the thought that I am doing a lot of good here, for the
standard of musical teaching is so low that it has become a
sort of trade. There is enough talent about, and the majority
of my lady pupils play such things, for instance, as Robert's
most difficult works, Op. 13, 17, Kreisleriana, sonatas, etc.
They very much want me to play at Leipsic, but I cannot
help feeling that I ought not to do it, because they received
you so badly. Do not laugh at me for this. . . .   The other
day I saw *The Taming of the Shrew*, and I was extremely
delighted with it. I only wish you could see such a piece here
once, perfect down to the smallest part. Next week Eckert
has promised to take me to *Fidelio* as a send-off. Please
write to me again soon, and think kindly and affectionately of
Your CLARA.

BRAHMS *to* CLARA.

HAMBURG, *March 26, Saturday morning.*

I am very sorry, dear Clara, that I can do no more than
write to you about our concerts here. Unfortunately I am
so unwell that I cannot enjoy things nearly as much as I
might. I am suffering badly from a swelling in my cheek
(and neck). Thursday evening went off very successfully.
The fact that Joachim and Stockhausen were encored was
natural enough. But I was encored too, and to-day we are
reading the most appreciative criticisms of my work by Heller.
The concert was packed. Hundreds were unable to get tickets.
Joachim practised my concerto extremely well, and played it
wonderfully. I do not know what more to say. Everything

was exactly as one would have wished it.   The gentlemen of
the committee were, for instance, highly delighted with the
concerto, and the rehearsals had good audiences.   In short,
the Leipsic critics have done no harm.   Hans von Bronsart
came over from Hanover.   He is a nice fellow and all I deplore
is that I cannot feel more sympathy for his compositions.

In a moment we shall be rehearsing my Serenade.   It will
make a heavy toll on the violins. . . .   I should be dancing
with joy if my cheek were not so painful, but I have to be
very careful in case fever or any other complication sets in.
I must close now and write more fully next time.   I am enclosing the criticisms.   Write soon.   God is my witness that I
have had to write to you three times about things which you
ought to have heard for yourself.   Affectionately yours,
JOHANNES.

BRAHMS *to* CLARA.
                                    HAMBURG, *Tuesday, March* 29.
DEAREST CLARA,
   How sad that I have to write to you and have always to
write to you ! Yesterday the Serenade was played to nearly
twelve hundred people and you were not among them, you
did not share our joy and I had to think of you as alone and
far away from me.   Unfortunately it did not go very well,
for the wind instruments, particularly the horn and the flute,
were weak, and the latter actually bad.   The rehearsals were
always packed and the people were pleased with it even then.
At the concert yesterday it appeared to have a telling effect
and the applause continued until I came forward.   I suppose
our concert was the most crowded they have ever had here ;
for, as in the case of the last Philharmonic Concert, only nine
hundred tickets are issued as a rule.   We shall most probably
do very well over it.   I am enclosing the programme.   Every
item was encored.   You would not have recognized the people
of Hamburg.

   At the beginning of May Stockhausen is to give a concert
in Leipsic (possibly with you).   He wants to do my Serenade
provided certain outstanding questions are settled.   I shall
be glad to do this and shall be there myself and force myself
upon you so that you will be obliged to hear something after

all. If you could be there I should be as happy as a king, otherwise I shall not care much what happens. . . . What pains Joachim has taken over my work! On this occasion I should like him to have had one or two better musicians, but in the future what I hope is that he will have better works to produce. For a long time I shall be unable to think of Joachim's presence here without real emotion. And now good-bye, dear Clara, be content with this and tell me if there is anything lacking in my letters. With heartiest greetings from all, Your JOHANNES.

[The following Programme was enclosed.]

Musical Soirée given by Joh. Brahms, Jos. Joachim and Jul. Stockhausen at the *Wörmer Concert Hall* on Monday, March 28, 1859.

Part I

1. Sonata for Flute and Violin by J. S. Bach.
2. Aria from Handel's Messiah (from the original score).
3. Sonata for Violin by Tartini.
4. Erlkönig by F. Schubert.

Part II

5. Serenade for a small Orchestra by J. Brahms.
6. *Cavatine de la fête du village voisin* by Boieldieu.
7. *Rondo Brillant*, Op. 70 for Piano and Violin by F. Schubert.
8. Songs.
    (*a*) Nuszbaum ⎫
    (*b*) Mondnacht ⎬ by Schumann.
    (*c*) Widmung ⎭

CLARA *to* BRAHMS.

DRESDEN, *March* 31.

Many thanks, dear Johannes, for writing to me so quickly. I was delighted to hear that everything had gone off so well, and also that you had made so much money. After all, this is a pleasant addition to all the other splendid things. I was broken-hearted at not being able to be there, and you were right when you imagined me sitting alone and miserable in my hotel. The programme is wonderful and I can well imagine with what love Joachim practised all the pieces, although I think it is only natural that he should do so. How often in life can a distinguished artist expect to have such a contemporary as you? If he has his heart in the right place, and with him nothing else could be possible, he must be deeply conscious of his good fortune. What with this and the joy of hearing your things produced by so sympathetic a conductor you must feel greatly stimulated. You could not help it, no matter how self-sufficient you were. But I shall not be able to hear the Serenade as soon as all that, for I shall not give the concert in Leipsic, or any concert at all for the present, —I cannot. Even if I still had the bodily strength for it, I no longer possess the musical ardour and freshness required, and as soon as I feel this, I stop immediately, because I regard artistic duty as higher than material gain. So I have told Stockhausen I cannot play at any more concerts. . . .

I was glad to get such an enthusiastic account of the concerto from Stockhausen, because the people of Leipsic had seriously prejudiced him against it. But if I were you I would not move a finger to let Leipsic hear another note from you. The day will come when they will clamour to hear you. Overjoyed as I would be to hear the Serenade I would rather forgo this pleasure than that you should produce it before such an unfriendly audience. You must strike Leipsic out of your map —this much pride you must and can have.

I had my concert in Prague on the same day as you, but not in the evening. I gave two and played before the Kaiser. I ought to have stayed longer, but, as I have told you, it was impossible. Besides, I know no one there who is the least bit sympathetic to me. In fact in the whole of Austria I hardly know anybody. The Austrians have fire but it is a flash in the pan. What I want is the fire that burns long and deeply. There is no lack of enthusiasm in Prague, but unfortunately the " music of the future " has begun to take root in the place and Liszt rejoices there, as everywhere else, in a following which works up enthusiasm for him.

I heard *Lohengrin* in Vienna once, and can see only too well how such an opera succeeds in imposing on people. The whole thing is full of romanticism and thrilling situations, so much so indeed that even the musician himself at times forgets the horrible music. Nevertheless, on the whole, I like *Lohengrin* better than I do *Tannhäuser*, in which Wagner goes through the whole gamut of abominations. They told me in Prague about the music of *Tristan and Isolde*. Apparently it is even worse than what has gone before, if that were possible. . . . What pleases me most is the thought of the joy your parents must have had. Greet them heartily from me and let me greet you affectionately too. Write to me soon and tell me whether you have quite recovered. I was terribly sorry that it should have come just at the time when you might have had such a thoroughly delightful experience. But all's well that end's well, and so it was with you. . . . Please keep a place in your heart for Your CLARA.

CLARA *to* BRAHMS.

LONDON, *May* 3.

I wanted to write to you directly after the Philharmonic Concert [1] yesterday, but I was so tired that the pen almost fell from my hands. I had been listening to the Concerto [2] with the very closest attention, the more so as I was unable to hear the rehearsal, for which I had hurried here, the reason being that owing to the latest regulations no one is allowed to be present at rehearsals. You can imagine how hard this was for me in my position. So after hearing it only once you cannot expect any considered opinion from me, all I can say is that in parts it delighted me, while in others I found it uninspiring, particularly through the frequently overloaded instrumentation, which often makes it heavy, although in its essence it is not so. Then a good deal of it seems to me Wagnerian, which displeases me somewhat. I think the motifs throughout, though, are wonderfully beautiful. The developments, particularly in the last movement, are extremely interesting and contain remarkable harmonic turns, as for instance at the return to the theme; and the whole thing is so homogeneous. The adagio (which you surely know?) is exquisitely profound, except that at the end the horns and clarinets repeat the theme a little bit heavily, which spoils the soft feeling. The other movement, however, is very long, and one is conscious of it,

---

[1] From the end of April to the 2nd of July Clara had been on a concert tour in England with Joachim and Stockhausen.

[2] Joachim's Hungarian Concerto, Op. 11.

which ought not to be so. If only I could just have a look at the score many things would become clearer to me. But one ought to hear such an important piece again and again to be able to form a judgment of it. Moreover it was not too well accompanied. In view of its great difficulties, it had not been sufficiently practised.

Of course the audience did not understand it, but what pained me was that they let him feel it, although not with actual hisses. But after all it will not have hurt him too much, because he knows what he wants. In fact I have just heard from him that he was glad the audience listened so quietly—I did not have a chance to speak to him again after it. I wish I could write to you more satisfactorily about it, but you yourself will be seeing it soon and when you do your two eyes will tell you more than I could hear with twenty ears. . . . The only other thing I can tell you about to-day is Joachim's first Beethoven evening which was quite wonderful. I have never heard such a quartet, although the others, in spite of all kinds of virtuosity, were miles behind him. With one single stroke straight from his soul, he beats them all. The only thing was that three difficult quartets like Op. 127, 95 and — were too much, all one after the other, and it was only his playing that made me endure it. . . . I enclose the flowers as a time-honoured form of greeting, Your CLARA.

CLARA *to* BRAHMS.

CAMBERWELL, *June* 5.

At last I am able once more to snatch an hour to myself —I did not mean it to have been such a long interval, dear Johannes, but I could not help it. I really have very little to tell you, for what is happening here is the same as what happened in previous years when I wrote to you about everything in detail. And then I could do so with pleasure, because it was all new to you, but now you know everything. . . . Our three matinées are now over. The second and third were better attended, and the audiences were really enthusiastic. . . . The matinées brought each of us three one hundred and thirty thalers [1] [£19.10.0.]. Isn't that miserable! And yet we

---

[1] Clara, Joachim and Stockhausen; the latter did not meet with any favour with the English public on this visit.

were glad that there was anything at all, for we had reckoned on nothing. I have only a few engagements, but I think I shall have a few hundred thalers over, though this is little enough for all the sacrifices I have made.

I have already told you that Joachim is very well. But he is frightfully busy and it hurts me to see such an artist work so hard. For after all, he is too good for that sort of thing and has not got to support a family as I have. You cannot imagine what his life is. From morning to night, rehearsal, concert, concert, rehearsal. And so it goes on day after day. He has just played the Kreuzer Sonata with me at a concert. He had hardly played the last stroke when he had to rush off again to rehearse it with Godard and others. He has never yet been able to stop to the end of a concert. The moment he has played, his violin is in its case, and he is off. Can one possibly keep one's mind fresh in such circumstances? I think not. Even the heart becomes callous and one hardly has time to feel. You can well imagine that as things are I see little of Joachim, and when I do it makes me unhappy, for here he is a different man from what he is in Germany. Over there, for instance, our artistic points of view were always very much in agreement, but here we differ so fundamentally from each other that now I never discuss anything with him. He thinks everything here is beautiful and is often so contradictory that if anyone told me about it I should not believe it. Stockhausen is frequently quite depressed about it. He too says that he finds him quite different here. He is now very intimate with Davison, and thinks everything right that he thinks right. The whole thing is a mystery to me. I can well understand how a man, or anyone with any intelligence, can find London intensely interesting. But how that can make him blind to all the darker sides is quite incomprehensible to me.

In my opinion the most beautiful thing in England is the country-side. How it invigorates and refreshes one! I could contemplate the sort of tree one sees here and which spreads its branches on all sides down to the very earth, for hours at a time and find a world of poetry in it—such varied and luxuriant vegetation is really wonderful. And now imagine whole parks of such trees about which one can wander for hours.   I saw the most beautiful of all these parks for the first time yesterday at Windsor and also the most beautiful of all castles.   I cannot attempt to describe it, but when you see it you live through the whole of Shakespeare.   How insipid a German palace seems compared with it.   What a magnificent piece of architecture it is with its beautiful Gothic windows, its large towers with their crenated battlements, all of it built out of rough grey stone, thickly covered with ivy in places. You would be able to wander about there for days.   When you have made a nice lot of money devote it to a trip to England. You could spend a month here comfortably on 200 thalers [£30].   But what I should like to know is how it would satisfy you artistically.   I cannot help feeling that an artist with very settled views would be unable to bear it here.   But one often makes mistakes in such matters.

The other day I heard the *Israel* at Exeter Hall.   Parts of it were quite wonderful, even overwhelming.   But Costa, the conductor, had the unfortunate idea of introducing the trombones everywhere, so that very often one wanted to run away and leave the place—and had it not been for the divine organ one would have done so.   But it riveted one to the spot, at least it did me, with its magic spell.   They are now preparing for the Handel Festival.   I shall probably hear one performance but more with the idea of getting an impression of the whole, than on account of the pleasure I shall get from the music, the effect of which is much clearer and more enjoyable in a smaller hall. . . .

The music festivals are now all cancelled, which is again a great loss for Stockhausen.   But how are things over there with you ?   Warlike ?   Here everything is upset by the unhappy war.[1]   Business men are all shaking their heads and not so long ago fifty firms went smash in a week.   I am very much looking forward to your serenade for four hands.   When I am back in Germany I hope you will send it to me quickly. Are you being very industrious ?   If you find Hamburg so boring why do you feel compelled to remain there ?   If you are not doing so on account of your parents, I don't under-stand.   Why don't you return to Göttingen ?   You can lead the most pleasant of lives there, enjoy everything, and live

[1] The Franco-Sardinian war against Austria.

cheaply. And you can get through enough work there too, if you seriously want to. It is only a matter of arrangement —morning, work ; afternoon, something different. I do wish you would do it. I hate to think of you cooped up in the town with the constant longing to be out of it. And perhaps you might find your exquisite balcony there again. But I must close. You will receive this letter on the 8th.[1] I know you will give me an affectionate thought on that day. Farewell, dear Johannes. Write soon and kindly to Your CLARA.

BRAHMS *to* CLARA.

HAMBURG, *July* 3, *Sunday Evening.*

I thought you had been back in Germany a long time, dear Clara, otherwise you would have had a letter sooner. I am very glad to know that you are on the Rhine,[2] and to be able to greet you there. . . . I felt just as happy about hearing that you were going to Wildbad as if I were going there myself. It must be very beautiful, certainly more beautiful than Wiesbaden. Frl. Wagner,[3] my favourite pupil here, is now in Wildbad. You have already met her here and, if you feel the least inclination to do so, you ought to see her there. She is an exceedingly charming, modest and musical girl and ought to please you very much. Occasionally she appears rather stand-offish, but this is merely superficial. She is the principal founder of my *Verein* here, and we sing at her house. If you like, I can send you the arrangement of the Serenade, and then you can play it alone or with Frl. Wagner. She can practise it beforehand. Incidentally she plays quite well and can do all kinds of things with her little fingers.

I don't like to hear, nor do I like to think, of Joachim's Anglomania. Is it all going to end in marriage ? If not, why does he wear himself out so ? I hope that he will remain as he is and that this is only a temporary aberration, which will not continue to take up his time and strength. I don't think for a moment that I shall ever go to England—at least not until I have been to Swabia, and wandered to my heart's content in the beautiful forests of Germany, nor before I have

[1] Schumann's birthday.
[2] In Düsseldorf.
[3] " Friedchen " Wagner, afterwards Frau Sauermann.

seen the Tyrol, Switzerland, Italy, Greece, Egypt, India, etc., etc. in spite of all the Handel choirs of three thousand voices, and all the wonderful scenes and battle-pieces in Shakespearean plays. With hearty greetings, and hoping you will write soon and recover quickly, Wholly yours, JOHANNES.

CLARA *to* BRAHMS.

KREUZNACH, *July* 16.

At last I am able to find a quiet moment for you, dear Johannes. I am sitting on a balcony overhung with creepers and am looking out in the direction of the Gans and the Rothen-felsen, etc. As you may well imagine there is much that moves me in the scene, and were it not that I have so long owed you a letter I would not write here at all, but it will take me five or six days to settle down in Wildbad.

I have brought Elise here on account of her eyes and want to stop a day or two with her so as to get her accustomed to the routine. Fortunately I have found a very nice family, where she will have the companionship of nine other girls; and I shall continue my journey to-morrow, reaching Heidelberg on the first day and Wildbad on the second. I am delighted that I shall find Frl. Wagner there, but I am afraid she will soon have to leave, as she must have been there for some time ? . . .

How delightful about your *Gesangverein*. I hope you have a large number of charming girls in it. But don't you include men as well ? I should think you would soon find women's singing alone monotonous. I should like to hear your songs. How did you like the songs which you tried with the organ on June the 9th ? Aren't they very difficult ? Did your girls sing them well ? Everybody is asking me why you are not publishing anything, and I really don't know what to say. . . .

After all I found it rather hard to leave London. Just for the moment there is something very attractive about the grand scale on which the whole of life is conducted. Without being aware of it one gets accustomed to regard everything from a grander point of view. But although outwardly one may appear to lead a freer life one remains dissatisfied at heart. But my principal reason for feeling low spirited at my departure was Joachim, and once again I was conscious of how dear he

is to me.   I don't know whether he wrote to you to tell you
that in September he is going with the Goldschmidts on a tour
in Ireland which will last from a month to six weeks.   He will
then probably go to the Isle of Wight.   Aren't you going to
write to him at all ?   Write to him on the 24th, his birthday [1] ;
it will please him immensely, and he did it for you.   A day
or two ago he wrote and told me that he was now seriously
setting to work (on a third Concerto), but I doubt whether he
will have the necessary peace for it.

I spent the day with Hiller the day before yesterday.   He
played to me a good deal out of *Saul*, canons with violin,
and solfeggios for three women's voices, etc.   I heard from
others that he is again engaged on writing a grand tragic
opera, I only hope it will not once again be tragic for him.
I always feel so sorry for him with all his incessant industry
and such little reward. . . .

Farewell, dear Johannes, and write soon to Your CLARA.

CLARA *to* BRAHMS.

WILDBAD, *Aug.* 5.

A thousand thanks, dear Johannes, for the letters and the
parcel.   As the latter took a whole week to come I was not
able to play the Serenade with Frl. Wagner, for she had gone.
But I almost preferred playing it alone to myself to playing
it with an amateur, as I can only enjoy music with people
who feel as I do about it. . . .   I saw Frl. Wagner often, but
Marie was with her more than I was.   They went out together
a good deal looking for bilberries.   I played very little to her
as she did not ask me to, and I could not offer to do so a second
time after having done so once.   I don't think that it means
much to her, and in those circumstances my inspiration goes.
If I am to play with pleasure to people, I must have eager
listeners, and often one can see this by a mere look in their
eyes.   But she is a very cultivated girl and the father is a
very pleasant man.   What is he really ?   I think I have
already told you that she once played something to me.   She
told me about your beautiful *Marienlieder*.[2]   What are the
words like ?   Have you not taken up the Deutsche Tänze

---

[1] This is a mistake, it was the 28th.
[2] *Ave Maria, Adoremus, Bone Jesu.*

again ? And what about the quartet ? I heard that you played it with Reimers at Frau Petersen's. . . .

Aug. 6.

Yesterday I was interrupted by Hartmann,[1] who told me so many interesting things that I wish you could have been present. He knows all sorts and conditions of men and countries and discusses them in a very enlightening way. Thus yesterday he told me about Uhland [2] whom he knew for a whole year. He confirmed what I heard about him in Stuttgart, to the effect that he was very ugly and never spoke to anybody except after he had met him several times, and then only in the evening at the public house. Then he would thaw and be most amiable and interesting, besides revealing much learning. He is very fond of wine and declares that he has not touched a drop of water for eighteen years. I should love to meet him, and from Stuttgart this would have been easy. But what would be the good if in the end he merely ran away ? . . . I am now looking forward to a letter from you quite soon, please quite soon, dear Johannes, and let it be a long one. Your life is fuller than mine. Affectionately yours, CLARA.

BRAHMS *to* CLARA.

HAMBURG, *Sunday afternoon, Goethe's birthday, Aug.* 28.

I got your letter early yesterday, beloved Clara, but I had lessons to give and then had to go to Bergedorff . . . This is the first chance I have had of writing to you. To-morrow my girls are rehearsing a psalm [3] which I have composed for them. I wrote it in the evening a week ago last Sunday, and it kept me happy until midnight. If you want to look at the text it is the 13th. As it has an organ accompaniment we shall sing it again in the church—this and my *Ave Maria.* You will be returning too late, otherwise how splendid it would have been if you could have listened, perhaps on the 13th of September, to the 13th Psalm. But I could arrange it later in the month if you like. I have at least forty girls now.

---

[1] Moritz Hartmann.

[2] Johan Uhland, German poet (1787–1862), the highest example of the Swabian school of poetry, famous for his lyric verse.—TR.

[3] Op. 27.

I don't think it is right that you should spare yourself so little. The winter is coming on and you ought to be gathering new strength. At least give up your practising for the moment, and don't persuade yourself that it is so frightfully necessary. . . . I feel ever more and more convinced that you are my friend and the thought fills me with the greatest joy. To think it has become a necessity of my life ! And you will sympathize with this and believe it once more. Write to me again soon and don't tell me that you are unwell or have no time. In Detmold I will tell you about the most beautiful girl in my *Verein* and many other things which I won't spoil by writing about. Addio, beloved Clara. Think of me kindly and be persuaded that you have no truer or better friend than I. Your JOHANNES.

CLARA *to* BRAHMS.

HONNEF,[1] *Sept.* 18.

I was overjoyed by your birthday greeting, dear Johannes. It reached me on the evening of the 13th when I was sitting alone at my window looking at the setting sun. The sky was full of the wonderful harmonies that you had sent me. Your Adagio only came on the following day, but your words were kind harbingers. Thank you most heartily. Now what shall I tell you about the Adagio ? It is not always true to say " out of the fullness of the heart the mouth speaketh." So great was my joy over the piece that I cannot find words to express it, and yet you want to hear all about it. To analyse it will be very difficult. In order to enjoy doing it I must imagine something very beautiful, as if I were examining one by one the stamens of a rare and lovely flower. For it is exquisitely beautiful. How softly and majestically the bass moves, like a noble personage, *à la* Bach, and the second theme begins so woefully (the mere sound moves one quite strangely), and then weaves itself so intimately into the other parts. And how magnificent the close of this first part is, with the organ point in the middle ! The *ff* later on is very fine and also the way it gradually subsides, while the whole of the transition

---

[1] From the middle of September to the middle of October Clara was at Honnef and Mehlem on the Rhine.

into A Flat major, the horn, the new theme, the liquid organ
point, and the entrance of the viola with the first theme again,
and the crescendo up to the G major—how glorious it all is !
But from there onwards it transports one to heaven (I always
play this passage :

pianissimo). It is so unspeakably gentle and stirring, and
the end, when everything becomes quite quiet, so carries one's
soul away that I really cannot say any more. The whole
piece has a religious atmosphere, it might be an *Eleison*. But
you know, dear Johannes, that I feel these things better than
I can express them.

The Minuet is very charming (a little bit reminiscent of
Haydn) and I can already enjoy the oboe in the Trio ; it
must sound quite original with the swinging melody. I might
have guessed at once what follows. I also liked the first movement very much, although one or two things in it, as I have
already told you, did not quite please me. I felt it again
this time. But they are only details compared with the
beautiful whole. It pains me to have to return it to you,
but I am not sending it back to you to-day, for you did not
mean me to, did you ? Let me know when you really must
have it.

The songs are charming and must sound quite uncommon.
How beautifully the *Adoremus* flows, in spite of its classical
form. I at once noticed how particularly tenderly the end
fits the words " *Dein köstlich Blut,*" before I had seen that you
yourself had called attention to these words. If only I could
hear all these things ! Won't you have the second Serenade
played in Detmold too ? Please do so, otherwise I shall not
hear it for a long time. I miss enough beautiful things as it
is. I did not know that you had spoken so seriously about

my playing to the family at Detmold.   Naturally I shall not retreat now for fear of treading on your toes.

[The end of the letter is missing.]

BRAHMS *to* CLARA.

DETMOLD, *Early Friday, Sept.* 30.

BELOVED CLARA,

My first quiet hour belongs to you.   I have just moved into a better room where I shall remain, and your little note w as the first thing that was sent on to me.   I must first write to you about my delightful Hamburg Girls' Choir.   Oh, my dear girls, where are you now !   I shall not even turn round when the beautiful things I have written for you are sung to me here.   The whole forty of you will stand before me, and in the spirit I shall see you and listen to you.   Believe me one of my fondest memories is this choir of girls.   Just imagine their attractive wedge formation, first of all the big ones, then the smaller ones, for whom I arranged the Folk Songs in three parts and practised them with them ;   and last of all the tiniest ones who only sang my one-part songs and to whom I gave red ribbons.

But on Monday in the church what a touching farewell it was !   Everything was sung twice over, and the audience could not help being pleased with such a concert.   When I got home in the afternoon I found a little box and in it, charmingly hidden among flowers, a silver writing-case inscribed with the words " In memory of the summer of '59 from the Girls' Choir ! "   What will next summer not bring in the form of psalms and songs of joy !   As a matter of fact I am becoming somewhat of a cult in Hamburg.   But I don't think that can do any harm.   In any case I am writing with ever more zest, and there are signs in me which suggest that in time I may produce heavenly things.

I should be very glad if Hiller were to produce something of mine, but I am not going to send the parts for the Committee to examine them, though I will gladly send Hiller the score for him to do so. . . .

I greet you a thousand times, and implore you to regard this as a rational letter in spite of its unpardonable sentimentalities regarding the forty girls. Spare yourself, and don't wear yourself out with Hiller's music. Wholly yours, JOHANNES.

BRAHMS *to* CLARA.

DETMOLD, *Wednesday, Nov.* 9.

BELOVED CLARA,

Your letter of yesterday delighted me.[1] I won't expatiate upon it, otherwise you will think me vain and imagine that I like to listen to flatteries. But I don't mind saying that I am very much pleased with my things. I really believe, dear Clara, that I am growing, but you will probably be able to understand how one " sings unto the Lord because He hath dealt so bountifully, so bountifully with one." Has He dealt so bountifully with me ?

But how delightful it is to work with buoyancy and strength, and to know that you and others are showing such keen interest. How sad I am when I think of the splendid man who did this so whole-heartedly and unreservedly.

I am sending my first Serenade to Hiller and should be highly delighted if he would produce it. A mere rehearsal would not please me so much. I would gladly place it at Dietrich's disposal too. I long for nothing more than to have my things performed. It would give me life (I mean it would add to what life I already have). If they would like to do so in Honnef I should be quite agreeable. The *Ave Maria* and the *First Psalm* are also at the disposal of whoever cares to have the parts copied out, although they will not be his property ! But I should have to have the first Serenade returned by the New Year, when it is to be performed in Hamburg. But it ought to be done in Cologne and Bonn before this and I would gladly come for the occasion. . . .

In a day or two, Sunday or Monday, I shall write to you and send you things, and then please do not be sparing in your use of paper, for I enjoy every word of praise from you. Affectionately yours, JOHANNES.

[1] On the 7th of November Clara had written to Brahms a letter expressing her heartiest appreciation of his *Ave Maria* (Op. 12), the *Psalm* (Op. 27), and the songs (Op. 22), and had asked his permission to show them to Hiller.

1860

AMSTERDAM,[1] *Feb.* 5.

Try how I may to arrange it, I don't think I can possibly come to you by the 10th, dear Johannes. If I left Rotterdam on the night of the 9th I could only reach Hamburg after the concert. But how about Hanover? If you are giving the Serenade on the 18th I may possibly be able to hear it. But, if later, I shall miss it, and that would be dreadful. And really if anybody has a first right to be present in Hanover it is I. Please let me hear as soon as possible when it is definitely going to be produced there. . . .

Unfortunately I must forgo the pleasure of having your Serenade at one of my own concerts in Berlin, as you have promised Joachim to let him produce it first, which I think quite right. Naturally I would make no attempt to deprive him of this pleasure. After the 18th, however, if all goes well, I must go to Vienna at once, otherwise it will be too late. I am glad to hear that your Ladies' Choral Society is again in full swing. What things you do write about it, to be sure! I am annoyed that you are once more on friendly terms with Otten [2] (I suppose in a sense I ought to say you've got

[1] On December 19 Clara had given a concert in Celle and returned to Berlin to spend Christmas with her family. Early in January Joachim and Brahms stayed with her for a short time, but on January the 21st she once more set out on a concert tour accompanied by her second daughter, Elise. They went to Hanover, Cassel, Brunswick and Düsseldorf, and then on to Holland, where during the first half of February Clara gave concerts in Utrecht, Amsterdam, Rotterdam and The Hague (*Life*, Vol. II, p. 177).—TR.

[2] In a letter of January 27 Brahms had told her among other things that Otten had the day before for the first time introduced works by Liszt at a first-class concert. He describes how irritated he was and goes on, " This plague will spread and spread. It will be sure to lengthen and deteriorate the donkey's ears of the public and of young composers."—TR.

to be). The musical fraternity in general are a miserable lot. But that is an old story. Nevertheless I think it is a reason why our little group of right-minded people should feel it incumbent upon them to maintain their self-respect.

I should like to tell you something interesting about myself. But you know my life. To many it may seem a happy one outwardly, but inwardly it is often unspeakably sad. Goodness knows, I have been honoured enough here. In Utrecht there was a torchlight procession, with Bengal lights, and the students serenaded me. I appeared at the window in the twilight and they cheered and would not stop shouting. On the one side there was enthusiasm and on the other deep emotion. It was very fine! And then in the morning all the torches were burnt out, as was also the enthusiasm—what was the good of all this display of feeling? It was symbolic of the whole of life. Here they gave me a flourish of trumpets and the enthusiasm was enormous. But you know the sort of thing: " Me to-day, you to-morrow " (I don't mean you literally!). I would gladly give up my place to you and much more besides. . . .

In Düsseldorf I spent a pleasant evening with Woldemar and Dietrich. They both paid me a visit and Dietrich brought Ludwig and Ferdinand with him, and I found them both very much improved (they looked quite changed). . . .

At present I am in a somewhat unfortunate position; I got a sudden pain in one of my fingers and it has already lasted two days, and I can think of nothing to account for it. I cannot play and have just sent for a doctor. If it is not better by the morning I shall have to cancel The Hague and Rotterdam, which would mean a loss to me of 400 gulden— just think of it! What extraordinary things happen to one without any warning! . . . But you have had enough of my chatter, dearest Johannes, so I will say adieu. Write me a nice long letter. Your devoted CLARA.

CLARA to BRAHMS.

VIENNA, *March* 3, *Evening*, 8 *o'clock*.

At this very moment, dear Johannes, your Serenade is being played; if only the sound of it could reach as far as me! It is very hard for me that I should have to be here at this moment. I am probably hardly in the thoughts of any one of you. What you say in your letter about your things not being good enough to receive more than a perfunctory and passing consideration from me, really does not deserve to be answered. Who knows better than yourself how every note of your Serenade, for instance, became part of my own flesh and blood, and how enthusiastically and deeply I absorb everything that comes from you. You ought to be thoroughly ashamed of yourself for uttering such meaningless phrases ; or did you want to hear what you already know all over again ?

What made you think of a harp and horns ? [1] I cannot imagine what the combination of these instruments would sound like, but it would certainly be something quite uncommon if not actually spellbinding. There must have been a very pretty girl in your choir who happened to play the harp and for whom you composed the piece. Provided the horns do not sound too harsh in the hall, I should think the general effect would be full of feeling. Please write to me about it, I am deeply interested, but above all tell me about the Serenade in Hanover. . . .

Just think what happened here the other day ! At a private concert in the large *Redoutensaal* Liszt's *Prometheus* and Mozart's G minor Symphony were played. Of course Liszt had his *claque* here as he does everywhere, but for a moment they were reduced to silence by hisses on every side. When, however, the Symphony began there were three salvos of endless cheers, the moment the first four bars had been played. It was far too spontaneous to have been organized, and everybody, even the most uninformed, declared that when the first notes of Mozart were heard they were, as Hanslick said, like a soft spring breeze suddenly penetrating a room reeking with fumes.

If only I had been there I would have wanted to cheer with the rest. But it does please one when for once the public has its heart in the right place. It was said that Liszt and Bülow had intended to come here, but all of a sudden the tongue of rumour was silenced. . . .

My first concert was on March the 1st and it was packed.

[1] Songs for a Choir of Women's Voices with accompaniment of two horns and a harp. Op. 17.

The best seats for all three concerts were sold long beforehand, and in the end every seat was taken. But what pleased me most was my reception. When I appeared the applause was unending, and I could feel that it came from the hearts of people who are fond of me. The audience consisted of the most cultivated people in Vienna. It is quite a pleasant experience to play here, for, after all, if one has to perform in public, it is gratifying to find the audience is stirred. In the *Carnaval*, for instance, there was not a piece after which I did not have, so to speak, to bring the applause to a close by beginning the piece that followed. However much this may harass one, at bottom it is very gratifying. You would hardly believe how the reverence for Robert is increasing here, and although in some respects I cannot help feeling sad about it, I am also very glad on his account, for it was here that he made so many vain attempts to be recognized.

At my next concert on the 8th I am thinking of playing two of your ballads, the one in D major, and the one in B minor.[1] The third is on the 15th, and what will happen then I do not know. It is a remarkable fact that the theatres and concerts have all been fuller this year than ever before, and the reason is that money has no longer any value. The people spend it because they do not know whether to-morrow it will not be worth even less. Just imagine, the thaler is worth tenpence more than usual; I shall feel this bitterly enough when I come to change my money in Germany. . . . Let me hear from you soon, dear Johannes, and with heartiest greetings, Your CLARA.

BRAHMS *to* CLARA.

HAMBURG, *Monday early, April* 2.

I have a fine week to write to you about, dear Clara; I wish you had been with us, or that you could come next time to see how well we can do things here. Grädener's second concert was on Friday. We had the *Genoveva* Overture, an Overture by Handel, a Cantata by Bach, a *Sanctus* by Em. Bach, etc. and the Concerto by Joachim.[2] How you will enjoy the

---

[1] Clara played them on the 21st of March. She says, "I played them very well, but they were a complete failure." *Life,* Vol. II, p. 180.   [2] *Das Ungarische Konzert,* Op. 11.

Concerto when you hear it again.   It has become magnificent,
particularly the first movement, which is now full of réstrained
beauty, and so calm, so deep and warm in feeling that it is a
joy.   Without any special changes being noticeable, last year's
version seems like a wild sketch compared with the present
beautifully fashioned work of art.   But you ought to have
heard it.   I cannot describe it.   Moreover it is so clear and
simple and makes such a delightful impression that it is bound
to please everywhere as it did the public here.

I had to show my skill as a conductor.   I had not seen
the Concerto since I was at Detmold and Joachim stepped
straight out of the train into the concert hall for the rehearsal.
I conducted it myself to my very special satisfaction.   Every
evening was spent quite merrily, but Sunday evening was
particularly delightful, and that was due to my girls, whom
I summoned to do honour to Joachim, or rather to do honour
to them.   I had really been intending to give the matter up
and had fixed to-morrow evening as the last of all.   But it
was charming.   I had spoken to Joachim about a certain girl
who wore a black dress, but when we arrived they were all in
black.   In spite of their joy over Joachim, they insisted on
putting on mourning because our evenings were over.   Wasn't
it sweet of them ?   Unfortunately we could not get a harp,
and two bad hornists accompanied us.   Joachim enjoyed the
whole thing very much and I was obliged to promise to go on
with it.

It is really quite pleasant.   The girls are so nice, fresh and
enthusiastic, without being soft and sentimental.   On the way
home (an hour's journey away) it unfortunately rained, otherwise we usually have a lot of fine singing and serenading on this
road.   My girls, for instance, will walk quite calmly into a
garden and wake the people up at midnight with their singing.
We wished every day that you could have been with us, and
I cannot help thinking that you must be here next time.   It
might be arranged very nicely for the 19th of April, when I am
playing my Concerto at Otten's.   The girls are always available.
I am sure you would enjoy them immensely and you do not
yet know Ossian, Shakespeare, etc. with harp and horns.[1]
With deepest affection, YOUR JOHANNES.

[1] Op. 17.

BRAHMS *to* CLARA.

HAMBURG, *April* 26.

DEAR CLARA,

I have just this moment received your letter and am over-joyed that the confounded journey will not take place.[1] I could think of nothing else and strange to say I had contemplated leaving here yesterday and did not even go to Berlin. As a matter of fact I simply couldn't go. So now let me implore you most urgently and solemnly to come here in the summer. I can do one or two things to make the time pleasant for you and it is just possible that Joachim may come too. You need not worry about me, for while I am writing (and I propose to be very industrious) you will easily find many other pleasant distractions which will crop up without any effort on your part.

Let me assure you, dear Clara, that I feel the greatest love both for you and for him who has left us, and it is a love that will last for ever. How glad I should be to prove it to you. I feel certain that you have enough youthful spirit to be amused by my Girls' Choir by which I have for once indulged in a conventional pleasure. It is not to break up. And I hope you will feel very much at home and thoroughly comfortable. Just imagine that I have been trying to persuade you for an hour to come here on Sunday or Monday (preferably Saturday). You will then be able to see everything. The Choir meets on Monday evening, after which the best alto will be leaving us, so you must hear it on that evening. Then we can run round and find lodgings for you. I have so much superfluous cash, my dear Clara, that I wish you would let me defray the expenses of this trial trip for you. Perhaps you might even be able to settle down here, let your children follow, and allow Frl. Werner to see to the rest in Berlin. Marie might come with you at once. Do your utmost, dearest, to come here to-morrow. It is only a short journey, why should you require to think about it ? But you absolutely must enjoy Monday evening with us, so that you can have a taste of the most important of our distractions. It is bright moonlight just now and we are living in a particularly charming house (half

---

[1] Clara had thought of going to England again, but she abandoned the idea for this year. See *Life*, Vol. II, p. 180.

an hour's walk from the town).   You will also be able to hear duets by me but only on one particular day owing to the departure of the alto.   To-day is Thursday, so I implore you, dear Clara, to leave either early Saturday or Friday evening. . . .   I would gladly set out now and be with you to-morrow early, but I trust you, my dear Clara, and feel sure that you will decide to leave on Friday evening or early Saturday. Telegraph to me and I may come part of the way to meet you.   Give me this proof of your love and I will return it a thousandfold.   Please be here on Saturday because Sunday afternoon or evening I have to call upon one or two nice girls near the town.   If you are there on Saturday you can walk a little way with me on Sunday and I will introduce you to some charming people.

I should like to begin all this begging and praying over again as I am so terrified lest you should reflect too long.   But what is this short journey to you if it gives you the prospect of a more or less pleasant summer ?   So come in any case. I shall be bitterly distressed if I do not see you on Saturday. . . .   Your JOHANNES.

If you are coming with Marie, you are my guests at the hotel. Please send me a telegram.   I am waiting with such longing. P.S.

I have nothing to do the whole day and no immediate work in view which will occupy me.   You can either stay at my place or go with Marie to a certain very comfortable hotel, where you will find the exceedingly pleasant lady who thinks so very highly of you and where I shall be able to visit you whenever you like. . . .   You will not see a note of my music the whole of the summer if you do not hear the perfectly charming new *Minnelieder* on Monday.   I will show you as much love as you can possibly want or demand ; so to-morrow early I shall get a telegram, shan't I, and you will follow the day after ?

CLARA *to* BRAHMS.

BERLIN, *April* 27.

How can one possibly resist such entreaties from a friend for whom one has the smallest attachment ?   I cannot, dear Johannes.   So you may expect me at midday on Saturday.[1]

---

[1] Regarding Clara's visit to Hamburg see *Life*, Vol. II, p. 180.

I am coming alone.   But would it not be better if you booked
me a small room in an hotel close to your house ?   It would
put you out less and I could spend most of the day with you.
Do you really want to come part of the way to meet me ?
Much as I should like you to do so it would surely put you to
unnecessary expense. . . .   All news when we meet.   With
affectionate greetings to you and yours, Your devoted CLARA.

CLARA *to* BRAHMS.

KREUZNACH,[1] *Friday, June* 21.
[DEAR JOHANNES.]   I have played nothing yet, in fact I have
done nothing at all.   I am leading a thoroughly lazy life, but
am beginning to feel that this is having a bad effect on me,
and shall start work again at once.   I hope very much that
you too are industrious and that you are able to work quietly
in your little room on the ground floor.[2]   Men like you are
always watching Nature and drinking in her charms and thus
refresh your minds.   This is proved to me by the beautiful
description in your letter.   In this way a fine stormy sky can
lead to a symphony—who knows what may have happened
already ! . . .   And now farewell, dear Johannes, let me hear
from you again soon.   Affectionately yours, CLARA.

CLARA *to* BRAHMS.

KREUZNACH, *July* 8.
Why no word from you, dear Johannes, not even a greeting
through Joachim ?   Can you possibly be so absorbed in a work
that you have no thoughts for me ?   I cannot send my letter
off to Joachim without at least adding a hearty greeting for
you and without letting you know something which I know
will please you—that I have given a concert which was brilliant
beyond expectation.   Just fancy, I cleared 340 thalers [£50],
which will pay for three-quarters of my cure here.   I also had
another stroke of luck.   Think of it, I was eating a sweet
omelet the other evening and was taking a spoon full of sugar
out of a bowl when, just as I was going to swallow a mouthful,

---

[1] Up to the middle of June Clara had been with Brahms and Joachim
on the Rhine at Düsseldorf, the Ahrthal and Bonn.   See *Life*, Vol. II,
p. 181.

[2] In Bonn, Meckenheimerstrasse 29.

I saw my lost diamond twinkling at me from the middle of the sugar ! For a long time I could not recover from my astonishment and could not believe that it was the stone until I had tried it in the setting and found it fitted. So for a whole week, while I had been mourning its loss, it had lain in sweet peacefulness. Afterwards I had to think of all the ways in which I could possibly have lost it a second time ! ! ! ! I have no news for you. Everything goes on just as usual. I have not played again since the concert, but I have gained one pupil (a Russian girl). I have begun my cure again, but I still feel seedy. Give me the pleasure of another nice letter, dear Johannes, my heart longs for it. Your old and devoted CLARA SCHUMANN.

CLARA *to* BRAHMS.

BERLIN, *Nov.* 16.

. . . I have only good things to tell you about Bargheer. He played magnificently and with a courage that I admired. He made a very good impression on everybody. Unfortunately the present moment is so unfavourable and there are such heaps of concerts that mine, although they are the most popular of all, are only just filled. But this is very bad for me, for I need money and am not only giving up my time but also my strength here. However I suppose I must keep on now. Bargheer has a beautiful tone which often reminds one of Joachim, but his playing still lacks energy and character. He played each piece like the other. I think that playing in public a good deal will improve him. . . . Your devoted CLARA.

CLARA *to* BRAHMS.

BERLIN, *Nov.* 19.

. . . Now for something that I forgot to write to you about the other day. At Dresden I was introduced to a young lady from Livonia who is staying there in order to study music. . . . She was most anxious to follow me about on my travels —but that would be absurd. She evidently has talent, so I thought you might take her on (she is really in earnest about music and I believe you would soon get some pleasure out of her). I promised her to write to you about it. In case you do take her on I have recommended Frau Brandt to her and want to ask you kindly to inquire whether she can put her up and on what terms. I have already told her your own terms (2 thalers [1] an hour). She wants two piano and two theory lessons a week. She is not a woman of means, but she has enough to provide for her education for a year. What a pity it is that she is not pretty ! Though as far as she is concerned it is a good thing. I also told her that you would try to give her every opportunity of learning and hearing all she can, and would make her a member of your *Verein*. Please do all you can for her ; I really think she deserves it. But above all write to me at once about it, because the poor soul has already been waiting ten days for my answer. . . . Things are not going very well with me here, I never feel quite fresh and go to great pains in order to earn little more than green laurels, on which one cannot unfortunately keep body and soul together. Moreover, the public is so blasé and devoid of artistic feeling that I have given up all my beautiful plans regarding Handel, Bach, Brahms (Var.), Schumann (*Davidsbündler*). I only give my soirées because they happen to be announced, but any pleasure I might have in them is entirely spoilt. I can only play the things I like to people who are sympathetic, so that I shall not play here again in a hurry. I am longing for a letter from you. Your most devoted CLARA.

[1] Six shillings.

1861

Brahms *to* Clara.

HAMBURG, *Wednesday, Jan.* 30.

Most beloved Clara,

There is a time for everything, including letter writing unfortunately.[1] Oh why am I not a musical conductor at a Royal Court ? If I had been in Detmold [2]—and I so often wished you could be there—what a very different holiday I could have given you from the one in Hamburg. . . . What a blank there was here after your departure ! It was impossible to get back into the old routine, and one could settle down to nothing. But we shall have to put up with it.

I am now beginning all kinds of new lessons. Whenever I enter a strange house to meet and to become acquainted with new people I always have a sort of presentiment or wish that they may be really fine examples of humanity, but everybody looks like everybody else ; how seldom is one deeply stirred by the sight of one's fellow creatures ! I often wish that I might be allowed to see this person or that, you, for instance, for the first time again so as to have a real thrill once more. But I am quite pleased with things as they are. You must feel the same. You must be able to count on the fingers of one hand the people whom you can rave about, who appear to you to be complete. But don't you also often wish there were more of them about ? I suppose you know of no address in Hamburg where I could call ? . . . I am thoroughly enjoying *Palleske*,[3] it makes beautiful reading. Please greet all the

[1] Concerning Clara's stay in Hamburg from the 9th to the 22nd of January with slight interruptions, see *Life*, Vol. II, pp. 189–190.

[2] Clara had gone from Hamburg *via* Osnabrück to Detmold.

[3] This refers to Emil Palleske's Biography of Schiller, which Brahms sent to Clara on the 11th of September, 1860, and which, in a subsequent letter, Clara suggested they should read together in Düsseldorf in the autumn.—Tr.

Court circle for me in Detmold ; I have very few acquaintances outside it. And recommend my songs so that I may
have some sales. . . . Aren't you delighted with young Bargheer ? He is a ruddier and healthier edition of his brother.
With a thousand affectionate greetings, Your JOHANNES.

CLARA *to* BRAHMS.

DETMOLD, Feb. 1, Evening.

MY DEAR JOHANNES,

Thank you for your dear letter of this morning. If only
you knew how much I needed it. Parting was such a sad
business that for days now I have found it very difficult to
talk to anybody. Yesterday evening directly I arrived I wrote
to you, but the letter was so sad that now your dear note has
come it is out of keeping. I spent my whole morning paying
duty calls in the castle, which meant a lot of running about.
Then Princess Friederike had her lesson, after which I took a
walk in the wood in most glorious sunshine. But I returned
feeling very unhappy, for I could not help thinking of you
the whole time and of how lovely it would be if you were here.
How different a walk in the woods would be then, and much
more besides ! Yes, you are right, it would be nice if one
could be more often inspired by really fine people, but I prefer
to love one or two really deeply than to rave about a crowd.
And so I have no wish whatever that you should see me for
the first time again in order to have a real thrill once more (if
that were at all possible). I should prefer you to love me
heartily and ever more and more ; that is surely the best of
all, isn't it ?

What a lot has happened between the last page and this—a
family tea and Robert's D minor Sonata played by the Princess and Bargheer. Oh that was a trial, as you may well
imagine ! As there is to be a Court concert to-morrow I was
able to get away quickly and can now chat with you a little.
As for the Court concert, what am I to begin with—Mozart's
G major Concerto ? I know what you are thinking—that I
am a woman and there is nothing to be done with me. And
what terrible levity I have shown ! I have only played it
through once to-day but it is enchanting. I shall think of
you when I am playing it to-morrow. I hope to be able to

do the other some time, but I could not do both to-morrow. Bargheer is playing a concerto too and I the E Flat major, that is three in all. What a pity it is that I have not got the score of the A major. When going through the G major to-day I saw how pleasant it is to have it (the Princess had it) and I always prefer to learn a thing from the score.

The Prince has behaved very decently to Bargheer and is giving him a fixed sum of 200 thalers a year [£30] for teaching the Princess, so he can now reckon on a regular income of 600 thalers a year [£90], and in winter he can often get away, which he could hardly have done in Hamburg. . . . I have not seen the healthy edition of Bargheer yet. . . . I am glad that you like Palleske, for I too read him with the greatest interest. I like his kindly tone, free from all exaggeration. One is made to feel Schiller's weaknesses, but only like filmy clouds passing overhead, and the fine noble creature always shines forth again in all his glorious brilliance.

Just imagine what the King of Hanover has done! To-day I received 100 Louis d'or [£80] with the message that the King was sending me this *important* sum for my artistic services since the last settlement in 1859, as also for musical evenings to be held later. What do you think this means? What does it really commit me to? Have I been shown a mark of favour or not? Fortunately Joachim is still there and I wrote to him at once to ask him whether I should have to write a letter of thanks. Isn't it curious? If it really were a year's salary for five performances, I should be quite satisfied. . . . I saw Grimm [1] for a moment or two in Osnabrück. He seems to be quite well but I can't tell you for certain. He had come over for the concert—he might have spared himself the pains, for it really was not worth the journey. It was as feeble as anything possibly could be, although the hall was full. They are still in their infancy there and the public is quite uneducated. The choir was terribly bad; some of Robert's songs, *Du meine Seele* for instance, were sung like street songs. After Hamburg, Osnabrück—what a come down! Very rarely, if ever, do I fail to be moved for one moment at a concert. But this is what happened here, and I was all too bitterly aware that I

---

[1] Ever since November 1, 1860, he had been Musical Director at the University of Münster.

was not in my proper place. You cannot imagine how sad I am when I feel I have not put my heart into my playing. To me it is as if I had done an injury not only to myself but also to art.

I have been talking as if you had been patiently sitting listening at my side all the while. If only it were so ! Oh, write to me often, my beloved friend ! You know how you can show your love in this way, particularly when I can feel that you do it willingly and from your heart. Greet your dear ones for me and for yourself a thousand greetings from Your devoted CLARA.

BRAHMS *to* CLARA.
HAMBURG, *Early Thursday, Feb.* 7.

I was delighted with your two dear letters, best beloved Clara, and your raptures about the Mozart concertos.[1] But I was well aware that you would rejoice over them, and that is why I was annoyed to think that you might in the end leave Detmold without having played them. How I should like to have been there ! It is impossible to experience a greater joy than to hear these concertos come to life. Merely to read them through is not enough. They seem to spring from a veritable fountain of youth. Unfortunately, however, one really enjoys them best alone. The very public, which is always pointing to Mozart and making fun of modern tawdriness, really only enjoys the latter and gets no pleasure whatever from the former. . . . If ever you should play one of these concertos in public choose the C minor.[2] It is the most effective and, moreover, still new to you. . . .

You will now have some idea of how attractive a post in one of these little Courts is. One gets plenty of time to play to oneself, but unfortunately one cannot always feel happy at heart, for, after all, one would become nauseated by the faces one sees there, they are enough to make anybody a misanthropist. One can enjoy the beauties of Nature alone, but

[1] In a letter dated February 5, Clara had written to him to say that she had played the two concertos and described her delight over them. See *Life*, Vol. II, pp. 191–192.—TR.

[2] Clara played it first on the 22nd of November, 1861, in Hanover, and then on the 12th of December, in Leipsic.

when playing music in the drawing-room before people one
does not wish to be alone.

The fee from Hanover would please me very much if I were
certain that the passage referring to future services were only
dictated by a certain modesty, otherwise it is not so much
after all.   If only I could hear from you that you had formed a
firm resolve to work no more than you are obliged to, that is to
say, to give no more concerts than you absolutely must in order
to make both ends meet.   Have you given up all thought of
England ?   You surely have enough money.   It would be far
more reasonable and better on your part if you were to spare
not only your beautiful self but also your health. . . .   Write
soon and think kindly of Your JOHANNES.

CLARA *to* BRAHMS.

DÜSSELDORF, *Feb.* 13.

. . . Thank you for your dear letter.   But you have written
me nothing at all about yourself, your life, your new lady
pupils, your acquaintances, Halliers for instance, and whether
you often see her.   And above all you tell me nothing about
your work.   I imagine you as very industrious just now—if
only I could peep over your shoulder from time to time at the
music paper on your desk !   I loved your beautiful words about
Mozart.   Yes, if only you had been there how I should have
rejoiced with you ! . . .   That promises to be a rather tedious
concert tour in Belgium [1]—I believe I shall meet with completely virgin soil there, as far as my music is concerned, perhaps even a desert.   I find it very difficult to come to a decision about it, but I suppose I shall have to go.

You think, dear Johannes, that because I occasionally lay
something aside I am giving too many concerts.   But think of
my responsibilities—seven children still dependent on me, five
who have yet to be educated, and next winter I shall have
them all at home again.   You know my views—I want them
to enjoy their youth as long as possible, not in idleness but in
each other's company as long as can be arranged.   Every year
the boys cost me more, and if they are able to earn their own
living by the time they are twenty I shall consider myself
fortunate.   I still have a lot to do for the little ones, to

[1] See *Life*, Vol. II, pp. 194–195.

mention only their musical education, and you know what that costs now.   And ought I not also to think of my own future ? How can I tell whether I have not got a long life before me ? Am I to spend it in perpetual anxiety about my daily bread, or to become dependent upon my children ?   I should certainly be able to spare my health more if I had to exert myself less. But, after all, does not every efficient worker give his life for his calling ?   So I am not overdoing it, for I feel that I have lost nothing in freshness and warmth.   On the contrary, I feel younger than I did twenty years ago, and cannot help thinking that a quieter life would leave too much time for brooding over my troubles.   Perhaps things will improve later on. Maybe we shall once more live in the same town and then I shall feel the need of a quieter life.   If I lived with a dear friend I believe I might recover peace and good cheer, although my happiness is for ever lost.

I have not yet come to any conclusion about England.   I shall let it depend on whether I can find quarters in a private house where my expenses will be small.   And even so I shall not try very hard, but simply take what comes along.   But I doubt very much whether this will be possible. . . .   On Tuesday I am playing again at Cologne.   On Wednesday I return here and on Friday the 22nd I go to Brussels.   I begged Hiller to let me play the Allegro in E minor instead of Robert's Concerto.   But he refused. . . .   Princess Friederike wishes to be remembered to you.   She broke her silence on the last morning in order to give me this message.   They were all very kind to me, but not a sign of any honorarium, except that the old Princess secretly sent me ten *Friedrichsdor* [8 guineas] by Frl. Kehler.   I was engaged to play at a Court concert, but I also played there on three evenings in addition without getting a halfpenny more.   The Princess sent me a bracelet.   I believe it was one she had discarded in her youth, for it was so hideous that I could not wear it, and the moment I got here I sold it, and in so doing discovered that it was filled with lead and zinc.   It really is incredible ! . . .   And now with most affectionate greetings, my dear friend, and expecting a letter from you soon, Your CLARA.

CLARA *to* BRAHMS.

DÜSSELDORF, *May* 29.

I should have thanked you for your parcel to Aix [1] long ago had I not had such a heap of letters to answer here that I really did not know where to begin.   Moreover I was so over- come with fatigue, from which I have not yet recovered, that to-day is the first chance I have had of thanking you, and I do so none the less heartily than I would have done a week ago.   I had just taken my letter to the post when, at the concert in the evening, Wüllner handed me yours which, short though it was, brought your Sextet [2] with it ; and, after the festival, I was able to play it with Wüllner.[3]   His way of playing made me miss you frightfully, but he was so pleased to get to know the work that I put up with it.   He was par- ticularly delighted with the first movement which, owing to the fact that we played it several times, he understood best. I will see to your slight alterations when I get to Spa.[4]   Up to the present it has been out of the question.

You were continually in my thoughts throughout the *Joshua.* It was a wonderful performance, and the splendid choruses were full of swing and go.   The means to hand (there were 500 performers) were so concentrated in the comparatively small space as to produce a prodigious effect which left nothing to be desired.   I don't remember having experienced such complete and unsullied joy for a long time.   The third day was also very beautiful—Joachim played divinely.   We both received laurel wreaths, but in addition he was literally bom- barded with bouquets by the ladies.   I don't think I have ever heard him play so magnificently.   But one always thinks that !   He did me the pleasure of remaining here half a day longer, which after all the turmoil was very enjoyable.   But we were both very tired.   Unfortunately on his return journey to Hanover he might have met with a serious accident.   His train ran at full speed into another, the carriages slipped the

[1] Clara had played at the music festival there with exceptional success.

[2] Arranged by Brahms for four hands.

[3] Franz Wüllner, teacher of the pianoforte at the Munich Conser- vatoire.

[4] She went to Spa for the cure on the 31st.

lines and the buffers smashed to atoms like glass. One or two passengers were severely injured but he came off with a blow on his head (caused by his violin falling on him from the rack). It is terrible to think that such a thing can happen in a flash to decide the fate of a beloved fellow creature ! . . .

I have again had an offer from America, this time for four months starting from the 1st of November, with a fee of 10,000 thalers [£1,500]. But I have refused it. It would mean my losing the whole year and spending at least half of the fee on my requirements, and so I should only have 5,000 thalers for all my trouble. It's not good enough. But I have been thinking over it for several days. All the same such matters are really nothing compared with the cares connected with my children which are never ending. . . .

On Friday I am going to Spa and will remain there in any case the whole of June. I have an engagement on the 1st of July, but as I am not allowed to play (I mean in public) during the cure, I shall stop it before then. I shall feel going there all alone very much, particularly as I am not allowed to work, to play or to write. But how dreadful it is to wander about alone—I really cannot do it, it makes me quite melancholy. Dearest Johannes, do write to me as often as you can, please, please ! Every day I have been secretly hoping for news from you, and would have been so glad to have had a note before my departure. You must know how much your letters cheer me up. You can also send me new compositions quite easily if you write your name on them and register them. My address is :—

Madame Cl. Sch.

Pianiste à

Spa

(en Belgique).

. . . Your devoted CLARA.

CLARA *to* BRAHMS.

KREUTZNACH,[1] *July* 15.

I shall not keep you waiting any longer for my thanks for your last two letters, although I cannot write to you at once

[1] On the 3rd of July Clara had left Spa and gone to Kreuznach *via* Bonn.

as I should like to.   I am so depressed by a thousand and one worries connected with my children, that I cannot think of anything pleasant to say.   It really is too much for a woman alone to have to endure this burden of care without a man to help her.   I am more particularly at a loss to know what to do with my boys.   According to Dr. Breusing and the tutor at Fr. Böcking's, who is an extremely cultivated man with a vast experience in educational matters, Ludwig cannot be sent to any ordinary school, and so he must be separated from Ferdinand who is now going to the Gymnasium.   How hard it is for him, and where am I to send him ?   He wants strengthening and I am advised to send him to a clergyman in the country.   But where on earth can one find all the requisite conditions ?   If only I could talk to you about it all you would perhaps be able to give me some advice.   But I should not like to bring my long face into your cheerful balcony-room.

I am so glad you have decided to move into the country.[1] But will you ever feel like work in such a charming and alluring neighbourhood ?   Are you also boarded in the house where you live ?   Could I take you by surprise some time in your balcony-room ?   Oh, but how far away it is !   And now you have all the magnificent songs and in such a beautiful garb. I am so pleased about it !   What I should like would be to find something that would give you pleasure.   What a delight that would be to me !   You have not written to say what works you are having printed now. . . .

I am now installed here for a few weeks and have all sorts of things to settle with Elise, Julie, etc. from here, very difficult things too.   I am not playing at all.   Nothing pleases me.   I often have to ask myself whether after all I am still an artist.   Do send me something again, and then perhaps I shall feel once more that I am one.

Farewell, dearest Johannes.   I cannot write any more, I am too miserable.   Write to me again soon.   I shall remain here for the present.   In August I shall go for a few weeks to Rigi, perhaps the air there will strengthen my nerves and raise my spirits.   Most affectionately, Your CLARA.

Greet your dear parents for me.   Are they not very sad that you should be leaving them ?

[1] To Hamm near Hamburg.

CLARA *to* BRAHMS.

KREUZNACH, *July* 29.

Really the pleasure you gave me was all too short. I hardly
had time to look the things through, that is to say I could
only take sips at the fountain of delight. And if only it had
been Joachim to whom I had to give up everything ! I am
so fond of him that I would give way more easily for him than
for anybody else. I am really very sad about it. I even had
to send the beloved Sextet with the rest. It was a good thing
that I happened to have it by me. I had brought it with me
because I did not wish to part from it. I hope you received
it all in time. I packed the things the moment your letter
arrived. I won't pretend to give you a considered opinion
but I can tell you about my first impressions. Would you like
me to do that ? I have often found that I remain true to my
first impressions.

There is much in the movement of the G minor Quartet
that I like, and much that I care for less. The first part seems
to me too little G minor and too much D major, and I think
that owing to the lack of the former it loses in clarity. The
passage after the second *motif*, where it becomes so full of
feeling

enchanted me with its swinging accompaniment. I do not
like the passage

so much, because it strikes me as too commonplace for Johannes
Brahms. The development in the second part is very fine, and
the crescendo up to the G major is full of life. But what has
become of the repetition of the second theme ? Does the motif
where the string instruments come in alone *p* take its place ?
Well, it does all right. And it is so beautiful where the piano
joins in in triplets. I think I could get to like the whole movement very much if only the beginning of the first part were

to keep more steadily to G minor and did not appear to be
so long in comparison with the second part. I cannot help
thinking that if you had me in mind at all when you were
writing it you must have known that I should be charmed
with the scherzo in C minor. In fact I should hardly call it a
scherzo at all. I can only think of it as an allegretto. But
it is a piece after my own heart! How passionate and profound
is the mournful passage

and how magnificently it carries one away. . . . I should
like to play the piece over and over again to myself for ever.
And how fine the organ-points must sound! You are certainly
smiling at me and thinking that I am not aware of the higher
musical value of the first movement. Certainly I am; but
in the C minor part I find myself so tenderly transported to
dreamland that it is as if my soul were rocked to sleep by the
notes. I don't know the scherzo in A major [1] well enough
yet, but I have followed the beautiful intricacies of the theme
with great interest. It winds in and out so wonderfully, and
one thing develops out of the other. The second motif reminds me very much of a passage in Robert's String Quartet:

not precisely in the melody but in its design and feeling. The
trio is very fresh and the rhythm is original. The sixth and
seventh bars struck me at first as unpleasing, but one gets
used to them. I think it is the same with this piece as with
many others of yours—one only gets to like it when one knows
it thoroughly and has heard it often.

Of course I was not able to form any idea of the *Credo* in
the short interval at my disposal because I require time to
find my way through such a labyrinth of canons. I marvel

[1] Op. 26.

at your skill in these ingenious and difficult things, but I really only enjoy them when I hear them beautifully sung. The song out of Ossian is enchanting. It must sound strangely wistful, but I think it would be difficult to sing. I was struck by one harsh passage in it but I cannot point out precisely where it is. It occurs where you go enharmonically into B Flat major and the progressions appear in the bass two bars further on. It could easily be avoided. I have kept back the choral piece and think that you have got out of the difficulty very ingeniously. But I cannot regard as beautiful such a chaos of harmonies following one on top of the other. And now, dear Johannes, let me thank you for all these things, which would have given me much more pleasure if I had been able to enjoy them a few days longer.

. . . I did not regret my journey to Aix,[1] and I thoroughly enjoyed the *Mass, Kyrie, Sanctus* and *Agnus Dei.* You cannot imagine how beautiful it was. The *Kyrie* is most stirring and as if cast as a whole, and in the *Sanctus* there are certain passages of such wonderful beauty that they make one's back go cold. Except for a few short passages, this music is really most religious and ecclesiastical, much more so than I had thought. Wüllner had practised the things well. Naturally I no longer feel any hesitation about printing it. If only I could hear the *Requiem* too !

I am so glad to hear that you are pleased with your summer quarters. You must now work hard at your composing. You wrote in the first place to say that you would only be able to stay there two months, and yet you think that I should still find you there if I came in the autumn. If I guess aright I believe that Joachim must have surprised you on your birthday. I don't think he was in Hanover at the time. . . . Stockhausen telegraphed to me to-day from Baden-Baden to ask whether I should like to play before the Grand-Duchess Helene of Russia to-morrow. I simply replied by asking what the fee would be. I am not after any honours at the hands of these grandees.

The other day I gave a very successful concert here at which my sister,[2] who is on a visit to me, assisted me, and also played

---

[1] Where Wüllner produced Schumann's *Mass* on June 22.
[2] Marie Wieck.

solo.　The proceeds came in very opportunely for my journey to Switzerland.　Up to the present Spa has done me more harm than good, and my only hope for this summer is the good air and the pleasant company I shall have in Switzerland. . . .　You have literally bewitched me with some of the melodies in your new pieces.　I have not been able to get them out of my head for days.　Let me embrace you in the spirit for them, dear Johannes.　How much I should prefer to do it in the flesh ! . . .　As always, Yours most affectionately, CLARA.

BRAHMS *to* CLARA.
　　　HAMM *near* HAMBURG, *Early Wednesday, Sept.* 11.
BELOVED CLARA,

I had again written a long letter full of descriptions and misgivings about lodgings and had carried it about with me in my pocket, when lo, I learnt that unfortunately we had had our summer and that we could now rejoice that quite a number of good things can happen in September, as, for instance, the birth [1] of aparticularly charming human creature [*nettes Menschenkind*],[2] or the arrival of the same in Hamburg.　Sometimes I think that both events might be celebrated together. If that could really happen and I were to know it and think about it, and Joachim came as well

we could try a quartet on the 13th.　If you do not come I will just play the Adagios quite sadly to myself, an exercise for which, unfortunately, they are well suited.　Furthermore, I will buy Mendelssohn-Bartholdy's wonderfully beautiful *Reisebriefe* for you on the 13th.　But perhaps you have them already.　They are splendid.　I shall also do all sorts of things for you, while in the spirit you will be constantly at my side, but I shall not go so far as to send anything, I am too much of a believer in surprises for that !

---

[1] Clara's birthday on the 13th of September.

[2] An expression frequently used by Avé.

[3] This is the music to the words *O namenlose Freude* (O nameless joy) from *Fidelio*.

I have not fixed on any lodgings and must beg of you to be as modest as possible in your expectations. I am sorry, but I am afraid you will not be satisfied. Won't Joachim come after all ? It would really be most delightful if he did. It would be easier to find something for him, of course. A man can do without many things that you women require. I shall probably have to ask you to put up at the Petersburg for a day, and then I shall be ready for anything. If you are not pleased with this place then I shall be just as happy to accompany you elsewhere for as long as you like in the Hartz or anywhere, where perhaps J. J. might come with us. After that I expect to spend the rest of my time until Christmas in Hanover. Honestly ! and if it were not for the King's,[1] I should have no misgivings because I am so very anxious to go. I should love to have a letter now in which I could find that you and Julie or Marie and J. J. would be here on the 13th. (My room in the town is occupied, that is why I cannot offer it to you.) If this letter should still find you at home it brings you the heartiest wishes for your birthday and for all times. Your JOHANNES.

CLARA *to* BRAHMS.

BONN, *Sept.* 17.

Your letter, my dear Johannes, was awaiting me in Godesberg, and, as you may imagine, gave me the happiest of welcomes when I reached there on the afternoon of the 13th. I was sorry, however, that you should have expected a surprise from me, particularly as the idea had been in my mind quite a lot, though I was unable to realize it. This month there are any number of things to think of and to do which leave me no peace. In the first place, I must take Ludwig next week to a country parson in Wissen near Siegburg, where provisionally he is to remain for a year. I was anxious to see to this myself, and to remain there for a few days in order to make the change (instead of Berlin) easy for him, and to give him a pleasanter first impression than if he had been fetched, for instance. What I chiefly wished to avoid was that he should feel any bitterness or suspect that Ferdinand was being put

---

[1] Here Brahms appears to be making a jocular allusion to the Court of Hanover.—TR.

before him, or taking his place. The latter will go to Berlin in the first week of October. Marie will go with him in order to take up her duties as housekeeper, and Julie will come from Schönau. So I have heaps to do and am now here (at Kyllmann's) to complete the outfits of the two boys. And all this means more time and money than one imagines. In addition I have to fix my plans for the winter and write all over the place. In short, I cannot possibly expect to come to you earlier than the first week in October, so must resist my heart's desire for a little while longer. But perhaps you intended going to Hanover as early as October. But of this I knew nothing, neither did Joachim. Write to me quite frankly about it. I can well understand that after you have put up with things for a whole summer in Hamburg you want a change. And this I know you enjoy more at Joachim's side than anywhere else. So if you would prefer to go to Hanover at once, please be sure to tell me, dearest Johannes.

My plan was to remain three or four weeks quietly in Hamburg practising, then possibly towards the beginning of November to give a concert in order to earn some money, because I have little to spare and still have to spend a lot, although I have spent so much already. But if you would prefer it I might perhaps come to Hanover too. I can also earn some money there. J. J. is not coming to Hamburg now because he is longing to get to work and does not want to leave Hanover. Would it not be a good thing if you were to pay a short visit to the Harz now and return in October ? Please write and tell me what you want to do.

I think you are right about the Hotel Petersburg. Perhaps it would be best if I stopped there, in which case please have the piano properly tuned. How I long for you, my dear friend, and how I rejoice to think of the many new things, the melancholy adagios. Had you already sent them to me ? I was really hoping a little that you had. I thank you heartily in advance for Mendelssohn's Letters. I have looked into them a little here and am quite enchanted. Every one of his words strikes such a vivid note in my soul. You have really given me a great joy. . . . But now I must say adieu. Answer me soon, so that I may know how matters stand. I greet you from the bottom of my heart. Your CLARA.

CLARA *to* BRAHMS.

DÜSSELDORF, *Sept.* 26.

With what a heavy heart I go to my writing-desk to-day for I must once again postpone my cherished plan to come to you. But I hope you will think I am right and then my heart will be lighter. As my domestic arrangements now stand, Marie is going to take up her housekeeping duties in Berlin next week. Frl. Werner had promised me that she would help her in every way, but unfortunately she is now in Weimar and will remain there until the New Year. Marie wanted to have a shot at managing alone, but when I put myself in her place I thought this would be rather hard, and the nearer the time comes the more my heart, which is always struggling between duty and desire, tells me that it would not be right to allow the poor child to go there alone. I must go there with her, at least for the first fortnight, to lend her my support and to establish her relationship to the servants from the start by my authority. I also want to take Ferdinand (who is travelling with us) to Dr. Planer myself, for it would make the boy feel more comfortable. And then there is Felix who has to be taken to a violin teacher (which is an easier matter for me than for Marie). So you see I have duties enough to fulfil. If you are remaining in Hamburg I shall be able to come about the third week in October. But I should certainly not be able to stay a month with you, but only a fortnight or three weeks at most. Then I shall go to Oldenburg, Hanover, (where I have asked for your Serenade to be played at the same concerts as I shall play in). I shall also play at Bremen and other places in the neighbourhood. I shall enjoy your company so much more if I know that I have neglected none of my home duties.

I feel sure my beloved and understanding friend will think I am right, won't he ? But do tell me where you are. You do not answer my letters. I do not know yet whether you are still in Hamburg or not. . . . Please let me have a word soon, a kind one, to let me know whether I may look forward to the middle of October in Hamburg. I have so much to do and so many thousand things to see to and letters to write that I feel quite giddy. So I must leave a good deal until we meet. After all, perhaps it is better that I should keep something back. So with most affectionate greetings to my good Johannes, Your faithful old CLARA.

BRAHMS *to* CLARA.

HAMM, *near* HAMBURG, *Early Friday, Oct.* 11.

DEAREST AND BEST OF CLARAS,

Your letter has just reached me and I am certainly not at all satisfied. My careless way of writing and my perfunctory manner of dealing with money matters is indeed largely responsible. So I will try to-day to be clear and settle matters. In all things that concern me you always have treated me, and always will, as though I belonged to you, and yet in all things that concern you I am allowed to do nothing. If I had not a farthing I should live with you. If I had a house you would certainly live with me. But now I have a purse full of superfluous pelf, which I shall scatter very shortly out of sheer anger (the Treasury Bonds) simply because it is of no earthly use to me as I am not allowed to spend it when as in this case it alone can serve. I can assure you that I shall be really furious if you refuse to be my guest here with Julie. If you will not do it, I shall throw all my money out of the window within a month. For what is the good of the trash otherwise ? But now let me offer a few less violent reasons.

1. I would make my hostess [1] here exceedingly happy if I were to give up my room to you for the time. I have never mentioned it to you because I did not want to make you feel under a sort of obligation to a stranger. And in that case I would have taken another room and paid for you in that way. For I pay ridiculously little here and it is only as a great favour that Dr. Rösing accepts any money from me at all for the room she kindly lets me have.

2. After your doleful letter I would have called on you at once in Berlin, if Grädener were not giving two concerts during the next few days at which I have promised to play. But if you do not come at once I shall be in Berlin in a day or two, and shall refuse to stay with you but will go to an exorbitantly expensive place, and will travel First Class from Berlin to each of Grädener's concerts here, and return each day with a most extravagant present for you, simply to annoy you and to show

[1] Dr. Rösing.

you how deeply attached I am to my money, because it is so useful to me for you ! After that you will be telling me that I could have managed ten times as cheaply here with two guests.

3. It is much nicer here than in Berlin but this does not weigh much with me because there is plenty for me to hear in Berlin, and provided I spend enough money I can find enough to amuse me.

4. I composed 'the Variations [1] for your birthday and you have not heard them yet although you ought long ago to have been practising them for your concerts.

6. I want to try my quartets here, but shall not move a finger unless you come.

7. It would be rascally of you if on the receipt of this letter you did not immediately send me an acknowledgment of the 200 thalers received and make your way here at once.

8. Otherwise I shall come to Berlin to-morrow and squander everything.

9. *Da capo.*

10. Hanover and Oldenburg constitutes the minimum of what I have promised myself when I see you again, for I want to enjoy your company at my ease and ultimately take a few drives with you, and you must be here on Sunday, early on Sunday, for on Monday you might perhaps not find me, while if you came on Sunday we might be in the Saxenwald etc. together on Monday, and that you would find very pleasant. Goodness me, but I believe Grädener's concert is on Tuesday, so we must have Sunday together first, otherwise the whole business will have no point. All I know is that there will be trouble if on Sunday I do not play my little Variations to you either here or in Berlin.

It is scandalous that Bargiel should have sent them off as early as September and that you whose name stands on the title-page have shown no interest in them. So once and for all will you have my money ? If not I'll throw it away so that you will see it glitter as it flies.

But now, joking apart, I should be only too glad to come to Berlin, but must first find out what Grädener has to say about it, and will then come back here with you and go on to

[1] Op. 24. Variations and Fugue on a theme by Handel for pianoforte.

Hanover and Oldenburg. Your concerts here, of which two will be in Hamburg, and one in Altona, will be quite successful. Things are not as bad as all that. You will earn quite a substantial sum.[1] In any case you must hurry up and send me a line or a telegram, otherwise I shall be packing up and getting into the train. Can you read my scrawl or are you going to order me to write more slowly ? Well then, hoping for the best and that you will be an angel of goodness for once and take my money (I shall wait two days longer), Your devoted JOHANNES.

CLARA *to* BRAHMS.

HANOVER, *Nov.* 21.

What pleasure you gave me to-day with your dear letter. It arrived just after the rehearsal of the Mozart Concerto,[2] during which I had you constantly in mind, just as I did at Detmold with the G major and the A major. It is wonderful but quite difficult enough. I am rather frightened of playing it in Leipsic, because David approaches Mozart in such a careless spirit that one would prefer not to begin at all, and things go badly if that's the case. We shall only start practising it in earnest to-morrow. Your cadenza pleases Joachim very much up to the unresolved 6/4 chord, which, as you have allowed me to make any change, I shall take the liberty of resolving. I was once more delighted with the orchestra (in Haydn's D major Symphony) and particularly with the conductor. What a joy it is to meet some one whose enthusiasm shines in his eyes and who seems to cast a halo about the whole thing the moment he steps up to his desk, so that from the very first note one feels all of a glow and full of fervour. You really must enjoy this treat next winter, dear Johannes ! I long for you to have it. . . .

I succeeded very well [3] with the G major Concerto.[4] I should so like you once to hear how I play when you are not

---

[1] Clara remained off and on from the 25th of October to the 9th of December in Hamburg. See *Life*, Vol. II, pp. 199–200.

[2] C minor.

[3] In Bremen, where Clara gave some concerts in the second half of November.

[4] By Beethoven.

there. When you are present I always make an effort to play particularly well, and this often makes me feel constrained. The audience was most enthusiastic and only Herr Töpken and Herr Möller refused to lay aside their severe expression of connoisseurship for a moment. I would have written to you from there on the first day, but it was a frightfully strenuous one for me. In the morning I paid visits and practised. In the afternoon at Fr. Möller's I again played for an hour, so that in the evening I was quite exhausted. The night was cold, my window was frozen up, and we could not get warm although we piled up all the rugs. In addition we were particularly unfortunate in all three of us having seats with broken springs, so that my poor back hurt me most dreadfully. Sleep was out of the question, so I thought of you most of the time. The moon shone brightly until seven o'clock in the morning and by means of it I sent you my morning greeting. How sad I should be if I were not to see you again soon, but things will be different shortly. . . . This evening we have to go to Herrenhausen.[1] We had quite forgotten all about it. So I must now leave you in order to go and practise. Early on Sunday I go to Oldenburg where I shall think of you a good deal. But this is always the case without any effort on my part. Joachim and Julie greet you heartily and I, beloved friend, close with a fond embrace from Your CLARA.

CLARA *to* BRAHMS.

OLDENBURG, *Nov.* 27.

Just a word, dearest Johannes, to tell you that I heard your Serenade yesterday and that it gave me the greatest pleasure. You know what I would most like to have done, beloved composer, if only I had had you there. If I could I would write to you pages and pages about every bar that enchanted me. But here every minute of my time is counted. You have many friends here, which makes Oldenburg dear to me. I have already played your Variations to Dietrich—of course he was delighted, as I knew he would be. You must come here this winter. I am sure you would be quite happy for a few days. The orchestra is quite good and Dietrich seems already to have exercised a very good influence over the place.

[1] The King of Hanover's summer residence.

What pleased me more than anything else was the musicians themselves, who seem to take so much joy in their work, and do not get through it like hirelings as they do in most places. . . . With a thousand greetings, dear Johannes, until Saturday. Your most affectionate CLARA.

1862

DÜSSELDORF, *Jan. 25, Saturday.*

DEAR JOHANNES,

First of all many thanks for your letter and the Variations. You see I am still in Düsseldorf. On the journey here I had the misfortune to get a severe attack of rheumatism in my right arm (I had been leaning out of the window on this arm) and I was hardly able to move it for several days. Of course I had to telegraph to Bonn and Frankfort, cancelling my concerts there. You can imagine how hard this was for me, the more so as up to the present my earnings have been very poor, in fact I have lost almost the whole month. Fortunately I was able to arrange to play at the Museum in Frankfort after all on the 31st. Last Tuesday I gave a soirée in Cologne (Stockhausen sang) and on Thursday one in Bonn. Both were quite successful. This is the first day I have been able to write at all, for I feel the rheumatism more in writing than in playing. I returned here yesterday evening, and my first thought to-day is to write to you.

Although my arm was in a sling I went to Cologne to hear *Faust* [1] and cannot remember ever having enjoyed anything more in my life. I feel convinced that this work will one day take its place among the greatest of masterpieces. The second part is at least as great as the third.

Seldom have I received such a deep impression from a new work as I did from this one. What a crescendo of delight from beginning to end, not a moment of boredom! And how can I possibly describe the moving quality of the harmonies? If one has not heard it, there are many things in it of which one can have no idea—Ariel, for instance, at the beginning of the second part, the sunrise, Faust's death and

---

[1] The first performance of Schumann's *Faust*, as a whole, in Cologne.

a good deal more.   I am sending you an article of Bischoff's
(I happen to have it here).   Let me have it back, it belongs
to Fr. Leser.   The beauty of Stockhausen's singing defies
description.   Unfortunately at the end and for fear lest the
public should get up and go, Hiller started the *Leonora* Overture
immediately on the close of the *Faust*, which made a very
unfavourable impression on everybody.   It was really terrible
—he hardly allowed the last notes of the *Faust* to die away.
I should never have believed that I could possibly listen to this
Overture except with the utmost delight, but to all us musicians
this was impossible.

All the musicians from the neighbourhood were there, even
Kirchner and Walter who had come from all that distance.
Everybody missed you and nobody could understand how you
could be absent when this particular work was being given.
I was very glad to hear that you derived so much pleasure
from your quartets and that Scholz is at last beginning to
appreciate your music.   Please greet both of them heartily
from me. . . .   And now with affectionate greetings, Your
CLARA.

CLARA *to* BRAHMS.

PARIS, *April* 6, *Sunday Evening.*

I am now able, dear Johannes, to tell you of the success
of my playing to-day at the Conservatoire.[1]   Beethoven's E
Flat major Concerto went very well and there was a storm
of applause.   It was beautifully accompanied and all the
players were delightful to me.   I have never had such a reception anywhere, except in Vienna, and you can well imagine
how this has stimulated me.   However poor our opinion may
be of the public on the whole, such lively sympathy is very

[1] In a previous letter from Paris, dated the 21st of March, Clara
wrote to Brahms as follows : " I heard a concert at the Conservatoire
the other day.   From the point of view of technique it was the most
perfect I have ever heard, but—cold.   Everything is calculated for
effect, and the whole composition is often sacrificed to that end without
scruple.   They often play a quite magnificent theme without any light
and shade or warmth, and then suddenly accentuate some point in
such a manner that the whole audience is electrified.   But nowhere
else can one hear such *pp* and *ff*, such *cresc.* and *dim.*" See *Life,*
Vol. II, p. 204.—TR.

inspiriting for the actual moment in which one is sitting there. On Tuesday I am giving my third concert. Whether it will be the last I cannot yet tell as the weather is so summery that the stifling air gets quite unbearable in the small halls, and when the trees burgeon outside there will be little enjoyment to be got out of concerts. In any case I shall remain a little longer as I give lessons every day and shall probably be asked for a few more soirées, for which I receive 20 louis d'or [£16]. There is also a lot I want to see which I hope to do in Holy Week. Up to the present this has not been possible, as I am tremendously busy, so much so that I often hardly have time for my lunch. To-day they have left me my evening free so that I have a little breathing space for once. I was asked to go to London, but I have definitely refused. Not that I think my stay here will provide me with a sufficient surplus to last the whole summer, but I will be frivolous for once. I am honoured here as only an artist can be honoured. Why should I go to London where I am regarded as nothing more than an ordinary craftsman !

There I have to call on the critics ; here I need not move an inch, they come and look me up—no, I can't do it, I prefer to spare my energy. Stockhausen wrote proposing a tour in the provincial towns, but the season is too advanced for this. . . . I should like to hear more about your stay in Oldenburg, and whether you played at the Court, also whether you were pleased with your honorarium. Did you also play at the concert where you conducted your Serenade, and what ? How did Dietrich get on ? Please answer these questions and look at them once more when you write. I am extremely sorry about your mother's trouble. I am so much afraid that it will leave her weak. It is always rather serious when old people break a bone. Do write and let me know how she is getting on. You will be glad to hear that Madame Erard has again presented me with a grand piano which I am to select before I go. I needed one so badly. Please send the Variations, the Songs and the Duet to Berlin so that I may have a nice welcome there. I shall probably go from here *via* Brussels to Berlin, as I have all sorts of things to see to for my children there. . . . Let me hear from you soon, and tell me what you are working at. May the

beautiful spring and the nightingales beneath your window
conjure sweet melodies from you and make you think sometimes
of Your ever loyal CLARA.

CLARA *to* BRAHMS.

BRUSSELS, *May* 1.

I have at last left Paris, and have been here since yesterday,
and I am snatching my first quiet hour to-day in order to
write to you, my dear Johannes. During my last weeks in
Paris things were so lively that I had not a moment from
morning to night. I had to give a fourth concert, then another
for the German *Hilfsverein*. After that I came on here, to
a soirée given by Princess Orloff to which I was specially
invited. The soirée was last night. Madame Viardot also
accompanied me here. To-day I received an invitation to
another soirée, and if they pay me well I shall remain here a
few days longer. I am staying with the Kufferraths, where
I am very comfortable.

Things went very well with me towards the end in Paris and
I did what no instrumentalist has done there for years—I
earned a lot of money. It is true that Madame Erard defrayed
my hotel expenses during my stay and that these amounted
to at least 400 thalers [£60]. But she did it in such a way
that I could not possibly object. The moment I arrived she
begged me to consider myself her guest. I have selected a
beautiful instrument, so that I have no reason to regret having
gone to Paris. But I am very tired and am looking forward
to the peace and quiet which awaits me. I don't yet know
what my plans are for the future. I shall in any case wait
until I reach Berlin and then I shall be able to settle everything. . . .

On the evening before I left Paris I had a little soirée at
my place to which only artists were invited and I played your
Variations. I had previously played them, together with the
Sextet and a Serenade, privately to one or two musicians,
and they were so moved that they begged me to play them
again. . . . I shall not ask you any more to tell me what
you are working at—alas ! I hear nothing about these matters
nor about your inner life in general. . . . I suppose you have
heard that Joachim often plays at three concerts on the same

day. I never expected anything else than that he would go
back to London again. Has he not invited you to the Exhibi-
tion there ? You ought to go and have a look at the place
one day. Not long ago I also heard that you were going with
Joachim to Vienna. Why is it, dear Johannes, that I hear
of these things through third parties ? Have you forgotten
how deeply interested I am in everything that concerns you ?
. . . But they are calling me to a meal, so I must say adieu.
. . . Let me hear from you soon. I shall be in Düsseldorf
from Sunday onwards. Your ever faithful CLARA.

CLARA *to* BRAHMS.

DÜSSELDORF, *Nov.* 3.

I am knocking at your door this morning, dear Johannes,
with a piece of news. But probably you have heard it already,
for people pick up every scrap of news about us. Well it is
this—in April 1863 I shall move to Baden-Baden, where I
have bought a nice little house in the Lichtentaler Allee. It
is just large enough for me to be able to spend the summer
there with my children.

I shall enjoy many advantages there both as regards society
and nature, and shall only need to see people when I want
to see them. For my house is in a quiet part behind the
Oos but with a view of the fine broad avenue. I shall also
be sure to have well-paid lessons there for so many foreigners
come during the whole of the summer. The girls will also
be able to find pupils, and what a lot of travelling about this
will save me. Not that I shall give up going to Switzerland
once every summer, but it will only be for a short time. You
have probably heard from Rieter that I went there for a week
from Guebwiller. We had a lot of beautiful music at Winterthur and Bâle, and I came away with a heavy heart in order
to take up my workaday life again. Among other things I
was particularly charmed with Kirchner's organ playing,
especially his *Phantasies.* He also understands registering
so well and conjures the best out of the organ.

I knew all along that you would be delighted with Vienna.
By now you will have visited Lewinsky, to whom I have
spoken a great deal about you, and perhaps have learnt to
like him. Julie Asten is now probably studying with you

and you will have been glad to take her on. Greet her for
me. It is quite impossible for me to write as I am so frightfully busy and have been for the last six weeks, so that I really
don't know which way to turn. . . . With ever affectionate
greetings, Your CLARA.

BRAHMS *to* CLARA.

VIENNA, *Nov.* 18.

DEAR CLARA,

I feel I must send you the enclosed letter.[1] It represents
a much sadder event for me than you can imagine or perhaps
grasp. As a man I suppose I am a little bit old-fashioned ;
in any case I am certainly so in this respect, that I am not
a cosmopolitan, but am as attached to my native town as
I might be to my mother. Now you must be aware that as
early as this autumn the *Sing-Akademie* were seriously thinking
of engaging a second Conductor, and it was a question of Deppe [2]
or myself, and just before I left Hamburg to come here I
was asked privately whether I would be inclined to accept.
And now this hostile friend comes and ousts me—for ever.
How rare it is for one of us to find a permanent niche and
how glad I should have been to find mine in my native town.
Happy as I am here with so many beautiful things to gladden
my heart, I nevertheless feel, and shall always feel, that I
am a stranger and can have no peace. You have probably
already heard about the affair and thought of me in connection
with it. But I don't suppose it occurred to you what a heavy
blow it has been to me. And yet I need only make a sign
for you to see how much I am losing. If I could not fasten
my hopes on my native town, what claims could I have elsewhere ? Where should I care to go even if I had the chance ?
Apart from what you experienced with your husband you
know that, as a general rule, what our fellow-citizens like best
is to be rid of us and to allow us to flit about in the desert
waste of the world. And yet what one wants is to be bound,

[1] From Avé.

[2] Ludwig Deppe (1828–1890) was a pupil of Marxsen in Hamburg,
where in 1860 he became a teacher of music and founded a singing
academy. He went to Berlin in 1870, where ultimately he became
Capellmeister to the Court. He enjoyed a considerable reputation
as a musical conductor.—TR.

and to acquire all that which makes life worth living. One
is naturally frightened by the thought of solitude. An active
existence in lively association with others and with plenty of
stimulating intercourse, the happiness of the family circle,—
who is so little of a human being as not to long for these things ?

If you want to be entertained by any more, see how my
friendly enemy mixes honey with the hemlock which he
gives me to drink, on the one hand he points to the future
which spreads gloriously before me, and on the other, forgetting all this, he looks forward to a future without me.

I am also sending a few lines to my parents, which are
intended for you too. Do not mention the contents of this
letter or even its existence to anyone, particularly Avé, Stockhausen and my parents. Affectionately yours, JOHS.

CLARA *to* BRAHMS.

HAMBURG, *Nov.* 21, *Friday Evening.*

I am writing to you to-day after the Philharmonic concert
so that you may hear about it soon and from me. Can I tell
you how much I have been thinking of you ? You must
know it without my needing to say so. I hesitated a good
deal before accepting the engagement here. But in the end I
thought I must overcome my heart's promptings with the
force of reason. But how difficult it is ! And now, on top
of it all, I received your sad letter yesterday. You know
how deeply I feel anything that concerns you, so you can well
imagine how pained I was by your letter. Until that moment
I had not taken the matter seriously ; for, although Avé
had often spoken of certain plans, I had never thought of their
being carried out. Now, however, I am suffering all your
pain with you just as I suffered it with my Robert years ago.
Avé received me yesterday with this news on his lips and we
sat talking together until deep into the night. I told him
frankly what I thought, that it had never entered my head
to regard such a thing as possible,[1] that it was a scandal etc.
etc. He replied with all sorts of reasons ; for instance, that

---

[1] From this and the previous letter from Brahms to Clara it appears
that the news which reached Brahms from Hamburg in March concerning Stockhausen's appointment to the post vacated by Grund, could
not have come as a surprise to Brahms.

there is a lot of spade work to be done here, and that this is not a task fit for such a musician as you are. He expected Stockhausen to do this after which you could step in. Altogether both he and Stockhausen seemed to speak as if they were quite confident that you and he would be able to work harmoniously together.

How it would answer I cannot tell—I find the whole thing rather obscure still. But who knows ? What artist has ever been so lucky as to be able to take up his abode in his native town ? That is precisely what is always so sad. And yet, dear Johannes, you are still so young. You will find a permanent niche yet and " if a man has a loving wife with him he finds heaven in every town." My husband said that so beautifully in the short poems, and you will certainly find not only a home but also domestic happiness—and everything. I can well understand that you still feel strange in Vienna. But you will certainly lose this feeling after a longer stay, and in time there will be many things which will rivet you to the spot. I wish you everything of the best, but in life it so often happens that what seems to one very hard turns out to be a stroke of good fortune. I am returning Avé's letter to you. No one, of course, will hear anything about it. But now before I write of other things I have a confession to make. In your letter to me you did not tell me a word about your first public appearance, etc., and nothing about how you live, and referred me to the letter to your parents as if the news in it were also for me. Now I was only able to see your people in the afternoon, which meant waiting half a day, so to make a long story short, I read the letter before I took it to your parents. As soon as I had done so, it occurred to me that I ought to have refrained, and that it would be better if I had closed it up again. But then I should have had to appear as if I knew nothing about it and I don't like such dissimulation, not only because I carry it off badly, but because it was connected with your own people, who are such lovable and straightforward folk. I went to them with my heart full of affection but noticed that their old friendliness was lacking,[1] and I can only surmise

---

[1] As it afterwards transpired, this lack of friendliness was not due to Clara's manner, but to disagreements between Brahms' parents themselves.

that this was to be accounted for by what I had done, and think it perfectly justified. But I can do nothing further at present except to regret what has happened and to resolve never to do anything of the sort again in similar circumstances, however difficult it may be for me.

I was delighted to hear that your first public appearance had gone off so splendidly, that you had played so well and are giving one or two more concerts. Are they to be chamber concerts or orchestral concerts ? And what is this C minor Sextet ? Aren't you going to send it to me, dear friend ? Am I not to know it ? And now just one request. Will you please send me at once your G minor Quartet. I am to play at Leipsic on a quartet evening, and would like to choose it as an ensemble piece. . . . I shall study it carefully and play it as well as in me lies. Unfortunately I have no ensemble piece of yours here and certainly no inspiring collaborators either. For our first soirée, therefore, I have chosen the *Variations* in B Flat. People can well hear that again, and so far from the scene and the sound I don't suppose it will be unpleasant to you.

This evening the Philharmonic concert went off most successfully and I exerted all my power to prevent my sad mood from affecting my playing. I need not tell you how beautifully Stockhausen sang. To-morrow we have to go to the Court at Hanover. . . .

I knew beforehand that you would be charmed with Lewinsky—I always told you that he is a genius. Greet him most heartily for me and anyone else who may ask after me. . . . You've said nothing to me about the house I have bought in Baden. Have you no good wishes for me ? And now farewell, dear friend. I hope you will soon be able to overcome the sadness which now fills your heart and do so more easily than other men could since you, as the darling of the Muses, must find the best comfort for everything in your art. Think of me as ever Your faithful and loyal friend CLARA.

CLARA *to* BRAHMS.

BERLIN, *Dec.* 18.

. . . I came back here yesterday after having played in Breslau, and let me tell you at once how delighted I was once more with your quintet. I think the last movement magnificent. It sums up the whole so well and is full of life. The introduction is also fine. The second motif works so pleasantly as a contrast to the first and the development again reveals such an ingenious interweaving of all the motifs. In fact it is quite masterly. If only I could hear it, for playing it at the piano is so trying and unsatisfactory. Did you hear it in Vienna ? . . .

I sent the Quartet direct to Simrock from Leipsic. I could not play it there, for in the first place the cellist (a pupil of the Conservatoire—they have no other) was so mediocre that it was almost impossible to risk so difficult a piece with him. And even if one had wished to venture upon it one would at least have had to be able to count upon the student's having a little love for the thing ; but N. behaved so hopelessly when we played it through that I gave it up, for one does not want to press upon such people things that one loves and reveres. A person like him is inclined to dwell on passages that seem to be a little bit hard, whereas we take them as they come and have all the more pleasure in other passages. But if I am to be quite frank I would say that I should like certain things eliminated from the Quartet, for instance the trio in the exquisite allegretto. Much as I like the intention, I feel unable to enjoy it as music ; and there are many other things. But what is the point of all this, seeing that it is now being printed ?

Bagge [1] told me some very pleasant things about your concert and particularly how beautifully you played—but I know this better than he does. But how was it that you did not play any of Schubert's pieces, on the very spot which was the cradle of his creations ? Are you still giving lessons and what do you charge for them ? . . . I have not spoken to your parents about the Conductor's post in Hamburg. As they said nothing to me about it I did not want to be over-hasty, or perhaps to call their attention to something

---

[1] Selmar Bagge, musician and critic (born 1823), trained in music at Prague and Vienna. He became professor of composition at the Vienna Conservatorium in 1851 ; resigned in 1855 and took to writing. Founded and edited the *Deutsche Musikzeitung*. In 1863 he went to Leipsic as editor of the *Deutsche Allgemeine Musikzeitung*. In 1868 he was appointed director of the music school at Bâle.—Tr.

they had not thought of and which would only have hurt
them.   They may possibly have known all about it, or have
only just heard of it, but they know me well enough to be
sure that I could have had no part in it, for on the contrary I
have not scrupled to tell Stockhausen himself what I really
thought about it.   He mentioned more than once that if only
you were to come back to Hamburg etc. etc.   But ought he
not to have spoken quite openly about it all, before he took
any steps in the matter ? . . .

And now with heartiest greetings and all good wishes for
you, Your CLARA.

1863

CLARA *to* BRAHMS.

BADEN, *May* 5.

DEAR JOHANNES,

. . . The children are very happy here and but for Julie, who is still in Nice and whose cough still gives me great anxiety, all are well. Ferdinand has been moved up to the Third Form with two First Class Distinctions and he will remain in Berlin as he is getting on so well there. Ludwig has also become quite industrious and to my joy is turning out quite different from what every one except myself expected. I always thought that the boy had more in him than appeared on the surface. I intend to study hard this summer and to get the girls well on with their playing. There is not likely to be any lack of other distractions in Baden which is full of visitors, so I am looking forward more happily to this summer than I did to last. The other day in Hanover I had the great pleasure of hearing Joachim conduct the *Orpheus* in which his *fiancée* [1] sang beautifully. I went there to see him once again before his marriage and to get to know his *fiancée* a little better. You will probably be there too about this time.

Have you been industrious during the last few months ? I was very glad to hear from Frl. von Glasersfeld and Julie Asten of the great appreciation with which you are meeting in Vienna. Are you going to stay in Hamburg now—probably in Hamm again ? Wishing you all happiness and with greetings to you and your people, Your CLARA.

CLARA *to* BRAHMS.

BADEN, *June* 14, *Lichtenthal* 14.

DEAR JOHANNES,

I have just heard from a reliable source that you have been

[1] In February Joachim had become engaged to Amalie Weiss (Schneeweiss).

155

given a post in Vienna.[1] This is splendid ! I must tell you without a moment's delay how delighted I am, for even if it is not a brilliant post, it is a step towards better things. And now you are settled down in a town which I hope has become dear to you and where one can live quite happily. As things are in Hamburg you could not have been content there for long. You would often have been overcome by certain feelings of bitterness—and so everything has turned out as you would wish. I suppose I shall hear from you in due course when you are going to take up the post, and what your duties and salary will be.

I was sorry to see that your letter was not at all cheerful and that dear old Hamburg no longer pleased you. And yet I foresaw that this would be the case when once you had learnt to know the life of Vienna, which, from the artistic point of view, is much more stimulating. As to myself, I have this much good news to give you, that my little house is at last in order and though small is exceedingly comfortable. In addition the whole of the domestic arrangements are just after my own heart. Each of the children (the big ones) has his own department and has to keep to it. I have quite got into the way of superintending the household again, though naturally I do not feel the same pleasure in it as I did when I had to make everything comfortable for my Robert. But I do it so that I may make the house pleasant for the children and help them to enjoy their share. . . . Will you please send me your Variations for four hands [2] and the Quartet,[3] or anything new you have composed. I shall send them all back to you whenever you want them. . . .

Julie has been here for a month and often speaks most enthusiastically about Nice. She is very cheerful though her cough is just the same. But what makes me most anxious about her is that from time to time she has a sort of cataleptic fit during which she will remain for several hours quite motionless. It does not happen very often, about every five or six weeks—but there it is. We must take great care of her and be particularly careful not to let her get excited. All the doctors

---

[1] As Choir Master of the *Singakademie*.
[2] Op. 23.
[3] Op. 31.   Quartet for four solo voices with pianoforte.

agree that the cough is purely nerves, for her chest and lungs are quite sound and her attacks are due both to her nervous condition and her tendency to anæmia. God grant that she will improve. I certainly do all I can for her.

Ludwig often comes over to us [1] and, odd though he is, his industry and fine character, which reveals itself in a hundred little ways, are a great joy to me. . . .

And now, my dear Johannes, farewell. Ever your faithful old Clara.

Clara *to* Brahms.

BADEN, *July* 10.

. . . Kirchner and I are both in raptures over your Quartet.[2] I have played it at two parties at my house, on the last occasion with such excellent artists as Jean Becker, Jaquart (cello), and Koning, a first-class viola player. Rubinstein heard it on both occasions, though he does not understand it yet. But Lachner [3] of Mannheim was most appreciative, which means a good deal for an old orchestra Conductor. And then there were Levi [4] and last of all Kirchner who from the first did not miss a single note. Apart from one or two passages which struck me as harsh or dull (the conclusion of the trio in the scherzo, for instance), it is a wonderful work in my opinion, and we enjoyed it thoroughly. I must admit that you are right after all and that it is more beautiful than the G minor, more important from the musical standpoint, and the first movement is much more finished. . . .

Levi has been here a week, Rubinstein three weeks and Jaëll and Moritz Hartmann also. The other day Dietrich came for a couple of hours just as we were having a musical evening. But he was not allowed to listen although he is very much better. He is now in Switzerland.

I am so glad you accepted the post in Vienna. I am full of hope and confidence that it will prove an ever more agreeable

[1] From the beginning of the summer Ludwig had been apprenticed to a bookseller in Carlsruhe.

[2] A major, Op. 26.

[3] Vincenz Lachner.

[4] Hermann Levi, at that time orchestra conductor at the Carlsruhe Theatre.

sphere of activity and source of joy to you. For there is hardly a town in Germany where you could find such ready appreciation as in Vienna. It is of course very hard for your parents, particularly your dear mother. But everything has its dark side. All the same she will also have reason to be pleased about it. For who knows whether your life will not pan out more advantageously there than it would have done in Hamburg ? How heartily I wish that this may be so. . . . So now farewell. Let me hear from you soon, and with reiterated thanks, Your CLARA.

CLARA *to* BRAHMS.

DÜSSELDORF, *Oct.* 18.

I should have acknowledged your kind parcel much sooner had I not been so terribly busy. The deluge of work with which I have been flooded is really almost too much. My correspondence about concerts is endless, while in addition I have to practise diligently. Unfortunately my conscientiousness is, I might say, increasing so painfully, that I always feel with every piece I approach as if I were only just beginning to practise it properly. I have been here for the last ten days, after having shut up my little house, which was no easy matter for me. . . .

Julie Asten and Hanslik must have told you a good deal about Munich.[1] It was very fine, but only in parts, for on such occasions one often forces oneself to partake of pleasures which, on that very account, cease to be pleasures. The one great defect of the festival was that there was too much of it. I should like to know what musician could listen to a concert lasting three hours (on the third day there was one lasting four hours) from beginning to end with the same zest.

But I have not yet mentioned the most important thing of all, which is your Rinaldo.[2] So let me tell you that I read it through with the same pleasure as I did in Baden. It is a splendid and vital piece, extraordinarily full of dramatic fire, interesting and arresting throughout. Its effect must

---

[1] I.e. about the Music Festival, which took place there between the 27th and 29th of September.

[2] Op. 50. Cantata for tenor solo, choir of men's voices and orchestra. Text by Goethe.

be wonderful, provided of course that you have very strong tenors. I am rather frightened about these, because you often make them go extremely high. I suppose the final chorus will follow very soon. . . . Thank you very much indeed for the *Hexenvariationen*.[1] I have started practising them most eagerly. But they don't seem to be suited for playing in public, the combinations are too surprising and laymen would not enjoy them the first time of hearing. I think it will be necessary to insert some with more simple harmonies, and then one (I mean the listener) would not find them such an effort. Just think this over. My favourites are the third, fifth, sixth, tenth, seventeenth, eighteenth and nineteenth. I shall no doubt add many others to the list when I can play them properly. . . . I shall think of you on the 15th of November.[2] I hope it will all be most successful. And now with best wishes for your welfare and happiness, with affectionate greetings, Your CLARA.

CLARA *to* BRAHMS.

SCHWERIN, *Nov.* 25.

I should have liked, dear Johannes, to write to you as soon as I received your letter, because I so much wanted to tell you with what deep pleasure I had heard of your splendid success. But only those who are with me can know how strenuous my days are now. To-morrow will be my fifth public appearance within a week in four different towns, and you know what this means in the way of exertions of all kinds. But I feel sure that you will know without any explanations from me that only the most pressing business could have prevented me from sending you my congratulations on such an occasion. But in any case you damp my ardour almost immediately by saying that you were not sure that you would keep the post after all, when all the time I imagined you were finally settled in Vienna. I can't imagine why you think Dietrich and Stockhausen's positions enviable. In your productions you also have to deal with an orchestra. Or would you perhaps prefer only to conduct orchestra concerts ? In

---

[1] Op. 35.   Variations on a theme by Paganini.

[2] The date of the first concert under Brahms' direction at the *Singakademie*.

view of the small appreciation he gets in Hamburg Stockhausen's position is on the whole certainly not enviable, for the public there is not nearly ripe yet for good orchestral performances. I think they may perhaps be soon. The productions of the Leonora Overture and Robert's C major Symphony were really wonderfully beautiful. I have never heard the latter sound so well anywhere, and if there were any criticism to make, I would only take exception to the restlessness which seemed to pervade the whole piece. Both the orchestra and the conductor seemed a little bit over-anxious, which after all is quite natural. They will get over this in time and Stockhausen will soon be able to conduct with masterly calm. It was again clear to me on this occasion how difficult your position would have been as so young a man and a native of Hamburg to boot. Your wings would soon have drooped with exasperation. But how different things will be in Vienna. I was not in the least bit surprised by your success there. I expected it. At the very moment when you were conducting there Rose [1] and Co. were playing your Sextet. Unfortunately they had not studied it sufficiently and they hurried over it too much.

I found your parents, particularly your mother, looking very well. We had egg punch on one occasion and thought of you a good deal, of course, while we were drinking it. Fritz also played me your Handel Variations which, however, are much beyond his powers. Although his technique is quite good, I think his playing is too dry and cold. I cannot understand it, seeing that he is so closely related to you. . . .

I am so glad you liked the Requiem [2] so much. I always did. The other day I played in Münster and had an enthusiastic reception. The ladies of the choir gave me a pretty surprise at the end by pouring a regular shower of flowers over me. It almost took my breath away. The public did the same thing to me here yesterday after Robert's Concerto, which pleased me very much. . . .

[1] Carlos Rose, later known in England as Carl Rosa, the founder of the famous Opera Company of that name. He changed his name to Rosa to avoid mistakes in pronunciation.—TR.

[2] Schumann's *Requiem für Mignon*, which Brahms performed in Vienna on the 15th of November.

It is now more or less settled that I am going to Russia at the end of January. I shall not dilate upon how hard it has been for me to come to this decision. In any case it would have been hard this winter, because I am not feeling at all well. But it can't be helped. I must go through with it. . . . So farewell, dear Johannes; I hope that your work will prove ever more and more stimulating to you. This and every other kind of happiness I wish you from the bottom of my heart. Your CLARA.

1864

ST. PETERSBURG, *March* 10, *Evening.*

Your letter, dear Johannes, greeted me on my arrival in St. Petersburg and gave me great pleasure, as you may well imagine. You must know that I came here almost a month later than I had intended. In the *Signal* I was reported as having arrived here when I was still quietly stopping in Riga ; for I heard in Königsberg that Easter falls five weeks later here than it does in Germany. And what was the use of my being here so long before the holidays and just spending money ? So I quietly gave concerts in Königsberg, Riga and Mitau, and was not only enthusiastically received everywhere, but also made quite a satisfactory amount of money. But the journey here, with its first lap from Königsberg to Riga and then from Riga on to here, was very trying, and during the first part of it I was so ill that on reaching Riga I had to go to bed at once and have really not recovered from it yet, although I got through my concerts with remarkable power and endurance. How I manage to get up my enthusiasm again and again I am sure I don't know. But it always gives me great pleasure to find so many devoted admirers of Robert everywhere, and I may say that Robert's things are among those with which I obtain my biggest successes. Thus a week ago to-day I played Robert's Concerto at the Conservatoire concert, and had such enthusiastic applause as I seldom experience. And the same thing happened with the Symphonic Studies at my second chamber-music matinée to-day. On the whole I find the public here much more musical than we Germans think they are. The Russians are by nature inclined to be musical, and that goes a long way, for although they do not understand, they feel a good deal. The day after to-morrow I shall give my third matinée. Then comes the week of silence during which the people do nothing but pray, after having spent this week in a regular whirl of pleasure (all the theatres had two performances a day). And then the concerts begin and mine on Tuesday the 22nd of March will probably be one of the first. It will be a very important day for me this time, for a great deal depends on this concert from the pecuniary point of view, and it is a terrible risk. Just imagine, it is to take place in a theatre capable of seating 3,000 people, and expenses alone will amount to seven or eight hundred thalers [£105–£201]. But it happens to be the tradition here that every artist should give his first big concert in this theatre. You have probably heard through Julie Asten (Frl. Hillebrand) that the Grand-Duchess Helene has invited me to stay in her palace, and here I have been installed quite comfortably for the last three days, although I found it hard to part with the dear family with which I was living. If only their house had not been so far away I should not have left them. It was the house of Dr. Stein, my sister-in-law's brother. I don't know whether you ever met him in Düsseldorf. You must not think that life is so very terrible over here. The cold is quite endurable, not worse than it is in Germany, although the whole of this vast city lies under snow, which will not disappear until the end of April. But while it is melting the streets are in a terrible condition. It is almost impossible to walk, one risks one's life if one drives, for one either drops into a hole or else gets driven into a lake, and all the streets have a sort of wavy surface, so that many people get seasick driving along them. But this city certainly has the most magnificent buildings one can imagine. They are long and low and a single palace, like the one I am in, takes up the whole side of a street. And then there is the glorious Neva which is now nothing but a sheet of ice and along which one drives as if it were a street. Whether I shall go to Moscow or not I do not know yet, as letters are already coming in from there.

Rubinstein is behaving very nicely to me and I get to like him more and more. He must be a most good-natured creature, free from any trace of jealousy, and he is the only person here who is perfectly sincere (but everybody is very hostile to him and endless difficulties are put in the way of his concerts). All the other artists are more or less two-faced.

Fortunately I have had no experience of this yet and do not wish to.

Alas, I have not yet seen the Grand-Duchess Helene but I expect to do so next week. I say " Alas ! " because after all I have heard about her I should very much like to know her better than was possible after only playing once before her at a soirée. Apparently there is no Grand-Duke or Duchess who does as much for art as she does, and whatever good musical institutions there are here are owing to her. For instance, she alone is responsible for the upkeep of the Conservatoire and all the Professors are paid by her, etc., etc. As for the Tsar, who by-the-by is very popular, he only gives a few instrumental soirées in the winter, but only as a matter of form, so they say.

I see with alarm that I have written almost two whole sheets of paper about myself although I wanted to ask so many questions about you. I am sorry that you do not seem to be as happy in Vienna as I had hoped. But the cause probably lies in yourself, for the creative soul with lofty aspirations seldom finds inner peace. I cannot quite understand what you have written to me about your Quintet. Did you produce it and was it a frost ? And did you on that account turn it into a duet ? [1] If this is so you cannot have been satisfied with it yourself in its original form or pleased with the way it sounded. Could you not have altered it quite easily and yet have left it as a Quintet ? Surely there were only a few passages which did not sound well and much of it at least gave the impression of being a quartet ? I should like to play it through with you but that will be impossible until next winter, when I really think of coming to Vienna. . . . So farewell ! Think sometimes of Your CLARA.

BRAHMS *to* CLARA.

                                          VIENNA, *April* 4.
DEAREST CLARA,

Heartiest thanks for your letter full of news, but which, alas ! had still to come all that long way to me. But what

---

[1] This refers to the String Quintet which Brahms converted into the Sonata for Two Pianos, and out of which he later evolved the Piano Quintet in F minor.

is even more regrettable is the prospect that the next one will
come from a still further distance and soon it will reach infinity.
Incidentally this sort of thing is only noticed by one like
myself who leads a quiet life.   By now your first concert and
probably many more big ones will have taken place, and I
hope they have been most successful.   I am not in the least
surprised that you should have met with such ready appreciation for your husband's works in Livonia and Russia.   As
early as his fiftieth year your husband might have seen how
universally his beautiful music was loved.   I wonder whether
it would have been different if he had lived, whether the spirit
of contradiction in men would have insisted on waiting for his
death.   No one is more popular than he is here and I mean
this in the best sense of the word.   I should like to hear Rubinstein more often.   I am inclined perhaps to expect more of him
as a man than people have expected of him as a composer, for
in this capacity he will probably achieve nothing greater than
he has done already.   In the autumn he played a piano quartet
here which caused a great stir.   Did you hear it ?   But he
writes so much that the quartet is already out of date.   I
have unfortunately to decide at once whether I shall remain
at the Academy next year.   If only somebody else could decide
for me !

The Christmas Oratorio went excellently at our third concert
(only parts one, two, four and six).   The choir and I enjoyed
it at all events, but a work of Bach's has a difficult time with
the critics here.   Hanslik may have suffered the pains of the
damned during the week, for two days afterwards Herbeck's
Johannes-Passion was performed.   Unfortunately we have
another concert on the 17th of April and still more unfortunately I had reasons to fall in with the proposal of the committee and to undertake to give only " Brahms "—the Ave
Maria, the Marienchor and other choral pieces, a motet, solo
quartets, the string Sextet, and finally my sonata for two
pianos which I shall play with Carl Tausig.   This will surprise
you most of all, for I expect you will have a terrible opinion
of Tausig.   But he is really a remarkable little fellow and a
very exceptional pianist, who, incidentally, as far as it is
possible for a man to do so, is constantly changing for the
better.   He often plays Rubinstein, Chopin, and particularly

Liszt, of course, very beautifully. He had already begged me to have the sonata for his own concerts, so we are now going to do it together. . . .

It is very nice that the people here should be so musical and should be able to sing from the score and practise so well. But life is too gay, and during the short season no person or institution can survive which does not rush to participate in the hurly-burly, instead of doing what they would like to do, which is to live quietly and find pleasure and culture in their own pursuits. But everybody wants to live, to dance from one concert to the other, and from one sensation to another. The financial and artistic side of my work are also jeopardized because no really distinguished personage with refined artistic feeling is at the head of affairs to help me. I could deal with the musical side adequately enough, but as things are here I ought to possess gifts of organization which I lack. Otherwise I have little to relate about my life. My real friends are the old ones. Unfortunately I am forced ever more and more to enjoy their company in imagination. Here I can find nobody to take their place—this was taken amiss early yesterday by my Viennese friends, and from that moment I was not allowed to write another line. One after the other came in, until I shut up my room and left with the last arrival.

This morning, I confess, that my next concert and the decision I have to make, are weighing heavily on my mind. If only one had money one could decide so much more easily and act according to the promptings of one's heart. Without it one is really always a prisoner. How glad should I be, for instance, if I could go to Hamburg very soon now and spend a few evenings in my old room (but before that I want to see some of the beautiful mountain districts round about here). On the other hand, when you come back, I shall be just as strongly drawn to Baden. I must try to find out boldly how much strain Härtel's gold bags will stand.

My Folk Songs arranged for choir have pleased the people here extraordinarily, and Spina very much wants them. But as Rieter rather insists on having them and does not care what he pays he will get them. I still have the Schubert Song lying here, which you saw at my place last year. I got it for you from a very pretty girl with whom God knows I might have

made a fool of myself if, as luck would have it, someone had
not snatched her up at Christmas.   My people are all well
but my love makes me feel anxious, for my mother is growing
old and who knows how soon a heavy blow will fall on me ?
Write to me soon and tell me a lot about yourself and your
children.   I always like to hear about them and to know that
they are well and where they are staying.   With heartiest love,
Your JOHANNES.

CLARA *to* BRAHMS.

MOSCOW, 17–24 *April.*

[DEAR JOHANNES,]

. . . One sees nothing but populace all round, dirty ragged
men and women, and what one hears about their habits really
makes one shudder.   The civilization of the people is on a much
lower plane than we outside Russia have any idea of.   And
yet with the suppression of serfdom things are already beginning
to improve.   At least the people are beginning to think for
themselves and to learn a few things—in short to be more
human.   It is only here in the provinces that one can form
any idea of the tremendous changes that have been inaugur-
ated by the present Tsar.   He is really admirable, for, in my
opinion, more courage is required for such reforms than any
general would need on the field of battle.

For the time being at least the nobility are completely
overthrown, which of course makes a good deal of difference
to foreign artists.   And yet, in spite of it all, I can assure
you that I am quite satisfied.   From the very start I made
up my mind not to expect too much, and now I find I have
achieved more than I anticipated ; for in Germany with the
same expenditure of energy I should not have earned so much
in three months.

My concert at the theatre, about which I wrote to you so
apprehensively the other day, brought me in a sum of 800
roubles [£86.18.0] after all expenses, amounting to 700 roubles
[£75.12.0], had been deducted.   And at my farewell soirée,
which was held in a small hall, I cleared another 700 roubles,
and the hall was so packed that a great many people had to
be turned away.   They are trying to persuade me to give another
soirée on my return to St. Petersburg from here.   But I don't

suppose I shall do so.   It is better to end up on the brilliant
success I have had.   The reasons for my still being here are
partly good and partly bad.   The very day after my concert
in the theatre at St. Petersburg I fell seriously ill and lost
almost three weeks.   I was still ill when I came here, but this
place soon helped me to recover, for the climate, the water
and the air are better here than in St. Petersburg.   Moreover,
I am living with a nice family, half German in nationality, who
look after me so kindly that nothing would be wanting to my
happiness if I were not so frantically homesick.   You cannot
imagine what struggles I have in my heart which often almost
bursts with longing   But if I had left before this I should only
have achieved half of what I can achieve.   I gave three chamber concerts.   Then came Easter in between, during which
no concerts can be given for ten days.   I shall have to wait
for this to be over in order to give another concert on the
4th of May (German calendar).   After that, on the 6th I am
engaged at a subscription concert (for Robert's concerto) ;
I shall play again on the 8th before the Grand-Duchess Helene
who is expected next week, and hope to leave St. Petersburg
on the 9th.

A day or two ago I had the surprise of receiving a deputation
from the orchestra offering me their services gratis at my
concert.   This really moved me very much indeed.   Such a
thing has never happened to me in Germany.   But if you ask
me what other artistic pleasures I have had, I must answer—
none.   I have come across nobody who is heart and soul an
artist.   They treat everything quite superficially, the good
with the bad, nothing moves them deeply, and of reverence
they know nothing.   I have often felt sad for days about it,
whenever circumstances have drawn my attention to it.   I
shall tell you about Rubinstein one day.   I cannot exclude
him from what I have said above, for, as a Conductor, his
attitude to music is just what one would expect from him as a
composer.   What he lacks above all is sacred seriousness, and
one feels this in his compositions and in his way of conducting
and playing.   But you are right, as a man he has rare qualities,
and were it not for his incessant and really feverish restlessness,
one could gain much from him.   I have heard the piano
quartet, and I must confess that it interested me more than

anything I have ever heard of his.   There are a lot of fine things
in it.   One even notices, particularly in the first movement,
how much pains he has taken.   But in the last he gets so wild
again that it is terrible.   The scherzo struck me as exquisite,
but the motifs all through are insignificant. . . .   With most
affectionate greetings, dear Johannes, and hoping that this year
and all that follow may be prosperous for you, Your CLARA.

CLARA *to* BRAHMS.

DÜSSELDORF, *June* 1.

. . . I am so glad that you are continuing in your post in
Vienna.   I thought the very same thing as you did, that many
people would put a wrong construction upon your leaving so
soon.   But you are quite right to insist upon a reform of all
the unsatisfactory conditions, for even if you do not succeed
all along the line, something will be achieved.   I am pleasantly
surprised at your wealth.   So you have about 400 thalers [£60]
and can spend the summer wandering about to your heart's
content, or look out for a nice little place to work in.   I also
have 22 thalers and 15 Sgr. [£3.7.5] interest for you.   I wish
you would allow the interest to accumulate so as to increase
your capital. . . .

We attended a great festival on the Kremlin on Easter night
and I shall never forget it as long as I live.   As far as my
own affairs, i.e. my success in Russia, is concerned, I must
say that in view of the present acute financial crisis there I am
well satisfied.   I could not have done as much in Germany.
It is true that the strain was often severe.   For instance, the
journey from St. Petersburg to Moscow lasted twenty hours.
I arrived at nine o'clock in the morning, had a rehearsal at
eleven o'clock and a concert in the evening.   Then followed
three concerts on three successive days.   When we returned
from St. Petersburg direct to Berlin the journey took forty-
four hours.   This was very hard on my poor back; but I
survived it all very well, in spite of the fact that I was never
really in the best of health in Russia (the climate and the water
did not suit me).

In Moscow I found Nicolas Rubinstein—the man has an
amazing technique, though his fingers are quite short and
thick.   He plays chiefly drawing-room pieces and thumps the

piano in the latest fashion, with a great deal of pedal work and no emotion beyond the soft pedal.   But he is a very lovable creature though with moral principles which I abhor.   It is really a bad business about these two brothers.   They are so highly gifted, yet they entirely lack real seriousness and respect for their art.   Anton R. is coming to Baden for two months. He wishes to work there.   For his sake one wishes he would. But I fear that he will only play again. . . .   I am now going to visit Hiller and Schmitz in Frankfort and then I go home, where Marie and Elise are making everything comfortable again for me.   I found Julie very lively and very much stronger, and I hope that after a month's stay with me in St. Moritz in Graubünden this summer (which both of us have been prescribed for the open-air cure) she will be quite well. . . . And now farewell, with most affectionate greetings, Your CLARA.

CLARA *to* BRAHMS.

BADEN BADEN, *June* 23.

Now at last you are back in Hamburg, dear Johannes. How glad I am for your people's sake and how well I understand your mixed feelings.   You must feel quite a stranger in Hamburg and yet it is the town which you have always loved so much.   Such experiences can make one feel quite sad.   And yet it has always been so, and men of note have always had to build their homes in foreign lands.   You have chosen Vienna, and this too pleases me.   What with your music and your books I feel sure you will soon be quite at home there.   But I was shocked to hear that you had given up your post there after all.   For when all is said and done, where is the post that has not got its drawbacks ?

I wonder what you have done.   Are you living with your parents or in Hamm ?   I heard the other day that Frau Dr. Rösing was looking forward to a visit from you.   Don't you think you would be comfortable there again ?   I have only been here a fortnight, but quite a number of pleasant things have happened already.   Rubinstein has been here for some time.   Kirchner paid me a visit of a few days, and Stockhausen and his wife took us by surprise the other day and stayed four days.

I have never seen him so amiable and so happy ; but he has a charming wife ; we grew to like her more and more every hour. She is naturally cheerful, and yet enters into everything very seriously. She is also refined and cultivated. In fact he has found a treasure which he ought to value, and he seems to be thoroughly aware of this. . . . And now let me hear about your doings in Hamburg and how you intend to scatter your gold pieces. The amount you have is really surprising. When do you think of coming to Baden ? And now farewell, dear Johannes, remember me to your people, and with most affectionate greetings, Your CLARA.

CLARA *to* BRAHMS.

BADEN BADEN, *July* 19.

I was so shocked and saddened by your letter yesterday that I feel I must write to you to-day. If you bear in mind that I had not the faintest suspicion of any discord in your family you will understand my alarm at your news.[1] Last winter when I was with them I certainly felt that there was something in the air, particularly in the case of your mother, but I ascribed it all to myself and thought that they were suspicious of me because I came to Hamburg and played under Stockhausen's baton, in spite of the fact that they must know that in my circumstances I cannot refuse any engagement. So you see that in any case I was quite innocent. In ordinary circumstances I should not be surprised at your standing by your father, but in this case, knowing as I have for years your preference for your mother, it is incredible to me. I think it terribly sad that two people who have lived so long together, who are surrounded by grown-up children and who are almost standing on the edge of the grave, should separate. Naturally I cannot form any opinion as to who is right or wrong, and yet I cannot help thinking that if a mis-understanding arises as the result of a number of trifles, it is the woman's rôle to be conciliating. She ought to remember that it is her husband who bears the principal responsibility for the whole of the home, etc., etc. But if the husband is unfaithful or neglects his wife, or is a gambler or drunkard,

[1] The letter evidently dealt with the disagreement and separation of Brahms' parents.

then the wife cannot be blamed if she refuses to endure it all. I know, of course, that there can be no question of this in your father's case and am longing to hear the truth about the matter. That you, who have been longing for a whole year to join your people should light upon just this unhappy juncture of affairs, grieves me very much, as you may well imagine. Wouldn't you like to cheer yourself up a little by joining Joachim who is with his wife in the Harz ? . . .

I have been studying the Paganini Variations diligently and the more I do so the harder I find them. But I shall not rest until I know them, as I am so much interested in their ingenious combinations. Let me hear soon how you are getting on. Perhaps you may succeed after all in conciliating the parties. Isn't that possible ? Have your family all dispersed ? Do they no longer live together ? You only hint at things, and I don't really know what has happened. And now let me greet you affectionately and hope that your sky will clear a little. If I had known about it this winter I might have done some good. With remembrances to your people, Your CLARA.

BRAHMS *to* CLARA.

BADEN, *Aug.* 15.

As I should like to make up for your absence [1] to some extent by a nice letter, I am writing this in order to get one. You ought to have written to me if only out of gratitude, for after all I came less to see Baden than to see Frau Clara, a fact of which I am now too well aware. Otherwise things are going on as merrily as ever. Rubinstein came here early this morning, and Hartmann and Szarvady from another quarter. The latter, incidentally, have grown very grey. After that Frl. Leser came to see me, and as I am probably seeing Hartmann again to-day, I will tell him what you write about Ludwig.

In Carlsruhe Ludwig was with us the whole day. I don't want to say much about him now, although his manner readily

---

[1] Brahms had paid Clara a surprise visit in Baden Baden on July 31st, and on this account she had postponed her visit to Switzerland, whither she went only on August 10th. Brahms lodged at the Bär in the Lichtenthal.

tempts one to do so, particularly as at present a man [1] who we have every reason to hope is very able will perhaps exercise an important influence over his career. All I can say is that a short meeting with him left a very deep, remarkable and quite pleasant impression upon me. Beneath his wholly original manner the most lovable and excellent character lies concealed. One cannot see into his mind, and anyone who knows nothing at all about what the hard years of life have taught him, might easily be led to fear or expect too much or too little in both directions. I can only hope that his training will be such as to make him capable of choosing his path himself. If it does I entertain the highest hopes of him. Our friends Allgeyer [2] and Levi have got very fond of him, which was only what I expected in view of my own enduring attachment to him. Be on your guard with him and don't do anything over-hastily. There are very few men who can force you to believe in them, and a man is soon spoilt. At present there is no obvious reason why he should choose a technical calling.

Otherwise nothing has happened except that my double sonata has not made its appearance and will be lost to the world in the end if my fingers do not exercise some patience. With heartiest greetings, and waiting to hear from you, Your JOHANNES.

BRAHMS *to* CLARA.

VIENNA, *End of Oct.*

. . . For the last few days I have spent every quiet moment at my quintet in order to be able to send it to you.[3] But I am never allowed an hour's peace. I am constantly being detained and interrupted by one thing or person after another. And now Rieter has come, and among others one of Rückert's daughters, who is tearing the last remnants of my time to bits, so that I have constantly to show the fine weather a long and dismal face. The winter drove me from Baden and now

---

[1] Clara had told Professor Moritz Lazarus about her anxieties concerning Ludwig. He expressed the wish to observe the youth, and Clara had sent Ludwig to Rigi for that purpose.—TR.

[2] Julius Allgeyer, the future biographer of Feuerbach.

[3] Op. 34.

I have to sit here and allow myself to be harried in this lovely summer weather. . . .

I am very comfortably installed here. You will enjoy it, I know, when I give you and Marie coffee here, or else treat you to some Austrian wine. I have three quite small rooms at 7 Singerstrasse up seven flights of stairs on the fourth floor. On Monday I had to conduct the Academy orchestra, as Dessoff was prevented from doing so. Apparently I was exceedingly lively. This is of course because I am not harassed by concerts and that Bach's Magnificat fires one with enthusiasm. I am glad now that I am free from the post, and on this occasion I was doubly so. . . .

If Allgeyer photographs you send me a copy and send me a photograph of Marie too. I have not got one yet. Has Elise already got a title ? I hope she will not allow herself to be bargained for and will only get engaged to the right man. . . . Dearest Clara, how glad I am that I can write gladly " dearest Clara."

Canone al rovescio, Your JOHANNES.

CLARA *to* BRAHMS.

CARLSRUHE, *Thursday, Nov.* 3.

I must at least send you a word of thanks to-day so that you may know how much you delighted me with your letter of welcome here, and also how charmed we are with the glorious quintet. Levi and David [1] are sitting copying as if they were riveted to their seats, and Levi tells me how wonderful the instrumentation is. Fortunately it has turned out that I am to stay here a few days longer and we intend to try it on Sunday at Levi's. And thus I hope you will be with us in your thoughts as we shall be with you in ours. The quintet is a very special joy to me, for apart from the fact that it afforded you the purest and highest of pleasures during its creation, it is now affording you another which cannot be reckoned among the least. I managed to seize the opportunity when the Princess [2] was enthusiastic over your dedication to suggest a beautiful present [3] for you, and the moment was so propitious that she

---

[1] Paul David, son of Ferdinand David, at that time second orchestral conductor at Carlsruhe.

[2] Princess Anna of Hesse, *née* Princess Anna of Prussia.

[3] The original MS. of Mozart's G minor Symphony.

commanded me to buy it then and there. You will realize
with what joy I did this when you see it. I hope she will
send it to you soon ; I have just taken it to her (she came
over here for the concert yesterday) and with a heavy heart I
surrender her the joy of being the giver.

I told her about the Sonata having now turned into a quintet,
and she asked me in which form it was dedicated to her, to
which I replied, of course, " In every form." Then she asked
whether she was getting the first copy, to which I, of course,
answered " Yes." . . . I have nothing but good news about
myself ; so far I have given three concerts and played with
such vigour and success that I wish I could have had you as
a listener. Unfortunately at Stuttgart the Viardot woman
queered my pitch by giving a concert at the theatre on the
very same evening on which my concert was to take place.
But it was not her fault, as it was in response to the Queen's
command, so that I had to give up mine entirely. But now I
have not only lost this one but many others in the neighbourhood, and must reckon that I have forfeited at least 500
thalers [£75]. But I have quite got over it, for with the bad
news there arrived also your letter about the quintet, and then
I was very glad indeed that I was able to stay.

Madame Viardot consecrated her Palace of Art (as she calls
it) the other day, and to the first ceremony she invited high
society (the Queen of Prussia etc.) when she naturally did not
want me ; and afterwards she had a reception for the populace,
for which I was considered good enough. The whole thing
was not very dignified, and the concluding scene of all was
revolting. The organ sounds wonderful though and might
have given one real pleasure if it had been adequately handled ;
but Madame Viardot cannot play with the pedal yet and opened
with the D major Fugue

 etc.

by Bach, which was a wretched performance, whereupon there
followed one or two quite pleasant songs of hers with organ,
violin, etc. I played a Beethoven sonata, and then came

an amateur, an officer with a tremendous voice, who sang
street ditties by Gumbert.   Finally we had Bach's Prelude by
Gounod arranged by her for organ, harp, violins and three
women's voices, and at the end the singers, after the style
of a Verdi Opera, *brawled unisono* so loudly that my ears and
eyes refused to function any longer and I left the Palace of
Art (! ! !) bristling with indignation.   After that I could not
prevail upon myself to return, and so left without seeing her
again.   Oh, why can't I have such an organ ?   How sacred
it would be to me !   And if you came and played on it for me,
what music fit for the gods we should have then !   I have often
wondered whether I ought not to go to America, where I
should immediately earn enough to purchase such an organ.
. . .   With most affectionate greetings, my dear Johannes,
and hoping you will remember me, Your old CLARA.

CLARA *to* BRAHMS.

HAMBURG,[1] *Dec.* 5.

. . . My heart was filled with anguish at your mother's to
see everybody scattered like that.   Oh what misery !   Your
mother and Elise were crying the whole time, and then there
was your father who unburdened his heart to me ; each of them
in turn said they could answer before God for every word they
had uttered.   I assure you it has made me feel quite ill, for
one's heart gets torn in two.   One soon recognizes the impossi-
bility of being able to do any good in the matter, but I certainly
convinced myself regarding the alarming condition of their
finances.   Things cannot go on as they are, nor can you possibly
provide for everything alone.   It will amount to more than
you think.   At all events your mother and Elise can manage
on 40 marks [Hamburg marks = 1 mark 20] a month, but then
they would have nothing left for the little extras which crop
up every day.   In addition to the 40 marks and the rent for
their lodgings therefore they must have a definite sum for
clothes, washing, etc.   So I earnestly implored your father not
to let the matter come to court and to contribute a little more.

[1] On the 11th of November Clara had returned to Düsseldorf and
had played in November at Cologne, Elberfeld, Bremen, Düsseldorf,
Brunswick and Hanover.   From the 30th of November to the 8th of
December she was in Hamburg.—TR.

But he absolutely refuses and declares that they can go to law if they like. But I doubt very much whether any court would uphold him, for the law says that a man must provide for his wife when he leaves her. I did not know what to do about the 100 thalers that you gave me for your people. You told me that I was only to spend it on the dentist and the rent, but the dentist business is not yet over and the rent only falls due after the 1st of May, while they are in great present need. They have borrowed and say they have not got a mark left in the house. I made them show me the accounts of what they have spent, and thought that instead of letting you send them a further 100 thalers now, it would be better if I were to give them the ones I have. I hope you will approve of this, as I really did not know what else to do.

Dec. **7.**

A whole day has passed between this and my first sheet. It was a concert day and can be reckoned among the good ones. It was very well attended except for the platform seats ; but to fill these a very different programme is required from what people of our sort give. We had a little mishap in Beethoven's F Flat major Trio. Hegar forgot the repeat and could not find his place again, so that I quietly stopped and began again. Rose got more rosy than ever with embarrassment. Hegar went white, but I was remarkably calm and had already forgotten the incident at the end of the first page. . . . I am so glad that you have at last got the G minor Symphony. The Princess seems to have found it hard to part with it. Isn't it written in a delightfully neat hand ? How triumphant you must have felt over the erasures ! [1] Well, in future I shall say no more about it, but it amused me. . . .

I suppose Joachim has written to you. He complained bitterly the other day that you never wrote to him, but from your letter I gather that you are expecting a letter from him. At the present moment he is touring in Holland, and in March is going to England for three months, where he has a very good engagement. They are paying him 8,000 thalers [£1,200] for none too many concerts.

The other day at an evening concert in Düsseldorf we had a

[1] When he had made a mistake Brahms used simply to rub the wrong note out with his finger.

curious experience. The gas suddenly went out, and they only succeeded in lighting it again at the end of a quarter of an hour. We started the last piece, which was the Kreuzer Sonata, but hardly had it begun when there was a flicker and the hall was plunged into darkness once more. We went on playing, however, by the light of a couple of candles placed on the piano. The audience kept their seats, and people said they had never enjoyed music in such a devotional atmosphere. Apparently the sight was a remarkable one,—we two looking ghastly pale in the light of the two candles. But we played with great animation and received such applause as I have seldom been given in north Germany. . . .

And now farewell, my dear Johannes, and let me hear from you soon, Your CLARA.

Marie greets you heartily. All the children are well.

CLARA *to* BRAHMS.

DÜSSELDORF,[1] *Dec.* 22.

. . . Joachim seemed very happy and is charming with his little boy.[2] He has not yet been christened because Joachim cannot fix on any name. He does not wish to insult the King, will not decide on the name George because we are all against it, and declares that for the time being there is no need to give him a name at all. I cannot understand this, for it is surely such a pleasure to call a child by its name for the first time, and I fail to see how anyone can deny themselves this joy for so long. But perhaps this is very silly of me. Are you actually a godfather ? I heard that only the King's representative had stood sponsor. . . . I hope I shall hear from you soon and get to know what you are doing. How about the quintet ? I had a letter from Levi with greetings for you and I am supposed to tell you how very much he honours and loves you. But such things mean nothing to you. You are perhaps more interested in the fact that he has a new coffee machine, a spare bed, and good cigars. . . . Let me hear from you soon. Ever your faithful CLARA.

[1] Clara had been here since the 20th of December, after having attended the Beethoven Festival on the 17th at Hanover.—TR.
[2] Johannes Hermann.

1865

Brahms *to* Clara.

[Hamburg] *Feb. 6, Monday morning.*

Dear Clara,

As this letter comes to you from Hamburg it is no good my trying to spare your feelings by breaking to you gently what has happened to us ; but it may comfort you to know that God took my mother away as mercifully as possible. Thanks to the fact that she always has plenty to do Elise is very well. She never has a moment to sit down and reflect and seems quite resigned to it. I am rather anxious about her as far as the future is concerned, but thank God the worst is over for the moment.

Last Tuesday evening my mother returned in quite good spirits from a concert and even joked with Fritz as she got out of the carriage. Hardly had the latter driven away, however, when she complained that her tongue felt heavy, and my sister saw to her horror that her mouth was all drawn sideways and that her tongue was swollen and protruding. In spite of the fact that she was convinced that my mother had had a stroke, Elise had to comfort her and remain quietly at her side while my mother complained that the whole of her left side seemed paralysed. After being brought home she believed herself to be quite well, and trusted Elise's comforting assurances that her chill would soon get better in bed. It was almost impossible to understand what she said and the doctor told Elise at once how serious her condition was. In bed she was still able to address my sister in the tenderest way and to press her hand. Then she closed her eyes and fell gently to sleep. Heavy perspiration now followed, then the death rattle, and at two o'clock on the following night she passed away.

Fritz telegraphed to me at once and I arrived here early on Saturday. I had naturally expected to find her dead, although

my brother had not said a word about it. We buried her yesterday at one o'clock. She had not changed at all and looked
as sweet and kind as when she was alive. Everything that
could possibly be done to comfort one for such a loss was done,
particularly for my sister. Her fellow-tenants in the house stood
by her in the most touching and self-sacrificing way, as did
also other friends, both male and female. . . . We surely have
no right to complain of the harshness of Fate for having taken
from us a mother who was seventy-six years of age. All we
can do is silently to mourn her loss and see to it that our sister
does not feel it too severely.

But what I am feeling ever more and more concerned about
is your hand,[1] and I am really anxious to hear how it is now
that the bandage has been removed and three to four weeks
have elapsed. . . . My father is quite well and it was a good
thing for the dear man that I came. Stockhausen and Avê
were very sympathetic and Avé and many young musicians
followed behind my mother's coffin. She had quantities of
wreaths and flowers and in spite of the bitter cold there was
music for her last farewell. Elise greets you heartily. She
seems to be quite well to-day and I no longer feel any anxiety
about her. If you have to spare your hand to some extent
in the future how would it be if at each of your concerts I
played one or two ensemble pieces so that you need only play
one or two solos ? And now farewell, and with hearty greetings
from us all, Your JOHANNES.

CLARA *to* BRAHMS.

Dictated.   COLOGNE, *Feb.* 8.

MY DEAR JOHANNES,

So the moment has really come when you must suffer the
sorrow which you have dreaded for so long. You can imagine
how deeply moved I was by the news, had I been able to
follow my heart's promptings I should have hastened to you.
It is so hard at such times not to be able to stand by one's
friends or give them some proof of one's sympathy. What
saddens me most is that the memory of your mother should

[1] On the 12th of January while walking in the *Tiergarten*, Berlin,
with Professor Lazarus, Clara fell and hurt her right hand.

have been so much spoilt by the unfortunate occurrences of the last few years. And yet I hope that in keeping with Nature's merciful plan this memory will be forced into the background in order to make room for earlier and more beautiful recollections.

Poor Elise ! She will be the one to feel the loss most, and I am constantly wondering how one can alleviate the first trying period for her. If it were summer and we were in Baden she would have to come to us at once. That would certainly have done her a great deal of good. Do tell me whether I can do anything. Could I help you at all by my presence in Hamburg ? I would come gladly. There must certainly be heaps of things to put in order. Are not Elise and Fritz going to live together ? Is she keeping on in the same lodgings ? Please write to me again at once, for it will relieve my anxiety until I can hear all details from you. . . . I can tell you nothing definite about my plans for the near future. I have only been able to move my hand a little since yesterday. This week I am to have a few more animal baths,[1] and then at the beginning of next week I may try to play again very gently. In the most favourable circumstances it will take at least another fortnight for my hand to get quite well. Give Elise all sorts of kind messages from me. Tell her how deeply I sympathize with you in your great loss, and if I can be of any possible use I should be only too glad to do anything. Aren't you in want of money ? You have had to take a long journey and must have a lot of expenses. I hope you provided yourself with warm rugs and felt slippers for your journey. It is so bitterly cold. Do for heaven's sake be careful ! . . . Ever your loving CLARA.

BRAHMS *to* CLARA.

VIENNA, *Feb.* 20.

Your letter made me feel you near to me, just as one wishes to be near to one's friends at such times. It was sent on to me here as I spent hardly a week in Hamburg, if that. I could

---

[1] The German is *Tierbäder,* or " animal baths." These baths, which consisted of laying an injured person's limb or limbs in the warm body of a freshly slaughtered animal, were given in the belief that the animal warmth possessed some specific curative principle.—TR.

do nothing more and was of no further use, and on the last afternoon of my stay saw only too clearly, alas! that there was no purpose in trying to arrange or worry about anything; for Elise got so excited when I mentioned my father, which of course I had to do if I wished to arrange anything. Avé witnessed the scene and saw only too plainly the terrible chasm which the years had gradually formed. He stood nobly at my side and urged me most emphatically to go away. For now that the first shock is over I could not hope to comfort my sister by my presence any longer.

Time changes everything for better or worse. It does not so much change as it builds up and develops, and thus when once this sad year is over I shall begin to miss my dear good mother ever more and more. I cannot write any more about it. The one comforting feature about our loss is that it ended a relationship which really could only have become sadder with the years, and at least I can thank heaven that it kept my mother as long as it did (seventy-six years) and let her go so peacefully. Elise will live with the Cossels (my old piano teacher), where Frl. Garbe also lives. She is of course at liberty to arrange everything as she likes, take her time, etc. Fritz lives alone, as does also my father, who I hope can now look forward to a pleasant and peaceful old age.

What is happening about your coming here? Alas! I still feel very anxious about your hand. But if it is fairly well and would allow of your playing perhaps a beautiful Schlummerlied, you ought really to give some concerts here. Then we could give them together. I am convinced that the moment is favourable and you know very well that the public is best pleased when you play your easiest and most familiar pieces. Certainly! And I shall arrange about the sing-song and other matters. It seems to me a most feasible idea. I am bullied enough for not playing and I would take a particular pleasure in filling out your programme. So please do not do anything hasty and cry off the concerts here. . . . Altogether, the kind of life I lead here makes Vienna as a whole seem every day more pleasant to me, but the people and especially the artists ever more repulsive. The way the latter behave towards the public and the critics, and play before them and depend upon them, takes away all one's desire to join in the swindle with them. . . . With affectionate greetings, Your faithful JOHANNES.

CLARA *to* BRAHMS.

NAUMBURG, *March* 23.

What I am going to tell you to-day, dear Johannes, will not please you. I found it hard enough to come to a decision, but I had no alternative. I am going to London from the middle of April to the end of May. Joachim wrote to me and offered me straight away so many engagements that I am insured against all risks. He also promised me that when once I am definitely there a good many other things will turn up. I have looked at it from every point of view. If I do not seize this opportunity of earning a little more money, I shall have to make up my mind this summer to encroach upon my capital to the extent of at least 2,000 thalers [£300]. If I were not strong enough it would naturally be out of the question. As it is, however, I regard it as my duty.

Thank God my hand improves every day, and although at times it makes me somewhat uneasy, this will all pass away when the weather gets a little bit warmer. The thought that when I return, after a successful tour, I shall be able to spend the summer quietly and enjoy your company more light-heartedly, gives me courage. . . . But I have formed the firm resolve not to stay longer than the 14th of June at the utmost, and then to remain quietly in Baden, and not to travel at all during the summer. This will enable me to take my ease for at least four months. You will scold me, won't you, dear Johannes ? And yet if you were the father of seven children you would certainly do what I am doing.

I am going to Prague on the 3rd of April, and shall play there on the 6th and the 8th ; and on the 9th I shall go direct to Düsseldorf to get all sorts of things ready during Easter week. I came here to-day for a concert this evening. Saturday I am going to Leipsic again, and on Sunday I am playing your A major Quartet in a quartet. We practised it very nicely this morning. . . . My hand has suddenly begun to hurt, so I would rather close. As a matter of fact I hardly ever write a letter now with my own hand. Farewell, dear friend, and be happy, and let me have a sign of life soon, Your CLARA.

CLARA *to* BRAHMS.

PRAGUE, *April* 4.

. . . This is too far away for a rendezvous, for if you came the journey would cost you almost as much as to come to Baden. So do not let us think of it but only of the visit to Baden. If only the land of mist and fog were already behind me ! But with Baden in the background it is easier to overcome present difficulties. This is always a pleasant feeling to me right through the winter. But just imagine, I have had to employ the builders there. There was dry rot in the dining-room, and to such an extent that whole joists had to be cut away and new ones put in. You can imagine how frightened I was. And yet this is said to happen in every house in Lichtenthal and is not serious provided one is sufficiently careful. But in moments of despondency I now often imagine my little house as a withering flower, though otherwise always as a beloved friend with whom alone I feel at home. Now don't laugh at me, I don't mean this altogether as a joke. . . . Your Quartet went beautifully. I can tell you so with a clean conscience, as also that it was most enthusiastically received. We were encored and what this or that ignorant critic may happen to say is no affair of ours. Certain people in Leipsic, particularly R., behave so stupidly with your things that one can only pity them, for they crawl like worms on the ground. . . .

I had some very bad news of my mother in Berlin. She is seriously ill. Woldemar, who wished to give her a surprise, found her in this state. We are all very much worried about it. . . . But now I must send my letter off and with it most affectionate greetings for you, dear Johannes, from Your old CLARA.

BRAHMS *to* CLARA.

VIENNA, *Monday, April* 24.

It is all very annoying that you should actually be in England now and that the beautiful spring weather should see nothing of you, and that I should be preparing all sorts of pieces of music to plague you with to no purpose. . . . If it is not already too late, let me beg you not to show the choral piece to Joachim.[1]   In any case it is probably the weakest part in the said *Deutsches Requiem*.   But as it may have vanished into thin air before you come to Baden, just have a look at the beautiful words with which it begins.   It is a chorus in F major without violins but accompanied by a harp and other beautiful things. . . .   I compiled the text from passages in the Bible [2] ; the chorus I sent you is number four.   The second is in C minor and is in march time.   I hope that a German text of this sort will please you as much as the usual Latin one.   I am hoping to produce a sort of whole out of the thing and trust I shall retain enough courage and zest to carry it through. . . .   I shall write to you from Carlsruhe or Baden soon.   I shall first of all saunter about Carlsruhe for a bit, then look for a place in Lichtenthal where I shall await you.   Affectionately yours, JOHANNES.

CLARA *to* BRAHMS.
LONDON, May 1, Morning.

The first greeting of May belongs to the May child !   To-day, my dear Johannes, you are on your way to Carlsruhe.   Oh, if only I could go off to Baden now !   Don't wander about too long but find a nice quiet place to work at.   I hope you will secure a pleasant lodging.[3]   But do not pay too much for it, for until the beginning of July the terms should be half, for the season only begins then—not more than ten shillings a week at the most. . . .   The chorus from the *Requiem* pleases me very much, it must sound beautiful.   I like it particularly up to the figured passage, but not so much where this goes on and on—

 etc.

---

[1] This piece, which formed part of his *Deutsches Requiem*, was sent to Clara in April just before her departure for England, in the hope that she might write to Brahms about it before she left.

[2] The full text, which is given on page 505 of the first volume of the German edition of the Letters, is merely an adaptation of some of the verses in the Sermon on the Mount.   The text to the second part seems to be a free rendering of some other Bible passages.—TR.

[3] Lichtenthal 316.

But that is a small matter. I hope you will not let the Requiem vanish into thin air. You surely could not after so beautiful a beginning. Of course I like the lovely German words better than the Latin. Many thanks for it all. . . . I could not show the chorus to Joachim because he is not here. . . . He is frightfully busy. He now has his wife and child with him here. She must feel most unhappy, because she cannot speak a word of English and that makes this country impossible. It would be a good thing for me if I had some of Joachim's engagements. It is true that I have a few, but they hardly cover the journey and the cost of staying here. I have played in public three times with great success. All the papers are full of the highest praise (the papers are all sent to one here). Everybody asks me to play Robert Schumann's compositions, etc., etc. But the engagements are few. In this place, if one really wants to earn money, the only thing to do is to place oneself in the hands of an agent. But something is sure to turn up and, come what may, if I can hold out till the end of this month, I can at least say that I have not shirked anything, and it will at all events make the summer easier for me.

I am once more charmed with all the green one sees here and the magnificent trees. The city is as beautiful as a big garden. We spent a day at the Crystal Palace a little while ago and I was once again quite overwhelmed by the magnificence of man's handiwork. We heard the Ninth Symphony there. It was very well produced, but the time was incredibly erratic; never have I heard this Symphony played so fast. . . . Joachim is seriously contemplating going direct to Baden from here, but I cannot believe that he will do so although you are a very strong magnet to him. It looks as if he intended to let his wife study under Madame Viardot. . . . Please tell Elise [Clara's daughter] that I have just received her dear letter and will write again soon. Greet her and Ludwig, whose letter I have also received, heartily for me. . . . But now farewell, dear Johannes, and let me hear from you soon. Think often of Your faithful CLARA.

Marie sends her love to Elise and Ludwig.

CLARA *to* BRAHMS.

LONDON, *May* 31, 1 ORME SQUARE, BAYSWATER.

It is already plain to me that I must write again, otherwise I shall not get another word from my dear Johannes. You really might have sent me another note from home, for there is not a moment of the day when I don't think longingly of Germany. But writing letters here is almost impossible ; the whole day is mapped out minute by minute, and at night one drops into bed almost dead. It is a most dreadful life. All artistic interest, in fact all idealism of every kind here is sacrificed to " bussiness " [*sic*]. Every one lives and strives only for himself, and I cannot describe to you how hard I find this. Nevertheless I suppose I shall have to decide to come here every year for three months in future (but from March to June), for it is the only way by which I can hope to secure for myself a more or less certain means of livelihood. But we shall be able to talk about this soon and about many other things as well.

I still continue to be received with the most extraordinary friendliness. The moment I appear the enthusiasm is so great that I usually have to wait some time before I can sit down at the piano. The day before yesterday at the Philharmonic Concert I received an ovation after Robert's Concerto, and to-morrow I shall play it again at the Crystal Palace. Wherever I go I have to play Schumann and although in regard to the general public this may be merely a matter of fashion, it probably takes its origin in a not inconsiderable number of genuine admirers of Robert's work, and this affords me great pleasure. I shall have to play a good deal within the next few days, and I find it a twofold strain in the very great heat. We are still having the most magnificent weather, which only increases my longing for Baden. We cannot enjoy it here very often because we never have any time for walks. Oh, if only these three weeks were over—I count the hours ! On the 20th I shall play for the last time. I hardly dare to look forward with certainty to my home, and yet how often does my heart not leap with joy at the thought of Baden !

I was overjoyed by your last letter of the 7th (I suppose you got mine of the 7th through Levi), and to hear that you had been able to make such excellent arrangements about your lodgings. . . . Please let me know soon how you are getting on and what you are working at. I imagine you as being very busy at present and expect you will have all sorts of new beauties to refresh me with soon. I expected to hear about you from Elise who had not written to me for a month, for I thought you often went to Carlsruhe. But yesterday her letter contained no mention of either you or Levi, except that the latter is going away for two months. For your sake I am sorry about this and also not a little surprised for I thought that he would spend his holidays with you. Or are you going away with him after all for a little while ? You must really write me a long letter very soon. Just think how badly I am in need of a warm greeting from home which I cannot get too often. I imagine you wandering the whole day in the woods and lying under the fir trees. Do you like Baden as much as ever ? . . .

I see Joachim only for a few minutes at a time. The way he works is inconceivable. He often holds a rehearsal immediately before a concert and is already dead tired for the concert itself. Poor fellow, he will probably have to do a good deal of such hard work in his life ! Little Johannes is delightful, he has a fine head. Frau Joachim has sung several times and has apparently met with much favour—as chance would have it I was unable to be present.

The morning is advancing and every minute I am interrupted. So I must part from you. With a thousand greetings, my dear Johannes, and let me soon see that you are thinking of Your CLARA.

Marie sends hearty greetings. She is very pleased with England but, like me, she is a little bit homesick.

CLARA *to* BRAHMS.

FRANKFORT, *Nov.* 1.

Thank you for your prompt greeting which gave me such a pleasant surprise. I cannot tell you how much it pleased me, for my heart was still aching at having to part from so much that I loved [1] and I found it dreadfully difficult to take up

---

[1] On the 28th of October Clara had left Baden Baden for Frankfort with Joachim, with whom she was going to give a concert. Her daughter Elise had accompanied them, as she wanted to settle down in Frankfort as a teacher of music.

my work again.   Had I been able to do as I wished I should
have thanked you at once, but I have had a terribly harassing time.   How delightful that we shall be seeing each other
again so soon ! [1]   I am having a real struggle with myself as
I should so much like to come to Carlsruhe for Friday [2] if I
had not a concert on the following day at Heidelberg.   But I
am afraid of getting over-excited, for we should remain talking together till late on Friday night and then I should have
no strength left for Saturday.   But Joachim will probably
come and I shall be with you in spirit with my loving
wishes. . . .   Our concert yesterday was very brilliant and
everything went wonderfully well.   We got tremendous
applause and at the end had to play the Haydn Finale over
again.   Instead of the Ballads (the subtleties of which would
have been entirely lost in the enormous hall) I played the
Andante with Variations,[3] and only hope I may play it
as well in Carlsruhe, for it was really very fine.   During
the whole evening I was in the most exalted state of mind
although I had just been through the most harassing day
a virtuoso could have, after which I scarcely hoped to be
able to carry it off.   I will tell you what these trials were by
word of mouth, it might be useful for you to know for next
winter.

Although she declares that she was trembling in every limb
Elise stood the test wonderfully, and played as if she were
not the least bit nervous.   This made me feel all the more
so, though of course I did not let her see it.   We were both
given a call.   I must confess that during the Variations [4] I
could not overcome my emotion when I thought what a fine
début this was for Elise to play a duet by her father with me
at the same concert as Joachim.   If only he had been able
to witness it, how lovingly his eyes would have rested on her !

---

[1] At a concert in Carlsruhe.   Brahms remained until the 9th of
November in Baden Baden or Carlsruhe.

[2] On the 3rd of November Brahms played his D minor Concerto
under Levi in Carlsruhe.

[3] Brahms' *Variations in D minor on an Original Theme for Pianoforte*
was not printed under this title, but became the second movement of
the First Sextet, Op. 18.

[4] Schumann's Op. 46.

. . . And now, my dear Johannes, with a thousand greetings, and how delightful that I can say *au revoir*, Your faithful old CLARA.

We have very good news of Julie.[1]

BRAHMS *to* CLARA.

CARLSRUHE, *Dec.* 3.

To the best of my knowledge I only wrote to you once from Switzerland, or did I do so more often ? But I had a very restless time, dearest Clara. You know how easily I allow my time to be taken up. I came here yesterday, and at Levi's this morning I will tell you in detail how successful I have been, as a matter of fact quite beyond expectation in every respect. What has pleased me most is that I really have the gifts of a virtuoso. I am entirely dependent upon the kind of piano I have. If it is good I play with the greatest calm and ease. The bigger the pieces, the better. I played the Phantasy Op. 17 twice, and also the Paganini Variations, in addition to organ pieces (D minor), etc. I brought about 1,800 francs back with me.

You may be able to gather how well I was received from the fact that after my first concert in Zürich, when I played the D major Serenade, one or two musical friends (particularly Dr. Lübke, Prof. Billroth [2] and Wesendonck) organized a private concert early on Sunday so that they might hear my Concerto and the A major Serenade again. They hired the Orchestra, telegraphed to all corners of the globe so that the parts, etc., might be certain to come, and everybody who had any interest in the matter was allowed to be there and to listen without further ado. So I first practised the Concerto with the orchestra, while Kirchner conducted it for me, and then finally the Serenade. The players were most devoted to me so that the whole affair was very gratifying. I had a beautiful Erard which belonged to Hug. It came to Winterthur with Hug and the tuner, and finally it seemed to thank me for the

---

[1] Julie was to spend the winter in Munich with Fr. von Pacher.

[2] This is his first connection with Theodor Billroth who, in his day, appears to have been an eminent surgeon. Lübke was the historian of Art, and concerning Brahms' visit to the Wesendoncks, see *Kalbeck*, Vol. II, p. 221.

honour without costing me a ha'penny. Hüni, whom I needed
for the orchestra, was just as obliging. In fact they all spoilt
me outrageously. . . . Did you get my letter (about the
concert in Bâle) in Berlin ? I don't pretend to understand
the calendar, but the concert was on the 19th and you asked
me about it on the 28th. The moment it was over I wrote
to you in Berlin that I had made 800 francs, etc., etc. . . .
But now I must bid you an affectionate farewell, as I have
other letters to write, and although I may have written to
you in a hurry I think of you often enough in the best of adagio
tempos and thoroughly *con espressione*. Wholly yours,
JOHANNES.

CLARA *to* BRAHMS.

Dec. 8.

What a delightful surprise your dear letter was to me, dear
Johannes. It came at the right moment, as I was just off to
my concert in Breslau, and what fine news it contained ! I
was so glad to hear that things had gone so well with you and
that for once the people had their hearts in the right place.
If only I could have been there and above all been able to
listen to you the whole evening at the concert when you were
really playing *con amore*! I should so much have enjoyed
hearing the Serenades again. You don't tell me how the
audience in the various towns received Robert's Phantasy or
what they said to your *Hexenvariationen*. I should love to
know. I was also very pleased to hear that you made so much
money. Be careful how you spend it. Remember that the
summer will be here soon and that you will certainly want to
wander among the mountains of Switzerland again. I wish
you would give me your money to keep for you ! Wouldn't
you like to ? Why do you always carry it about with you ?
. . . Tell me, how is it that you want to spend Christmas
precisely with the Bargiels ? If you don't want to spend it
at Hamburg surely Joachim is a closer friend ! But you promised your sister to go to her, and for weeks she has been
looking forward to spending the festival with you.[1] She will
be wretched if you disappoint her. Remember it is the first
Christmas without your mother—how hard for her ! Wouldn't

[1] On the 5th of November Clara had given a concert in Hamburg.

it be much better if you helped her as kindly as possible to get over that evening and then went on to Joachim's ? Please tell me what you think about this. I need not tell you how glad I should be to see you in Düsseldorf at Christmas, but I should have a guilty conscience as regards your sister, particularly as I had the pleasure of seeing you the whole of the summer and hope to repeat it often again. Let me hear soon, dearest Johannes, what you have decided to do. . . .

I found your second letter about the Bâle concert on my arrival here from Dresden. I had sent off mine from there in the morning, but where yours came from I could only guess, because it had neither place nor date. But after your last letter I know everything and in such detail that I can tell where to find you now, which is always a pleasant feeling to me. . . . Have you heard that the concert in Hanover (the first subscription concert) was such a failure that the Royal Family are quite concerned about it and are now leaving no stone unturned to lure Joachim back again ? Now with heartiest greetings, my dear Johannes, and hoping that things may go well with you, ever Your devoted CLARA.

CLARA *to* BRAHMS.

DÜSSELDORF, *Dec.* 23.

I feel I must send you my most affectionate greeting with the little Christmas present I am giving you. I hope, dearest Johannes, it will seem less prosaic to you than the gift is this time. I thought of many a book but was afraid that with your present wandering life anything of the sort would only be a burden. Besides, you always get any book of importance at once. On the other hand your old grey travelling-bag hovered before my mind, and it struck me that to replace it by a new one would not only be practical but also pleasing to the eye. I should be so glad if you would take it on your travels with you together with all my good wishes. . . .

Thank heaven we have fairly good news of Julie. She has got over the danger of typhoid, but it will be a long time before she has completely recovered. Ludwig wanted to leave Frau

Wills [1] at a moment's notice and to my great sorrow I was forced to conclude from what I saw how muddled all his ideas are. So you see I have my full share of anxiety again. But I shall now practise diligently for Vienna and this will strengthen my soul. . . . Let me hear from you soon, my dear Johannes, Your loving CLARA.

[1] Frau Wills had been looking after Ludwig like a mother for three or four years, but he gave her an enormous amount of trouble and wounded her feelings constantly, though probably quite unintentionally. In a letter of the 10th of September to Elizabeth Werner, Clara writes very sadly about her anxiety concerning the dreamy youth, and declares she is at her wits' end to know what to do with him.—TR.

1866

[DEAR JOHANNES,]

. . . Heartiest thanks for your last dear letter. It gave
me a lot of pleasant news and I suppose that you are now
sure to be giving concerts with Joachim all over the place—
for the present he has nothing in view. . . . Things seem to
be in a bad way here as regards finance, and yet concerts
are well attended. I hope mine will be also ! My first is on
Saturday the 27th, the second on February the 1st. I should
be much obliged if you would send me the Horn Trio [1] which
I want to play on the 4th of February at Hellmesberger's.
He seemed to jump at it at once and spoke to me about a
remarkable hornist (not Levi). . . . Up to the present Hanslick is the only one of your acquaintances I have seen, and he
is going to bring Nottebohm to me in a few days' time—the
man who has written such wonderful variations for four hands
on a theme by Bach, and who from sheer modesty has kept
them hidden away for ten years. . . .

Just fancy, I have had another stroke of misfortune, for in
Brunswick the other day I had such a fall that I might have
broken every bone in my body, and this was at a concert too,
before a whole audience. Four temporary steps were resting
against the stage, because the latter and the steps to it were
not yet finished, and the steps were not fixed to the stage but
only put there for show. Now when I had finished playing
and wanted to listen to the Symphony, a gentleman led me
towards the steps in question, but, the moment I put my foot
on them, the whole thing collapsed with me on top. I was
terrified and it was a long time before I could get up, for I
had hurt my foot very much indeed. In fact I am still suffering from the effects of it and cannot walk but have to drive

[1] Op. 40.

everywhere.   Meanwhile the sun is tempting me with all its might to go out and I am feeling rotten for want of exercise. And yet I don't like to express my annoyance about it all, for really it was only a miracle that things were not worse.

I also want to tell you about your stocks and shares.   I bought 500 thalers' worth [£75], but paid only 495 thalers 15 Sgr. and therefore have laid aside 9 thalers 15 Sgr. for you, to which I shall also add the interest later on (you gave me 505 thalers).   I should have liked to get you 6% stock, but one cannot realize these at a moment's notice, and I did not know whether you would like that. . . .

I am longing to have news from you and above all to hear how you got on in Hamburg.   Are you still there ?   And how is your father [1] and when is he getting married ?   How do you like her ?   Greet Elise for me.   Poor soul, how she must have enjoyed your being there !   I only hope you were not too much depressed by her unhappy circumstances.   And now farewell, dear Johannes.   Let me soon have news of you. Your old CLARA.

CLARA *to* BRAHMS.

VIENNA, *Feb.* 4.

DEAREST JOHANNES,

Day after day I have been waiting for a quiet moment to thank you for your two dear letters, and so to-day I am sitting up late, otherwise I should never find time to do it.   I wish I could stretch out the days like a piece of elastic and do the same to my mind and my body.   I have good news of your friends here and your ears must often burn for we talk a lot about you.   I have to send you greetings from all of them.

I received the Horn Trio the day before yesterday and also the Quintet which I had left in Düsseldorf, for I took it for granted that I should find it here with Hellmesberger as it has been on his programme for months.   What a hornet's nest of intrigue and pettiness I fell into !   I was so angry !   Just think of it, we were to practise it on Friday (it had just arrived an hour before the rehearsal).   But all the players seemed so indifferent about it that at last I said to them, " Gentlemen,

[1] Brahms' father had become engaged to Pauline Schnack, a widow, in October, 1865.

I must ask you to tell me when you will have time to study
this piece with me, because I refuse to have anything to do
with a perfunctory rehearsal." Whereupon all of them (with
Hellmesberger at their head) declared that they had no time,
that the rehearsal on the following day (the last) would be
before the public, and so it was impossible to study any more.
So I had to leave the Quintet out of account and urged them
to do the A major Quartet. We played this, but oh, how
they played it ! I still don't understand how I controlled
myself so as to play it to the end, for I was really not prepared
to meet with such hostility. In short they declared that they
had played it with you and really did not need a rehearsal,
and then Hellmesberger came and said that it really did not
suit his programme and that it would be better if we did not
play it after all. So there was nothing left for me to do except
either not to play at all (which is certainly the course I should
have adopted if I had not needed H. in my concerts) or to
play something else.

I then heard that from the very beginning H. had said he
would not play the Quintet, and a lot of other gossip besides,
and I think he has by no means heard the last of it, more
especially from Hanslick, who was very angry. I need hardly
tell you how wounded I was by the whole business, both on
your account and my own. I do not know yet what I shall
do with the Horn Trio, for you can imagine how much all this
has upset me ; and, whereas at the beginning I looked forward
to it so much, I really do not feel as if I had the courage to
expose myself to another such affront. I have found it hard
to tell you all about it, but it was better you should know it
all through me, besides it won't upset you as much as it has
me. Men can rise superior to such things.

Of your pupils I have Frl. Wittgenstein [1] and Frau Rosen-
garden, who really plays very well. Frau Bruch also came.
But what a woman ! She is not stupid, but never in my life
have I known anyone so eccentric. Just imagine, before she
began her first lesson she drew a little packet out of her bag,
laid it on the piano and said that before she embarked on her
polyphonic tour with me, for such it was, she would lay this
on the altar of Art, etc., etc. She then begged me to let it lie

[1] Anna Wittgenstein.

there unless I wished to make her so nervous that she could not remain a moment longer, and so on. I left it lying there and sent it back to her on the following day through her friend Frau Streicher, but without breaking off with her. I have not seen her again! (In the little packet there were twelve ducats!)

I have now given two concerts which have gone off most brilliantly in every respect. One could not have wished for a warmer reception than I had, and both concerts were packed. I am giving the third on Friday the 9th and the fourth probably on the 17th. On the 19th I am to give a big soirée at [Baroness] Sina's, so in any case I shall stop till the 22nd or 23rd. There is little likelihood of my going to Pesth as the political situation there is too unsettled, but I am rather relieved for I shall be able to spare my strength for England if I do not exert myself too much now. . . .

I have seen a good deal of Nottebohm. Yesterday I played his Bach Variations with him. One can tell very well from them that he is a capable musician, but the real thing—originality—seems to be lacking. I am simply longing to hear from you again and especially to know what your immediate plans are. . . . And now good-night, my dear Johannes. Think of me as I think of you. Your CLARA.

Please let me know some time how Ludwig is getting on.

CLARA *to* BRAHMS.

PESTH, *March* 15.

. . . You will be surprised to hear that I have given up the idea of going to England this year. As a matter of fact I am suffering with my liver and the trouble has increased so much this winter that the doctor in Düsseldorf made me promise on my honour to take the cure in Carlsbad or Kissingen this spring (at the very latest at the end of May). As I have been detained so long in Vienna I could only go to London after Easter, and then I should only have five or six weeks left for England. It would not pay me to go there for so short a time. It would be doing the thing by halves. So a week ago I made up my mind to give it up. But I shall take all that offers in the neighbourhood here, and shall therefore go after Easter to Graz and Trieste and, if it is not too expensive, from there *via* Venice and Milan through Switzerland to Düsseldorf for the music festival.

So now you know all my plans. Please let me hear yours in return. My address until the second day of the Easter holidays will be the same as before in Vienna. Do you know that poor Frau Joachim is still in bed ? She was even said to be dangerously ill for a few days. Apparently poor Joachim had a dreadful struggle to decide whether he should go to London or not, until at last the doctor calmed his fears. It is really wretched to think what women have come to nowadays, they can no longer endure anything. So far I can give you good news of the children. Elise has so many pupils that she cannot take on any more. Julie has quite recovered. Ferdinand will go into business in the autumn, and as to Ludwig —you know more about him than I do. He seems to have pulled himself together a bit recently. . . . Greet my Ludwig and also Levi [1] for me and remember Your devoted CLARA.

CLARA *to* BRAHMS.

GRAZ, *April* 8.

At last you see I have really left Vienna, but it was hard to do so and I stretched the time out like elastic. I came here yesterday. The magnificent journey over the Semmering in the most wonderful spring weather was delightful and refreshed my poor heart so that I arrived here much refreshed. To-day I gave a brilliant concert (midday), and in the afternoon we went for a charming walk—Graz is really beautifully situated. To-morrow I go to Klagenfurt in Carinthia, which I am told occupies a magnificent position on lofty rocks amid snow mountains. The people are moreover said to be very intelligent. A concert has been arranged for me there and on Friday I shall be back again here, when I shall give my second concert. I shall not go to Trieste or Venice. Conditions in Trieste are too primitive for concerts and to my joy I shall get to Baden all the sooner—the sooner the better, for I feel ever drawn to the old familiar scenes and the things I already love, and I am naturally anxious to have my home comforts again as soon as possible. Everything has turned out very much as I wanted.

[1] Brahms was remaining in Carlsruhe until the 18th of April.

I agree with you about doctors, but this time I had really
thought my trouble worse than the doctor did.   It is certainly
liver trouble. . . .   But I know it is, you can take my word
for it.   Before I decide to appeal to a doctor I have to be very
bad. . . .

Herewith I am sending you your *Trio* and a few things by
Schubert, which Flatz has had copied for you.   I have seen a
good deal of him, and the evenings which we have spent either
at his place or more often at mine with his wife and Lewinsky
were most agreeable and belong to my most pleasant memories
of Vienna.   I really think that in future I shall spend every
winter from the beginning of November to April there.   Certainly in no other city could I find so much to make me happy.
I do not know of a more musical community, while even in
the provinces I find an extraordinary amount of enthusiasm
for music.   Vienna, of course, has its drawbacks, but not more
than other places, and it has more good points, the *Burgtheater*
for instance !   What pleasant times I have had there !—they
have remained with me for long afterwards and enabled me
to face every exertion cheerfully.   What splendid things I
have seen there—Phædra, the Niebelungen, Wintermärchen,
Nathan, etc., and how wonderfully they were played !   I cannot understand why you did not enjoy it more. . . .   I
received the portraits of Robert, but they are so bad I cannot
use them, nobody will look at them.   I shall return them to
Allgeyer and ask him for others. . . .   With most affectionate
greetings, ever Your devoted CLARA.

CLARA *to* BRAHMS.

BADEN, *July* 8.

DEAR JOHANNES,[1]

. . . This place has only begun to fill up during the last
few days.   Numbers of people fled to this really peaceful valley
where they can hear no echo of the din of war.   Until just
lately we too have been very quiet, but three days ago Mamma [2]
arrived, and I also have two of the girls and Ferdinand.   Dr.
Planer, alas, could not let Felix come because his return would
be too uncertain and he must not miss the reopening of the

[1] From Carlsruhe Brahms had gone to Switzerland.
[2] Clara's mother, Frau Bargiel.

school.   You can imagine how sorry we are for the poor little fellow.   Ferdinand has now left the Gymnasium, will remain here until October, and then probably go into some firm in Hamburg.   I have put my mother up at the Bär where she is most comfortable.   She comes to me regularly every evening, but I insisted on keeping my days free so that I could do all that I wanted to do without being bothered.   As I have not yet finished my cure I am not playing at all except a few duets with the children just to give them practice.   I also give them lessons regularly.   But otherwise I am kept quite busy, particularly lately with correspondence, chiefly due to the sad state of affairs.   I also work at French every day so as to make some progress in that language.   Stockhausen has been here a week and has been taking the milk cure, but to-morrow he is going to Zug in Switzerland with his parents and brothers.   His wife is in Kiel.   He is planning all kinds of productions for next winter.   He wants some time, for instance, to give one or two acts out of the Genoveva, which we have gone right through together.   I thought all the time what a joy it would be to hear this opera performed once by a group of singers like him. . . .

I was sorry that you told me in your letter that I was afraid of scores.   It really isn't true.   If only I could have a little leisure to get some practice in reading them and some one to help me to learn how to do it I would certainly not lack the will.   But I am too conscious of my incompetence in reading any complicated score.   I hope some day to be able to find time to practise it and then I trust you will be glad to send me your scores.   But I am getting none of your printed things —Waltzes,[1] Cello Sonata,[2] Horn Trio,[3] etc.   Wüllner asked me the other day whether you had no *a capella* works.   Every Sunday they sing their Masses only *a capella*, and I had told him about yours.   You have told me nothing lately about Kirchner.   But you see a lot of him, don't you ?   Stockhausen told me something that pleased me very much—that your father was so happy now.   How are things between him and Elise, and what news have you of your brother ? . . .   Your affectionate old CLARA.

[1] Op. 39.   [2] Op. 38.   [3] Op. 40.

CLARA *to* BRAHMS.

OLDENBURG, *Nov.* 24, *Sunday.*

At last, dear Johannes, I can find time to write you a letter, but where to send it I really don't know, for I fancy you must be in Switzerland,[1] as Julie told me you had returned there. Your concerts must have been wonderfully lively and I wish I could have heard more about them ; I should have been so glad to follow you in spirit from place to place. Thank you so much for your letter, dear Johannes ; it is true it came late, but I know your roving habits and am only too well aware of what happens when one is travelling. One makes up one's mind every day to write a letter and never does it. It was the same with me about this one. If I had followed my own inclinations you would have had a greeting from me long ago. But the trouble with me is that on days when I have to play a good deal I may not write, for I immediately feel a stiffness in my fingers. And then I dictate almost everything. But I don't like doing this to people who are close to my heart. I am so glad your concerts were so successful financially. Now you need not worry about money matters at all for a whole year, and without encroaching on your capital you can give your father some extra pleasure. That is really splendid.

I shall not get to Hamburg this winter and for Friedchen's sake I am very sorry. Stockhausen certainly telegraphed to me the other day asking me to come. But in the first place it is difficult for me to arrange it, and then the inducement was such a peculiar one. He wanted me to play Beethoven's Phantasy with chorus before the Peri. What an idea ! It would simply mean destroying the listener's mood for the Peri. I afterwards got a letter which was so confused that I was doubly glad I had not gone, and when I heard how poor the production had been I was trebly glad. Böie conducted the thing in the most boring way, which was only to be expected, and only the solos by Stockhausen and Frau Joachim were any good. Stockhausen has already given ten concerts in Hamburg. I am afraid he is overdoing it and wearing himself out. . . .

---

[1] Brahms came to Baden on the 17th of August and remained until the middle of October. He left there with Joachim to go on a concert tour in Switzerland.

I came here three days ago and was most kindly received by the Dietrichs. The wife is charming in her really childlike devotion to her husband. But he does not seem to appreciate the treasure he possesses. Dietrich gave me a great musical treat with Robert's Third Symphony, which I had not heard for a long time and which again afforded me great delight. The only thing was, the brass instruments blared so earsplittingly in the hall that one was almost deafened. Yesterday among other things I played your Waltzes at the Court with Dietrich, and the audience seemed very much impressed. This afternoon he is having a few people and I shall play your Quartet in A, which I am very much looking forward to. . . . Now, dear Johannes, I think I have told you all my news and I hope you will do the same soon by Your CLARA.

CLARA *to* BRAHMS.

COBLENZ, *Dec.* 22.

In order that you may not be without a Christmas greeting from me, dear Johannes, I am writing to-day, although I have very little leisure, for every minute of my time has been occupied for weeks. . . . If only the critics in Leipsic [1] were not more stupid than the public, and malicious into the bargain ! Now I know who the donkey was who told Härtels that your second Sextet was too mad for him, upon which they returned it to you. They must already be savage about it, and he must be feeling ashamed. There is no need for me to tell you his name. I feel less angry over the stupidity of such people than over their infamy in thus passing sentence of death upon a work on which a composer has spent all the strength of his soul. But fortunately it has not succeeded and the tide is now turning.

Yesterday your letter came with its beautiful promise [2] for Christmas which I am very much looking forward to. But I wish you had left out the bitter pill which you added to it in the form of a few remarks. Is it kind, for instance, to say, as you did, that a fortnight ago the idea of giving me the

---

[1] Clara had left Oldenburg to stay in Berlin, and on the 9th of December went to Leipsic. Here she had played Brahms' *Horn Trio* at the Gewandhaus between the 9th and the 16th.

[2] The pianoforte arrangement of the *Requiem*.

pleasure of having your Requiem seemed quite right and natural to you, but that now it strikes you as unnecessary ? Why spoil my joy in this way ? But I will try to imagine that you really did not mean what you have written and shall once more revel in your Requiem. You wrote the other day that you liked it more when you played it to Joachim in Switzerland for the second time. Why ? I hope I shall find it to-morrow in Düsseldorf.

I have been wondering for weeks how I should be able to give you a little treat and my attention was called to the recently published translation of Byron by Gildenmeister, which is said to be wonderful and has delighted all who know it. I hope nobody will steal a march on me by giving it to you. Unfortunately I could not get it bound before Christmas and could not make up my mind to send it to you unbound. So you must be satisfied with this simple greeting for Christmas, which, however, from the point of view of heartiness is substantial enough.

I had a great joy in Cologne. Rudolf had been studying the Manfred, and produced it very beautifully in a small hall before an invited audience. Dr. Bernays [1] of Bonn recited much of it wonderfully well, and from the musical point of view everything was perfect. Wendelstadt had offered to defray all expenses. Farewell, dear Johannes. Your Viennese friends will see to it that you have a merry Christmas. Please tell me about it soon and remember Your CLARA.

CLARA to BRAHMS.

DÜSSELDORF, *Dec.* 30.

. . . The pianoforte arrangement of your *Requiem* has given me unspeakable joy and I have revelled in it again. If only I could sing all the voices together as I should like to do ! Your arrangement, moreover, is beautifully done, it is not hard to play and yet it is rich in material. I congratulate you most heartily on it. . . .

We spent Christmas very quietly here, and in Coblenz it was very hard for me not to go to Mannheim where Julie, Elise, and Ludwig (Levi also joined them) were together. But

---

[1] Michael Bernays (1834–1897), a historian of Literature. He was Professor of the History of Literature at Munich.—TR.

as Rosalie had been expecting me for months to spend Christmas here I could not disappoint her. . . . Your description of *Lear* made my mouth water. Oh, if only I could see a play like that again at the Burg ! The other day we saw *As You Like It* beautifully acted, and we could not help remarking how wonderfully effective Shakespeare's plays are on the stage and how much more enjoyable they are than when they are read. . . . Rudorff is now in Berlin. Stockhausen took part in a concert there the other day, and Scholz played a quintet of his own and many other things. Auer also took part. But the concert was badly attended and the applause was feeble. The audience was annoyed because although Stockhausen had charged one and a half thalers [4/6] admission, he only sang short songs, and gave the Löwenbraut as a first item instead of an Aria from Handel for instance, which would have been more suitable.

But one cannot help thoroughly despising a fellow like Hellmesberger. He plays me the dirtiest of tricks and then proceeds to crawl before you. I am leaving on the 10th. Heaven grant me a safe return ! That is my constant thought in connection with this journey. For the first six weeks my address will be C/o Mr. Arthur Chappell, 50 New Bond Street, London. . . . I called on young Rieter in Leipsic and as he said he had been doing good business with your *Waltzes* I had recourse to entreaty and got him to give me three of them for the children who were to get them all for Christmas. With my most affectionate greetings for the New Year and hoping you will think of me often, Your CLARA.

1867

DÜSSELDORF, *Jan.* 11.

[DEAREST JOHANNES]

. . . The donkey in question is Bagge— ! Of course I did not speak to Härtels about it, I have your pride too much at heart.

Julie is not going with me. She feels very comfortable at Frau Feidel's.[1] She is learning a good deal of ensemble playing with Lachner and also with Koning.[2] But, alas, she has been ill again for a fortnight, because she has over-exerted herself with all kinds of work. We were all the more shocked to hear about it because she had been quite well all through the summer. So it will do her more good to be quiet than to go on this journey. We have again had all sorts of trouble with Ludwig,[3] but Levi has smoothed things over and as long as Ludwig is under his supervision I feel easier in my mind than I otherwise should. I have had my full measure of anxiety in other ways as well just lately, and I often feel as if I no longer had the courage to go on. But, thank God, such a state of mind is only temporary. My little house, with everything that it contains in the summer, soon brightens my horizon again. I could not show Hiller your Requiem because he was not here, and I only saw him once for a few hours before I received it. He showed me a number of his own things, and to my real joy there were some quite nice pieces for four hands among them. It is true they were only trifles, but he is always so exceedingly friendly to me that I was glad to be able to praise him for once. . . .

[1] Hermann Levi's aunt in Mannheim.

[2] A viola player.

[3] The close of the year had been saddened by bad news of Ludwig, who had not settled down as he should, and Levi had taken charge of him in the most unselfish and noble manner.—TR.

Farewell, dear Johannes, and with the most affectionate greetings, Your CLARA.

CLARA *to* BRAHMS.

LONDON, *Feb.* 26,
17 HALF MOON STREET, PICCADILLY.

How glad I am to be able at last to find a quiet hour this evening for you, dearest Johannes, all the more so because I am able to inform you that your Sextet was produced with great success at the Popular Concert yesterday. Joachim had, of course, practised it well and played magnificently. The reception was most enthusiastic, particularly after the first three movements. The Scherzo was encored, but Joachim wanted to keep the audience fresh for the last movement and so did not respond to the call. I enjoyed it thoroughly, and should have loved to have been the first violin. I really wanted to play the A major Quartet but Joachim insisted on the Sextet, which he thought more suitable for the first perform-ance of one of your works in England. I gave way, but most unwillingly. After all it went splendidly, and that is the chief thing.—I really played with them in spirit. . . .

I was glad to hear that your Sextet [1] had been loudly ap-plauded in Vienna. Were you pleased with the way it was played ? And where are you now, in Graz or Pesth ? I had a most unpleasant surprise when I heard that you had given up all serious attempts at producing your Requiem. I thought the arrangements were in full swim. What do you expect of a musical production in Zürich ? You always said that you were particularly anxious to have it produced either in Vienna or Berlin. And now I must tell you something or rather give you a message from Joachim. It is this—an Englishman [2] who is a great lover of music, whom he met in France and to whom he spoke about your Requiem, asked whether you would allow him to subscribe 1,000 francs towards defraying the expenses of its production. I can see nothing to be said against this. In Germany artists and even composers are, after all, not in a position to be able to defray the expenses of such productions out of their own pockets. What do you think about it ?

[1] Op. 36, G major.
[2] A Mr. Behrens of Glasgow, of German origin.

The news about myself is so far good that I have been most
enthusiastically received wherever and whenever I have
appeared. I have also had great success in the provincial
towns, and although travelling was often very tiring, things
were made as comfortable as possible for us. Chappell is
behaving as generously as one could possibly expect from a
regular business man. The concerts themselves have always
been just what one would have wished, and only good things
were chosen. It is true that we often performed the same
programme two or three times in succession, but there were
business reasons for this arrangement. We have seen many
fine places on our travels, above all Edinburgh and Torquay,
each of which is magnificent in its way. Unfortunately we
spent too short a time at both places, so that we were not
able to see enough of the beautiful surroundings. But next
week I am going to Edinburgh for a couple of days, and then
we shall make up for it. I am going to give a recital at which
I shall play alone for an hour and a half. But we did manage
to see Holyrood, the palace of Mary Queen of Scots, and the
wonderful Shakespeare monument,[1] to which the whole country subscribed. Thank God, I have fulfilled most of my engagements. The strain was often very great, for, as a rule, the
concerts were so arranged that we had to play three days in
succession in different towns, and in addition had from four
to six hours' travelling every day. Joachim has accepted a
longer engagement ; he often plays five times in a week, and
in addition attends any number of social functions. I cannot
conceive how he survives it all, but he often looks terribly
haggard. I make it a strict rule here not to squander my
strength at futile social gatherings, and spare myself as much
as possible on concert days. It is only by this means that I
am able to hold out and to remain always fresh and enthusiastic
for my music. What one has to complain about least here is
the public, but artistic stimulation of any kind is entirely
lacking, for people take up music in order to earn money, and
that often makes me feel frightfully depressed. I really believe
I should die if I had to stay here. They are strongly advising
me to remain here for the season, but I have emphatically

[1] Clara probably means the Scott Monument in Princes Street.—
Tr.

declared that I will not do so.   But it is not easy to stick to
one's point, for I would earn a good deal here during the season,
although I would injure my health and spirits ; and, after
all, I should like to keep the little sanity I have left.

So I shall remain here until Easter week and then I shall
have earned sufficient to be able to look forward calmly to
next year.   But I shall hardly be able to put anything aside.
I have had nothing but good news from my family.   Ferdinand
is turning out very well and Ludwig's master is also pleased
with him.   Felix often gives us great amusement with his
letters in which his vigorous nature stands revealed.   Julie is
being well looked after and cared for, and is studying diligently
with Lachner ; and Elise is doing a lot of music apart from
her lessons.   On the 26th of March Joachim is going to France
again, and this time to the provinces.   He has earned a lot
of money this winter, for which I am very glad.   I only hope
he has laid a good deal aside.   He is seriously considering
moving to Berlin. . . .

I am longing for news from you.   I hope you are quite well,
dearest Johannes, and may you sometimes remember Your
CLARA.

CLARA *to* BRAHMS.

LONDON, *April* 15.

DEAR JOHANNES,

To-day I am able to tell you that I have at last finished
here, but latterly I have been so harassed that I could not
write to you as I should like to have done.   I gave my second
recital the day before yesterday.   To-morrow I shall go from
here to Brussels, where I shall stay with the Kufferaths for a
couple of days, and then on to Düsseldorf for the holidays.
What will become of me then I do not know.   I must try to
consult a homœopath, for my trouble, which gets worse at
night and thus prevents me from sleeping, is becoming more
acute every day, and I am beginning to realize that I can't
ignore it.   It is just possible that I may have to go to Carlsbad,
which would annoy me very much, because what I would like
most would be to go to Baden. . . .   Unfortunately I am not
so satisfied with the financial side of my visit, in spite of all
the strain it has been, as I was last winter in Vienna.   Never-

theless things are more certain here, and there they are precarious. . . . You can imagine how busy we are to-day, but I want to let you know that I am leaving. I should like to be able to look forward to something pleasant during the holiday in Düsseldorf. You know what I mean, dear friend, with most affectionate greetings, Your CLARA.

Marie insists on my telling you how brilliant my farewell to England was. Well, it is true, and I am very pleased about it.

CLARA *to* BRAHMS.

DÜSSELDORF, *April* 26.

By a happy accident the letter you wrote to me when I was in London reached me here on the second day of the holidays, and the good news it contained delighted me—the splendid concerts,[1] the enthusiastic audiences, and heaps of money, what more can one want? And now I hope it will be the same in Pesth. . . . What shall we do with all this money? I wrote to Wendelstadt at once about buying stock for you and for me, but he replied that he preferred to talk to me, for I wanted to buy Railway stock which is now very low. But if war really breaks out with France it is a little bit risky. On Monday I am going through Cologne to Mannheim to see Julie and then I shall speak to Wendelstadt, and shall in any case buy the same securities for both of us. You can always let me have the money later on—I have enough by me for the summer and I shall pay for yours out of that. So I shall simply spend a thousand thalers [£150] for you, as you are sure to earn some more in Pesth. But don't forget to change your *guldens* into Prussian money in Vienna, otherwise you will lose too much on them here. Spina always looked after this very well for me, so that I had as little loss as possible. If one can earn a lot of money in Vienna, it is certainly a very different thing from England in spite of all the exertion. After all I have done I can't put any more aside than you have done after two concerts. But of course one must remember that I spend very much more, particularly in England where every-

[1] Concerning Brahms' series of concerts in Vienna—17th of March and 7th of April, Graz, Klagenfurt, Pressburg and Pesth, see *Kalbeck*, Vol. II, p. 210 ff.

thing is so frightfully dear. . . . Unfortunately I cannot give you very good news of myself. I shall certainly have to go to Carlsbad. My pains are not very great, but I feel that if I do not go they will get more serious. . . .

I think your idea of settling down in Vienna is very good. Just you do it. When once you have all your music and your books about you you will feel so much more at home, and with all its drawbacks Vienna is after all the best place for an artist. If I could do as I liked I would go there every winter. You must have misunderstood me about Joachim. He is only going to Vienna in the autumn. He is now giving concerts in Paris, and his wife is said to be singing much better than she used because she has learnt so much from Stockhausen.

I ought to be playing in Hamburg to-day, but I have told you my reasons for refusing. I could not forget the infamy [1] that has been perpetrated against you and Grädener and so could not bring myself to go. . . . And now, my dear Johannes, with most affectionate greetings, Your CLARA.

CLARA *to* BRAHMS.

CARLSBAD, *May* 6.

I only arrived here last night and my first thought this morning is to send you my heartiest wishes for to-morrow, my dear friend. I hope they may reach you in time in the morning, but if they do not, you do not need this sign from me to know that I am still thinking of you with the same loyal affection. . . . I should naturally like you to join me here, dear Johannes, but it would upset me to think that as you know nobody else here you would be thrown entirely on me for entertainment, and I should be afraid that you would get bored and headachy from wandering about. I would much prefer you to give me the pleasure of a longer visit in Baden, for I should be able to appreciate it much better there, and so would you.

Did you earn much in Pesth ? I have bought you three Rhineland Railway shares in Cologne for 750 thalers [£112.10.0].

[1] The fact that after Stockhausen's resignation of the post of Conductor to the Philharmonic Concerts and the *Singakademie* Brahms was again overlooked.

. . . I should like to have bought 1,000 thalers' worth of securities for you, but I did not know whether you would like me to, as I should have had to pay about 1,200 thalers for them. They are now standing at 111 and in good times reach 120 and over and pay 6½%. I paid about 845 thalers for them. I hope it is all right. If you want me to buy another share (so as to spend the whole of the 1,000 thalers on securities) write, and I will see to it through Herr Wendelstadt. Until I return to Baden I have placed the securities in safe-keeping. . . . What my trouble is neither I nor the doctors actually know. One says it is nervous, another that it is rheumatic and another something else. But I feel pretty sure that the liver has something to do with it, and as three out of the four doctors whom I have consulted during the last few years recommended Carlsbad, I soon made up my mind to come here. As a matter of fact the doctor was here a moment ago, and he says I must lead a thoroughly lazy life and have no brain work at all, and not much writing or playing. You can imagine how hard this is for me. With most affectionate greetings, Your CLARA.

CLARA *to* BRAHMS.

BADEN BADEN, *Oct.* 3.

And now all the beautiful things have come, and what a mass of them—so like Brahms ! My first feeling, I must confess, was one of horror at the expense to which you have put yourself, and beautiful as the baskets [1] are (they went like hot cakes), I still feel a little bit pained that you should have spent so much money. With the rest, however, I was thoroughly delighted—the song, the garland, the violets—that was a charming idea. My heartiest thanks for all this. I am not answering your last letter to-day. I don't wish to in any case. But I feel I must say this to you, that I have never read any of your letters except with friendly feelings, and so have never expected to find anything unpleasant in them. But at times it is very hard, almost impossible. But I won't say anything more about it, so let us change the subject. . . .

I suppose you have heard that Rubinstein will be touring Germany this winter ? He is also going to Vienna. His wife

[1] Glass baskets from Venice. The song was Op. 49, number 5, *Arbenddämmerung*.

and child will remain here this winter. . . . A few days ago Julie left for Divonne where she has met Frau Schlumberger. She is to take the open-air and cold-water cure there. She was very bad this summer, but all the doctors (even the one in Divonne) are agreed that her organs are all sound and that she only needs to have her nerves strengthened. Heaven grant her a speedy recovery! We drew so close to each other this summer that I found the parting terribly hard, as she did too. I must say that altogether I find my intimate relationship to my children a source of ever greater happiness to me. Felix is now rejoicing my heart with the most affectionate letters from which it is easy to see that he has brains. He has now been moved up to the Lower Fifth and when he is sixteen and a half he will probably have got through the *Gymnasium*.

I have again been detaining you with my chatter and it will probably be the last really quiet hour I shall have for a long time. Correspondence about concerts is once more in full swing and all the other preparations for a tour. I leave here on the 11th, remain three days in Frankfort, and reach Hamburg on the 15th, where I hope to go and see your people at once. I suppose your father will call on me? With affectionate greetings, ever Your faithful CLARA.

CLARA *to* BRAHMS.

HAMBURG, *Nov.* 13.

. . . My heartiest thanks for what you have sent me. I was particularly pleased to have them here although I have not yet succeeded in playing through the F Sharp minor song [1] without bursting into tears, which you will say I do very easily. I can only believe that its mood was your own while you were actually writing it, but I should be pained indeed if I believed that you often felt like that. No, dear Johannes, a man like you with all your gifts and in the prime of life, with his career still before him, ought not to harbour such gloomy thoughts. Make a home for yourself soon, find some well-to-do girl in Vienna (there must surely be some one of this kind whom you could love) and you will become more cheerful. Although you may continue to have many cares of some sort,

[1] Op. 48, No. 7. *Herbstgefühl.*

you will also learn to know joys which you have not experienced hitherto, and will embrace life with fresh zest. For after all the idea of earthly bliss will then become concentrated only on your life at home. I do wish you would think about it, the time is ripe.

I have seen a good deal of Elise [Brahms] and I am glad to find her looking so well and so happy in her lonely life. She is extremely pleased that you are coming for Christmas. Do you seriously intend to do so ? You are probably having a fine time now with dear Joachim. Please greet him heartily for me. Your first concert certainly turned out splendidly. If only I could hear the Requiem on the 1st of December ! [1] All my thoughts will be with you on the occasion.

I leave here to-morrow, after having given some well-attended concerts. The public here are certainly remarkable. They have a great love of music and they come again and again. But they show it so little that sometimes one feels all cold inside, particularly over pieces with which they are unfamiliar. But you know this as well as I do. . . .

Joachim has perhaps told you that Marie and Elise have been to Paris. They were full of their stay there and lived and enjoyed themselves like gods. The news of Julie is very comforting. The cure is apparently doing her good and she is to remain in Divonne until Christmas. Everything is all right except that I am not feeling very well, but as long as I can be active I shall not complain, for that is the chief thing.

Do not repay silence with silence. You know when I am silent that it is not because I am lazy but because I have no time, and that it is either the result of too much rush or of over-fatigue when I feel least inclined to write to you. Farewell, and may everything go as you wish. Send as much money as you can to the new Government Stocks. Your faithful old friend, CLARA.

CLARA *to* BRAHMS.

FRANKFORT, *Dec.* 22.
. . . In the first place I hope and wish that you may at least be spending your Christmas with nice people. But you

---

[1] The production of the first three movements under Herbeck.

will have no lack of attentive friends about you. I hope you will also think of us. We have suffered a rather severe disappointment through Julie having to be away (the poor child suddenly fell very ill again and so cannot be here until a week after the holidays). So we three are together (Ferdinand also arrived yesterday) and it would be ungrateful if we did not try to enjoy what we are vouchsafed ; for at least we hope to see our beloved Julie again soon. It makes me so happy and grateful to think that I still have all my children.

I have fortunately heard another account of the Requiem [1] than the one you gave me, and I was particularly pleased with what Joachim and his wife wrote to me about it. Oh, if only I could hear it some time, what a treat I should have again ! . . . As regards the playing of your compositions in public, he feels the same about it as I often do. One cannot take it amiss when a composer plays his own things a good deal. But a third party has often to fight a hard fight with the opposition, and so one has to go more cautiously about selecting works. Moreover one often dreads sacrificing works which lie very near one's heart to a crude uncultivated and irreverent public. This may not perhaps always be right, but the feeling on which it is based is well founded, and we surely do not deserve to be treated with so much suspicion on account of it. You only offend your friends in this way and this you should not do, for in the end one simply holds one's tongue and says nothing—I don't do so because I always think that I can make you understand. I should like to see you more cheerful and contented, for I notice that you so frequently ascribe to others what you should partially at least lay at your own door. Don't take what I say amiss ! You know I mean well by you.

About myself I have hardly anything new to tell you. I have played a good deal and for the most part successfully, but physically (and morally too very often) I have felt the strain very severely indeed. Besides, the concerts excite me a good deal and take a lot out of me. Now I am resting for a fortnight here before going to England. On the 22nd of January I play for the first time in London. But I shall not

1 It had been hissed in Vienna.

go to the provinces much, only at the beginning (the first fortnight), to Edinburgh, Glasgow, Bath and Torquay.   After that I shall stop in London. . . .   Think kindly of Your old CLARA.

1868

CLARA *to* BRAHMS.

BRUSSELS, *Jan.* 14, 13, RUE DE LA CHARITÉ.

MY DEAR JOHANNES,

You would have had an answer to your last letter long ago if I had followed my inclinations. But we have been going through hard times and I have only just this moment got a little breathing space. Our Julie has been very ill in Divonne, so ill that she was not able to come for the holidays and in the end I sent Marie to her (a twenty-four hours' journey), so that she could see for herself how she was. The doctors still say that organically she is quite sound, and that only her nerves are below par. But isn't that bad enough ? No one knows how to get at them. She has been taking the cold-water cure and has been rather overdoing it ; in spite of my most earnest entreaties that she should not do so, she insisted on taking two plunge baths a day, and I feel certain that it is owing to this excess that she has become so weak that she has not been able to walk for a month now, and has to be carried from the bed to the sofa. The terrible part of it was that she always had an aching desire to be with us, and was in a constant state of excitement as long as I was in Frankfort because she thought she would be able to come to us. But they are quite mad on the water cure where she is, and the doctor says that she has reached the crisis, etc. For the last few days the news has been better and I am feeling a little bit more easy. I was very unhappy at not being able to go myself, but I could not put such a tax upon my strength in view of the exertions awaiting me ; for long journeys take it out of me very much. So although Ferdinand was with us we did not have a very jolly Christmas, for the thought of our poor suffering Julchen depressed us. It really is too sad that I can see so little of her, for we do love each other so much. Her devoted, enthusiastic nature is tremendously sympathetic to me and when I am with her I feel as if I were a girl again. But enough of this! My heart is full to overflowing.

But now to turn to you and your letter, dear Johannes. How could you ever think that I should misunderstand it? All you said about J. is exactly what I have always felt whenever I have been associated with him, and last winter in England in particular it often made me extremely sad. What I fear is, the more he lives in the world the more this sort of thing will take the upper hand. I utterly fail to understand it, for I find that it is precisely one's life in contact with so many different people that confirms one in one's own philosophy of life. The more one knows of the life of shams, the more it nauseates and repels one. This feeling increases with me daily, and my own struggle is to get myself to do enough of what Joachim does too much of. But I cannot agree with you that Joachim is only giving concerts with you because you happen to be there, for I know how often he has invited you to join with him and you have refused. I also know that there is no man with whom he is more pleased to play than you—I admit that this is no merit.

I should prefer to tell you about my own concerts by word of mouth. I often feel exactly what you say, but you know how much depends upon me and I should like to accomplish enough to make myself at least independent. On the other hand, as far as music is concerned, I feel as strong as ever— nay, I often think that with many of the things I play I show greater mastery, both in the spiritual and technical sense, than I have done for years, and that therefore I can still be of use in many ways. For instance, a few days ago I played Robert's Concerto which had been a failure here before, to an audience of 3,000 people with such success as I have seldom had. This was not only a joy to me but a fresh proof that there is life in the old horse still. As a matter of fact I can very well claim that in the last few years public appreciation for my playing has greatly increased. I press Robert's works on nobody, but to be able to do as much for their popularity as everybody insists upon my doing now is of course a great joy to me. Let me hear from you soon. Your old CLARA.

BRAHMS *to* CLARA.

HAMBURG, *Feb.* 2.

Your Brussels letter was just going to Vienna when I was coming here, so I have had to do without it for some time. If only you could be a listener on Good Friday [1] I should be more happy than I can say. It would be as good as half the performance for me. If it goes at all as I wish it to, you would certainly have good reason to marvel and rejoice. But unfortunately I am not the man who succeeds in getting more than people deign to give me of their own accord, and that is always very little. So I am resigning myself to the thought that this time, as in Vienna, it will go fast, too fast and too sketchily. But do come ! ! I never thought that you had spent your Christmas without Julie. How sad for you that the poor girl (of whom one cannot think without a certain emotion) was so far away and ill into the bargain.

For when one sees Julie one thinks of all illness as being far away, although she is so delicate. But I still hope that at a certain period of her life she will improve. It is true that she is now grown up, but if I were in your place I should still have this comforting hope. Only I can't very well talk to you about it. I am now feeling sorely tempted to find an unfurnished apartment for myself in Vienna, and that means making up my mind for once. How much it would help me to know whether you may not be thinking of moving there sooner or later. I think there is a lot to be said for it, and that next year the time will be ripe for you to go. In spite of what you told me [2] I should like to implore you to bear in mind that your unsettled way of living must come to an end in time. There is only one thing you have to consider, and it applies to everybody, to me as well, and that is, whether it is necessary for you to earn money in this way. No other consideration should have any weight either with you or with other people. [3] Neither is what you think about your strength anything to do with it, etc. Just ask yourself how much of this may be self-deception and habit. I don't ask you this because I do not hear you in public, and in any case would not venture to

[1] For the first production of the *Requiem* in Bremen.
[2] See footnote on p. 72 *ante.*
[3] Compare Brahms' letter to Clara of February 7, 1861.

express an opinion for many reasons. I certainly am and shall remain the only one who will speak to you about this matter. But I should like to implore you always to bear in mind the inevitable and to consider only the above reason in coming to a decision. Take an example from those in a similar situation, and don't believe in exceptions. But I hope we shall soon be able to have a talk together again, and I am sure you are convinced that it would be impossible for me to harbour the smallest unsympathetic or unfriendly thought about you.

Frau Rösing of Hamm is now moving (May) to Hanover. Please tell me what to do with Robert's grand piano which the good lady has kept for us so long. I cannot, of course, have it here because space is money. But you have no room in Baden either for this precious but bulky memento, and as Heins was telling me, it would be impossible to hope to sell it here, nor would we want to. Write to me soon about it. If I lived here I would not dream of giving it away, but as it is I must come to a decision. What say you ?

Oh, and another thing,—in case it may be worth your while, I should like to tell you that I have quite grown out of my fur coat which is still perfectly good, and for a long time I really have not been able to use it. Could not Ferdinand or Felix make use of it ? And where do they live in Berlin any way, for I think of going there some time ? . . .

And now for a matter which as a good son and brother I ought to have started with. I found everybody here well and happy. I am living with my father and up to the present have quite enjoyed sauntering about. But my sister threatens to give me further serious trouble, for she has got a most unsuitable marriage in mind. I only hope this bitter cup will pass from me. Surely it is enough that I should have refrained from putting this sweet draught to my own lips on her account ! Let me hear from you soon and hold out some hope that you will be a listener on the 10th of April. I am not only anxious that you should listen but also that you should see. Your loving JOHANNES.

CLARA *to* BRAHMS.

LONDON, *March* 19, 186, PICCADILLY.

DEAR JOHANNES,

It has taken me a long time to find a moment to answer your letter and how many sorrows and joys have I not had in the meantime. It has been a time of sore distress,[1] about which you will probably have heard something in Berlin. I really cannot begin to talk about it for it is endless. As regards Felix, I have good hopes that this summer with us he will get quite well. But what is to happen to Ludwig I am utterly at a loss to know. At present he has actually got another situation in Leipsic, but how long will it last ? What a difference there is between them. The one causes me anxiety through his idleness and refusal to work, the other because he works too much. What a good thing it was that I insisted on sending Felix to a first-class doctor, because I was worried about his looks in the autumn, and the doctor at once took a serious view of the matter. Julie has been in Frankfort for three weeks and seems to be much better than she was last summer. And so it goes on, up and down, and my poor mother's heart never gets a moment's peace. It was doubly hard that all these troubles should come upon me precisely here. But the struggle certainly increases one's powers of tension, as I have once more discovered here. . . . I am so weighed down with care again and shall have so many extra expenses this summer that I hardly dare think of any pleasure or joy that may be awaiting me. . . .

You really seem to be living under the illusion that I have enough and that I am touring for my own pleasure. But surely one would not make all these exertions merely for pleasure ! But apart from this the present moment when my powers and success are at their zenith is hardly the time to retire from public life as you advise me to do. The whole of the past year I have been received so enthusiastically everywhere, all my concerts have been so packed (and people hardly

---

[1] The troubles had been about Ludwig and Felix. Felix had begun to show the first symptoms of lung trouble, and Ludwig had again lost his situation in Berlin owing to unpunctuality. Raimund Härtel obtained another post for him in Leipsic at the firm of Rieter Biedermann.

pay to go to concerts out of pity), and with but few exceptions I have played so well, that I can hardly understand why
I should stop precisely now. I cannot conceive what could
have led you to think that I am no longer what I was, it surely
could not have been unfavourable criticisms. Artists by pro-
fession can be my only guides in this matter, and it is precisely
from them that I have had the joy now more than ever before
of being assured that they have never heard me play better
or show more spiritual and technical mastery over the works
I produce than I am now doing. And they were people who
had absolutely no ulterior motive for speaking as they did,
and who I knew spoke from their hearts. When you say that
I ought not to think of wishing to be an exception by suppos-
ing that I can remain for ever young, this reproach is so unjustified that I hardly feel inclined to defend myself against
it. Surely you know only too well that I should never dream
of such a thing, for how often have I not expressed my views
about the matter to you ? But I will think the matter over,
for I cannot weigh it properly until I know what reasons you
could have had to say all these things to me, and why you
should have done so at a time when they might possibly make
such an impression upon me as to paralyse all my powers, if
what you said were not disproved on all sides by the extraordinary appreciation I have met with, which has confirmed
my confidence in myself. It was inconsiderate of you, I shall
say no more. . . .

You can send the fur coat to me some time in Baden, or
if you want to be rid of it now send it to number 12 Lichtenthal
for me. I shall know what to do with it. I was surprised
about your sister. And yet, when one thinks it over and
remembers how lonely the poor girl is, one cannot blame her
very much for the idea, though the question certainly is what
sort of choice she has made. Our stay here is drawing to a
close. Joachim and I will play for the last time in public
on the 30th, and on the 3rd of April we are going together to
Brussels. . . .

Farewell for to-day ! May things go well with you. Greet
Stockhausen for me and with love to yourself, Your
CLARA.

CLARA *to* BRAHMS.

CARLSBAD, *May* 5, *At* KÖNIGSTEIN.

Your birthday is drawing near and as I have never missed one yet I don't want to do so this time, as my wishes for your welfare remain ever the same. The close of the past year brought you great satisfaction in the general appreciation of your Requiem [1] and the joy it gave to all your friends. May many such days fall to your lot. I hope that the second performance of it went off as you wished. You will probably have missed the organ sadly at times, but in other respects I am sure it was all very successful. I now imagine you preparing the work for press. . . . I have found a good place for Robert's grand piano, but only in the autumn, for Elise has begged me to let her have it as she has a fine large room. So I shall let Heins know later on when he can send it (he has probably still got the crate ?), if you will kindly tell him about it some time. . . . And now farewell, and go on creating for the joy of lovers of music. Your CLARA.

CLARA *to* BRAHMS.

BADEN BADEN, *June* 24.

My thanks for your *Traurigkeit* [2] are late in coming. But after your beautiful and refreshing piece arrived all sorts of difficulties arose as well as work, and I had very little energy and strength. Meanwhile, however, you will long ago have heard so many comforting things about your *Traurigkeit* in Cologne [3] that mine will seem to you unnecessary. Nevertheless I feel I must tell you how wonderful I think the piece is, not only in its feeling but also in its artistic development. I am so glad that it is not left out of the Requiem or out of my copy either. Once more my heartiest thanks for it. Your two letters were sent on to me and dear Joachim had carried the last about with him in his pocket for ten days. We spent some delightful days together in Coblenz. I had not had Joachim to myself in peace for a long time, and after all the

---

[1] On April 28 in a concert hall.

[2] *Ihr habt nun Traurigkeit*, the fifth movement of the *Requiem*, composed after the rest of the piece in May.

[3] At the music festival on the 1st and 2nd of June.

sad things that I have been through [1] I found being with him a regular tonic. . . .

My present plans are very simple, I really have only one, and that is to go to St. Moritz in the Engadine in a few days' time, chiefly in order to strengthen my nerves with an open-air cure. I hope it will do me good and will inspire me with fresh courage, for after all my endless anxiety about Ludwig I am badly in need of it. But I must get it back, if only for the sake of the others who are such a joy to me (Julie is now very much better, but alas! we shall have to be without her all the summer). I don't know how long I shall remain in Switzerland. Felix will stop with Marie here, as the journey is too expensive for us all. And now I want to ask you a few questions about business. Your interest now amounts to about 150 thalers [£22.10.0]. Eighteen months ago I bought you a few Rhineland Railway Shares which paid a good dividend, the last being about 8%. Now I think it most advisable to buy some fresh shares with this interest, and I will gladly see to it if you wish me to do so. Why do you want to spend the interest? You surely have enough! Another thing I wanted to ask you—I hope you have invested the money you made last year. Couldn't the person who has charge of your latest investments also take charge of the securities I hold for you (including the 100 thalers' worth which I bought some time ago)? For these papers are a real problem as I am out of my house the whole winter. I always take some of them with me and leave the others with Frl. Leser, for it would be too risky to leave them here. But the present arrangement is also risky. I could not very well leave the first securities with Mendelssohns, for it would give them all kinds of trouble and this I should be sorry to do, because they are only looking after my papers as a favour to myself. So it means that I have everything now in my own keeping. If you have nobody whom you can trust I will go on keeping

[1] News had reached her on the 30th of May that Ludwig had not been able to keep his post in Leipsic, and for the first time Raimund Härtel told her frankly that Ludwig's mind was obviously unhinged. Although this was abundantly confirmed during the next few weeks, she was unable to bring herself to believe it. Meanwhile Ludwig was sent to his grandfather Wieck in Dresden.

your papers. But if you have some one who is looking after your latest investments, who is always on the spot, and who can watch the market to see how they stand, I should be very much relieved. What an easy matter it would be, for instance, for me to overlook an announcement that certain securities are to be redeemed—what a fright I should have ! It happened to me a little while ago with my own securities and I lost a lot of money on account of it. It was for this reason that I asked Mendelssohns to look after them for me. Write to me about it and let me know whether you want the interest, or whether I am to buy some American Government Stock of 1881 (issued in 1864 and guaranteed by the Government) which pay good interest of about 6% to 8%. I should like to know this before I leave. I shall remain here until Sunday of this week. I could then see to the matter before I left or send you the money. But this would be rather silly. Just think of it, you are already getting 120 thalers a year in interest [£18]. Now this is not at all bad, and it can go on increasing without giving you any trouble and may be very welcome to you some time. I hope you are happy in Bonn. Farewell, and may you be as happy as possible—this is the constant wish of Your CLARA.

CLARA *to* BRAHMS.

BADEN, *June* 30.

In great haste, for I am off to-morrow, I am sending you your papers. They consist of 1,000 thalers' worth of Prussian Government Stock with coupons, 750 thalers' worth of Rhine-land Railway Stock with coupons, 400 thalers in two Rhineland Shares, 100 thalers' worth ditto ditto with coupons, 100 dollars' worth of American Stock.

Interest held by me . . .	157 Th. 15 Sgr.
Paid for securities just purchased .	114 Th. 23 Sgr.
	42 Th. 21 Sgr.

I am sending you the balance herewith, except the 21 Sgr. which I will give you some time, as it would make things complicated here. I also enclose the receipt for the American Stock purchased. Please let me have word the moment you receive everything, and write here (as I have already given you various receipts for the papers I am sending you) and please sign the following receipt with your name (kindly add date). . . .

I also wanted to tell you that I would certainly not send you the papers if I were convinced that you were not merely fooling when you said that you would only shove the securities away among bundles of music. I feel sure that you will look after them properly and not regard them as trifles. Divide them up by all means, so long as you keep them by you. For instance, place the coupons in a different place from the securities and make a note of your securities in your note-book so that you can have the numbers in case you were to lose any of them. It is a good thing to be prudent. And now with most affectionate greetings, Your CLARA.

BRAHMS *to* CLARA.

BONN, *July* 2.

I will just write a line so that you may know I have received the papers. I have not only got to thank you for having looked after them so carefully, but it seems to me that you have also attended to their increase with loving care. I thank you most heartily. It is even a little bit painful to me now to think that you have looked after them so long, for I know how very much more anxious and cautious you are than I am. Although I cannot hope that you will believe me, I still main-tain that I do not boast and also never lie to you. Towards others I may certainly get so far as not to be able to swear that I am telling the truth, although I believe that I really intend to do so more than they do.

It may interest you to know, therefore, that in Vienna I always kept my money in my music cabinet. I let a friend keep some Austrian securities of mine, and the remainder, quite a large amount, lie in Hamburg mixed up with a lot of music. My father knows the packet in any case. I cer-tainly wish I could be more careful and will make up my mind to be so at once. But meanwhile I don't wish to be suspected of having told lies, and it is precisely on that account that I am able to appreciate the sacrifice you have made in looking after these things for me and realize how grateful I should be to you. . . . You know that the Jubilee of the

University is to be celebrated here very soon and Hiller is to be made a Doctor ? That is the kind of honour I should like, better than titles and orders. At the beginning of the winter I am to produce my *Requiem* in Hamburg and also in Bâle. I hope that repeated performances will double my fees (110 Naps.[1]), otherwise I shall not be over-keen to play my funeral music too often to myself. Adieu for to-day. May you prosper, and I hope the beautiful mountain air is doing you good. Affectionately yours, JOHANNES.

CLARA *to* BRAHMS.

BADEN BADEN, *Aug.* 17.

So here I am again at last in my dear little house and am sending you a greeting. I was not able to find time to write to you at St. Moritz, dear Johannes. The days slipped by so quickly,—in the morning, bathing and a walk, and in the afternoon, until dinner-time, out in the open air. So I really only had a little time for writing in the morning, and then I was pleased if I could manage to get through what was absolutely necessary. But the stay has done me a lot of good, particularly the magnificent air. There was not a trace there of the heat we feel here, but we certainly had a snow-storm once and a week of rather severe cold. . . .

Things are getting lively here now, but I keep as much as possible to myself. Levi often comes over to see us and that is always a great pleasure. Schmitt, the Orchestra Conductor of Schwerin, was also here for a couple of days, and now we have Auer, Cyprian Potter from London, and many others. Next week we are to hear Madame Viardot's new operetta *Der Menschenfresser*, which I am looking forward to very much. She is having a stage built in the concert hall. My chief concern now is to get to work, and how pleasant it is after nearly four months of idleness. I think loafing is hateful. Unfortunately I have only a little time left, for October will soon be here and then one has to get ready for touring again. This time I really intend to get to Vienna and hope that nothing will prevent me. . . .

On the whole I have only good news about ourselves. Felix is very well, Julie's condition varies, and as for Ludwig he

[1] £88.

is working fairly well, which is as much as one can expect. The result of a number of medical examinations have certainly proved that his nervous system is badly affected, and the trouble with his eyes is believed to have exerted a great influence upon his thinking capacity. So he has to be treated with the greatest care. This is a terrible grief for me and I pity the poor boy and will do all I can for him. But I shall also try to overcome my grief. I must not become absorbed in him, for the other children also have claims upon me and give me a lot of joy. And now with my heartiest greetings, dear Johannes, and hoping soon to hear from you, Your CLARA.

CLARA *to* BRAHMS.

BADEN BADEN, *Sept.* 4.

Your last letter compels me to refer to-day to certain matters which I would much rather leave alone,[1] but you force me to do so because you seem inclined to ascribe my attitude towards you to a circumstance which has nothing whatever to do with it. How can you speak of hatred when after that most offensive letter of yours (over.which no man of sensibility would be able to laugh if he read it) I gave you fresh proof of my deep interest in your work by not hesitating to take that journey after I had only just returned from another

---

[1] The disagreement between the two as evidenced by this and the following letter was not of recent standing. From Clara's Diary, which unfortunately at this period has several gaps, it is clear that she had had to suffer more than usual from her friend's rough and blunt ways, and more especially on his visits to Baden Baden, had his lack of consideration for her children been regarded by her as an affront to herself. It was for this reason that during the previous year, for instance (1867), when Brahms was in Baden, she had not invited him, as had been her custom, to take all his meals with them, because in the long run she could not endure the uncomfortable atmosphere which he always created, and from which, above all, she wished to protect her children. Brahms' unfortunate letter of the 2nd of February, 1868, in which he had not the remotest intention of wounding her feelings, and which was dictated only by his solicitude for her, had, clumsily worded as it was, and sent off at a most unpropitious moment, only served to widen the rift between them. But in spite of this she had gone to Bremen. Their meeting there, however, had left a thorn in her soul owing to Brahms' behaviour the day after the performance.

very fatiguing one. So it is all nonsense to speak like that. But in any case I can assure you that, thank God, no such ignominious feeling as hatred has ever found a place in our hearts. The fact that for the last two years—that is to say, long before the letter in question—I have held aloof was owing to your last visit here. You appeared to be so uncomfortable with us and were so disagreeable, not now and then, which among friends would have been passed over, but continuously day after day, for weeks at a time ; and gave so little thought to cheering me or to making your visit as a friend at all pleasant, that it really was a most uncomfortable not to say miserable time for all of us. Such a relationship was too abnormal for me to wish to repeat it—it would have been beneath my dignity. I have told you frankly what I think. I do not understand the art of expressing myself in diplomatic phraseology and besides I would regard it as unedifying and not at all friendly. . . .

But now for other things. I was very much shocked to hear of Hiller's illness which appears to me to be something like a stroke. I hope he will feel no ill effects. I know nothing about Stockhausen and have no intention of giving a concert with him in Vienna. It would be quite unpractical for the two of us in that small hall and would do neither of us any good. Unfortunately one has to think of these things. I have heard the name of Rieter's charming daughter coupled with yours. They say she has grown up wonderfully pretty and is rich into the bargain, which, for a composer, is very necessary. Haven't you ever thought of her ? If there is any possibility of this union, which is so suitable from every point of view (and I gather she is very partial to you), I hope for your sake that it may come off, for it is high time in my opinion. For many reasons you ought not to remain alone, that is what I feel. . . .

The other day I heard a violoncello concerto by Eckert,[1] a good deal of which appealed to me very much. He might certainly make a fine piece out of it if he would polish it up, but he is surrounded by so many flatterers that I think it will

[1] Carl Anton Florian Eckert (born 1820), more famous as a conductor than as a composer. In 1868 he succeeded Dorn as head musical director in Berlin. He died in 1879.—TR.

remain as it is.   And now farewell, and let me hear from you soon, Your CLARA.

BRAHMS *to* CLARA.

Sept.

I cannot get the matter out of my head, dear Clara.   I should like to answer your letter, which certainly contained many hard things, without any anger, and quietly survey such ruins of the temple of my friendship as still remain standing without disturbing them.   But I cannot.   My ill-fated letter keeps running in my mind.   Let me say quite briefly that I have thoroughly understood what you write about your interest in my art.   But it seems impossible that you should not have felt how willingly one would do without this kind of interest.   I speak through my music.   The only thing is that a poor musician like myself would like to believe that he was better than his music.

You refer to my moods in Baden.   Here again there is no matter for dispute, each of us has an opinion and insists on being right.   I too had reason to complain that I had not been as successful as usual in my endeavour to win sympathy in your house.   It always seemed to me as if I had first to overcome some obstacle.   But I cannot get my letter out of my mind.   I see it as a great wall standing between us. Again and again I should like to run my head against it, although I know that it would be no good.   I cannot hope to convince you.   But just read what I am writing now and later on perhaps, much later on, you will think more kindly and leniently about me.   In any case the thought will occur to you—he is the only one with whom I have had to be angry in regard to such a matter.   There is certainly one thing that should have prevented me from writing this letter, as it should every letter—I have no patience for writing.   You were always aware of this failing in me, and surely I have the right to expect the same or even more indulgence from you now than before. But what else have I done ?   I never gave expression to any doubts about your art or repeated anything others had said. All I did was to utter a few words of truth by way of warning and to beg you to think over them and to turn them to account.

For the matter—no, but, for the manner, a good friend can surely expect to be treated with indulgence and be forgiven. I acknowledge that I may have spoken those words of truth perhaps at the wrong time, and perhaps in the wrong way. What I chiefly wished to imply was—if your circumstances force you to do what you are doing then my letter was to be regarded as not having been written, and I had no right to question anything. In every respect I may have made the biggest blunders—in my whole grasp of the question. But I have often heard you discuss such matters and in doing so mention such names as Garcia, Rettig, and in another connection Fichtner, etc. I may be mistaken as far as you are concerned, but I expressed no personal opinion nor did I listen to anybody else's views. I simply called your attention to yourself, not so much to your own feelings and habits as to your general experience of others. Time may show that I have been mistaken. I ought to have written in the autumn instead of in the spring. But even now I should have some difficulty in finding an opportune moment for such an admonition. I might have written in 1878 instead of in 1868. But in any case my reminder ought to have come before the need for it arose, and the mistake about the year and the day does not seem to me now to be very serious. In regard to myself my judgment may err. I thought that one readily allowed a good friend to say things for which an outsider would be turned away.

So please forgive this friend for his overdose of truth. All he did was to inform you of a perfectly familiar universal fact, to use it as you liked. He said nothing harsh to you and, moreover, neither obtained secretly nor did he repeat to you any gossip from others. But so much of the good friend remains over that you can surely forgive him what needs to be forgiven. The crux of the whole matter is his old besetting sin—that he cannot write letters and cannot write diplomatically either, as you so tauntingly remark.

Incidentally I do not expect any answer to this. As I have said, I tried in vain to write differently, but the whole of this letter cried out to be written and it ends as disconsolately as it began. Always and in all circumstances, Your entirely devoted J. B.

BRAHMS *to* CLARA.

Sept. 12.

Thus blew the shepherd's horn to-day :

Hoch auf'm Berg, tief im Tal, grüß' ich dich viel tau=send=mal! [1]

CLARA *to* BRAHMS.

BADEN BADEN, *Oct.* 15.

. . . I should like to have answered your previous letter at once, but I should have had to do so with businesslike brevity, and that I did not want to do. You said you did not wish for an answer at all, and yet you have made a mistake which I am all the more anxious to clear up as it is important for our friendship. That letter of yours is not the wall that stands between us, as witness the fact that even last summer (that is to say, long before it was written) I did not invite you to pay me a visit here, which I should have been so glad to do in other circumstances. It is not a matter of destroying any wall between us, but only of showing a little more friendliness and a little more control of evil moods, particularly when the latter last such a long time (to this I would also add something that grieved me very often,—your lack of trust in us). This would be enough to make our relationship a much more beautiful one. What a terrible suspicion is implied when you refer to my children's aversion. Let me remind you of the correspondence in which Marie apologized through me for a remark she had quite thoughtlessly made (an apology she would have tendered on the spot if you had not rebuffed her in the most dreadful way). And what was your answer on that occasion ? So where is this aversion you speak of ? When one is conscious of such a feeling one does not ask forgiveness for a trifling offence. But I confess that my children

[1] " High up in the mountain, deep down in the wold, I greet you, I greet you, a thousandfold ! "

were often angry when they saw how I suffered from your unfriendliness on many occasions, and when they found so many an hour pass sadly by, which you might have made happier for us—hours of which I have all too few in the bosom of my family. Think over all this and ask yourself whether it is conceivable that a friendship can continue with the mother when it does not extend to the children. How can there be any question of such a thing (as I understand it and wish it to be) when for whole periods at a time you ignore my children ? It really depends entirely on you, dear Johannes, whether things will improve between us, or whether a wall should be allowed to grow up, which would be a source of the deepest sorrow to me. As for that letter, I had long ago put it on the shelf. It is you who refer to it again. But I am glad all the same that you have made your meaning clear. So it was only a question of the manner and the time ! But the time remains unalterable and for years I have thought about it more often than was good for me. So let us regard this as settled once and for all.

But I cannot help thinking that your view of my concert tours is an odd one. You regard them merely as a means of earning money. I don't ! I feel I have a mission to reproduce beautiful works, and particularly those of Robert so long as I have the strength to do so, and even if I were not absolutely compelled to do so I should go on touring, though not in such a strenuous way as I often have to now. The practice of my art is an important part of my ego, it is the very breath of my nostrils. But on the other hand I prefer to starve rather than appear before the public with waning strength.

But now, before I turn to other things, I want to thank you heartily for the exquisite present with its bright and cheerful Alpine greeting. I have taken the little casket into use at once. So you are now back in Hamburg ? I might almost have seen you there, but I had to refuse the Philharmonic Society, because I should have had a rush to get there, and I must avoid such strains so that I may be fresh for Vienna. My concert there is on the 21st of November. Will you be there by then ? I heard that you wanted to produce your Requiem in Bâle. How does this fit in with Vienna ?

. . . Felix went back to Berlin a week ago.   He has made
a splendid recovery and given us a great deal of pleasure with
his charming ways.   He seems to be showing a singular combination of energy and good nature.   In many ways he reminds
me every day of Robert, and I always felt happy when I looked
into his soul.   For the last month we have had nothing but good
news from Julie, but it is not certain yet when she will come
back to Germany.   She is at present in Venice with Frau
Schlumberger.   Otherwise everything is all right.

And now something else occurs to me.   Do you intend to
publish your Rinaldo now ?   Forgive me for appearing to
question the advisability of this so soon after the publication
of the Requiem.   Is it important enough to follow the Requiem ?
But now I must go to my boxes which gape entreatingly at me.
Farewell, dear Johannes, and let me hear from you soon, Your
CLARA.

BRAHMS *to* CLARA.

HAMBURG, *October.*

I should have required a thoroughly quiet hour, dearest
Clara, to be able to thank you heartily enough for your letter.
And as I cannot find it I will at least reply to you in my usual
rapid and brief epistolary tempo.   With all due penitence
and regret I must confess that there is a tremendous deal
of truth in your letter,—if it is not all true.   And with much
joy and deep emotion I see how kind it is, just as kind as
an angelic soul like yours could make it.   So let me thank
you a thousand times.   Am I to believe or merely to hope that
there will be no further cause for you to show me your kind
indulgence ?   Life is a mad jingle of sounds and very often a
good woman like you can bring about such a wonderfully soft
resolution of these discords. . . .

My Requiem will be produced here at Easter, but I don't
know when it will be done in Bâle or Vienna.   I should like
to get the Rinaldo produced in Vienna as well.   I really do
not altogether care when it is published.   At all events it
would not have been so practical to sell it before the Requiem,
for now it has brought me in 100 louis [? £80].   But in any
case it has been very carefully polished and looks much better
with its great finale.   Have you found the Variations for Two

Pianos,[1] and could we not play them together in Vienna ?
I must go there anyhow and would like to go in November.
After that a symphony of Dietrich's will be played to you in
Oldenburg, and on that occasion you will require rather more
tact than sincerity. . . . Kirchner's wedding took place on
15th of October, as his fiancée informed me it would some days
before the event. At the present moment I am plagued with
proofs and revises and in addition I am practising the piano,
so *addio* for to-day and hoping most heartily to see you in
Bremen, I am and remain for ever wholly yours, JOHANNES.

CLARA *to* BRAHMS.
                                    DÜSSELDORF, *Oct.* 24.
    I was just going to write to thank you for your dear letter
which pleased me so much, when your kind surprise arrived,
so I now also have to thank you for your musical greeting,
which I do with a hearty shake of the hand. If only I had
the proper bass for the pieces ! I have given them to Marie
to look through and I hope she will soon manage to play them
with me. That is a fine idea of yours to come to Oldenburg,[2]
but if you could only spare the time that you expected to
devote to Bremen it would be all too short. I shall be there
only for a day ; my rehearsal is in the morning, in the afternoon
I must rest before the concert, the concert is in the evening,
and I must go on further the following morning. So the
journey would have to be a night one and would hardly be
worth your while. If you can't make yourself free for a longer
period when in Oldenburg, it would be better if we were to see
each other only in Vienna where we should have more leisure.
What do you think ?
    I am glad that you are going to Vienna in November. I
have got the Double Variations with me and should be only
too happy to play them with you. . . . I shall probably hear
from you what is happening, so with reiterated thanks and
heartiest greetings, Your faithful old CLARA.

---

[1] By Schumann, Op. 46. *Andante and Variations for two pianos,
two violoncellos and horn*, which she played with Brahms in Vienna on
November 28.
[2] From the 30th of October to the 4th of November Clara gave
concerts with Brahms in Oldenburg and Bremen.

1869

FRANKFORT,[1] *April* 28.

DEAR JOHANNES,

What a long silence this has been. . . . But do not be angry with me, and do not think that it has been due to carelessness. I should like to have had direct news of you again, but had to content myself with the newspapers. I gather that you have spent the winter very pleasantly and also profitably. You have had some beautiful concerts in Vienna. . . . As you see, I am once more back in my beloved Germany, although I must say I left London with a heavy heart, because I have made many dear friends there. . . . And the public too are almost like friends to me now. I never appear without feeling that I have the warmest sympathies of my audience, and for an artist this is, after all, extraordinarily gratifying. It was not at all easy to call a halt. But I abide by my conviction that the sort of life an artist leads in London can only last a short time without leading to both spiritual and material damage, and that is why I always set myself a limit.

But I do not do so without making a certain sacrifice. For instance, this time I had to refuse all lessons although I might have got one and a half guineas an hour for them, because I felt that they consumed too much of the mental and physical energy which I required for my concerts. Thus I only gave lessons during the two Easter weeks when I was not playing in public. But at least I had the satisfaction of always feeling inspired at my concerts, and that sort of spirit gets transmitted to one's audience. You can well imagine how much I am looking forward to my little home. Marie and Eugenie have gone on ahead to get everything in order, and I shall follow

---

[1] In November and December, 1868, Clara had given concerts with Brahms in Vienna, and from January until April had played first in Holland and then in England.

with Julie in the course of the next few days. So at last we
shall again spend the whole of May there, when Baden is so
particularly delightful.

. . . The other day I was in Cologne where Hiller and
Joachim gave a *soirée populaire*, which unfortunately, owing to
the fact that Hiller's resignation had annoyed all his acquaintances very much, was practically empty—at least empty for
the *Gürzenich*. I am curious to see how the affair will end
and whether they will succeed in getting Hiller to stay. He
has only two supporters, Wendelstadt and the Mayor. I very
much fear that Hiller is deceiving himself and was misled
by the reception he got in Vienna. . . . That is really the
worst of Vienna. Out of pure friendliness the public immediately acclaim every composer without waiting to find out
what his compositions are like.

So far the news about ourselves is good. I frequently
feel rather out of sorts, but how few people are not as they
grow older ? I found Julie looking much better and her old
troubles seem to have disappeared. She is able to work and
run about, etc., etc. Ludwig is studying slowly and doing
as much as his health allows, and seems quite contented now.
I shall at all events let him come to Baden Baden this summer
for a while. I am very pleased with Ferdinand and Felix,
the latter has now been moved into the Upper Fifth, which
is very high for his age. Eugenie has now left school and
seems to me to have grown into a very nice girl. Now you
know all about us. Let us soon hear all about you. Do not
repay like with like. Let the interval be a short one. And
so farewell, with affectionate greetings, Your CLARA.

CLARA *to* BRAHMS.

DÜSSELDORF, *Oct.* 23.

DEAR JOHANNES,

I am trying, though my hand is still bad,[1] to send you
my thanks and a greeting to Vienna. I was glad to know that
you had left Baden, for I often thought how you must have
been shivering in the morning and evening there, and how bad
it is to sit in a cold room doing brain work, for the blood

[1] Shortly before leaving Baden Baden, Clara had had an accident
in which she had injured her right hand.

surges to the brain all the same. So I hope that you will soon feel at home again in Vienna. You can surely bear life better there. I have had to postpone my visit on account of the trouble with my hand, and yesterday I had unfortunately to cancel my Leipsic engagement, which means that I have already lost 500 thalers [£75]. What trouble my carelessness got me into! The doctor declares that the hand will be all right in a few days. But then I shall have to practise again for at least a week, for my fingers have got so stiff. For the moment it is a matter of being resigned and reason helps me with this. I received your Waltzes [1] and still regard them with the same genuine delight. They are so beautifully got up. . . .

Bruch's piece was a complete failure in Cologne the other day, and I think unjustly. A good deal of it sounded very beautiful. I was afraid that after this débacle Stockhausen might be a little bit hoarse, but he sang the songs (Schubert's *Nachtgesang*) with such power and feeling that I thought I had never heard him sing so well before. One was carried into the seventh heaven. . . . With most affectionate greetings, dear Johannes, and hoping you will not forget me, Your CLARA.

[1] Op. 52, *Love Songs, Waltzes for Solo-quartet with Piano Accompaniment for Four Hands*. On the 6th of October at Carlsruhe Clara had played them with Levi at a concert at which Brahms was present.

1870

DÜSSELDORF, *Feb.* 5.

DEAREST JOHANNES,

Thank you for your kind greeting which I have found here on my return from Cologne. I had secretly been hoping for it all the time. . . . You have probably heard from Betty [1] about our cold return journey. [2] We were hardly out of Vienna when it turned bitterly cold. We spent a ghastly night with the windows all frozen up, and were so miserable that the words withered on our lips. We found it very hard to leave Vienna. . . . As you may imagine my meeting with Ludwig [3] again was in every respect a very depressing experience for me. When I first saw him looking pale and neglected I really felt quite sick with pain, but I managed at last to overcome my feelings so as not to destroy his pleasure at seeing me again. It is really dreadful to feel so utterly incapable of contributing one iota to the happiness of a child, or even to be able to shield him from sorrow. In view of his condition he works much too much, but the most loving admonitions of his hostess, who is extremely kind to him, are without avail. He has but one thought, and that is to earn money, and she told me that he often spent hours of the most dreadful suffering owing to his incompetence. She tries to comfort him as much as she can and I also tried in every conceivable way. My parents are allowing him to go and see them again, and my father is very kind to him, but has not the faintest idea of what is wrong with him. My mother and sisters are not really well disposed to him ; all they feel is that they are

---

[1] Betty Oser, Clara's pupil.

[2] Clara had left Vienna on January 21.

[3] What Clara heard from and about Ludwig on this occasion could only awaken the gravest misgivings, for he showed obvious signs of mental aberration. He had given out that he was a teacher and seriously contemplated giving concerts, etc.—TR.

in duty bound to put up with him. But I may be doing them, my mother at least, an injustice.

Here I got very good news of Julie,[1] who writes among other things about the children who are so fond of her that she often does not know how to get away from their caresses. How glad I am of this, both for the children's sake and Julie's. . . . I must tell you that the other day your Dances (I played five of them) made a furore, although I had some difficulty in carrying Agnes [2] along with me ; but I believe her lack of spirit doubled my own. I was tremendously full of go.

I have received Dietrich's Symphony from him, and a few other things—a Sonata for four hands, and a Sonata with violin. He would like to have the symphony produced in London and begs me to put in a word for him. It might possibly be given at the Crystal Palace. Gernsheim [3] played only one Quartet of his own composition. It pleased me quite well, better than earlier things I have heard of his. It is, of course, utterly lacking in originality. Indeed, where could this come from all of a sudden ? But it has a good deal of feeling, a certain amount of colour and here and there some charm. I met Max Bruch in Cologne and enjoyed his *Schön Ellen* although it was indifferently produced. But what pleased me most about him was the way he spoke about your Rhapsody.[4] What he said was so intelligent and so enthusiastic that it quite melted me. You will say, of course, that that is not very difficult in the case of a woman, but it only happens when a woman feels that a person is really sincere. . . . With the same affectionate greetings, Your ever faithful CLARA.

CLARA *to* BRAHMS.

LONDON, *March* 6, 14, HYDE PARK GATE, KENSINGTON.
DEAR JOHANNES,

. . . So you have found nice quarters ? I cannot tell you

[1] Julie had become engaged to a certain Count Victor Radicati di Marmorito, in June, 1869. They were married in Baden Baden on September 22, 1869.

[2] Agnes Schönerstedt.

[3] Friedrich Gernsheim, at that time a teacher at the Cologne Conservatoire.

[4] At the time of Julie Schumann's marriage Brahms had brought this piece to Clara as his *Brautgesang*, and it had moved her very deeply.

how glad I am to hear it. I did not like to tell you before, but I thought your old rooms very gloomy and never liked to think of you in them. If you could only find a nice young wife now with a little money you would really begin to find life quite agreeable. Of course I know your ideas about this matter, but I return to the subject again and again because I am so anxious that you should have a home. After all, we women are made like that. We keep on beginning all over again when we have our hearts in anything. I hope you will keep your present rooms and that next winter I shall find you in them. But before that we shall meet in Baden. . . . This year we are feeling the cold less than before, as the Burnands are making us as comfortable as possible. They will not let us go and we are only too glad to stop. In other respects, too, things are going extraordinarily well. I have been received more enthusiastically than ever, and in spite of all my nervousness I have played with great success. But I am dreadfully troubled by certain symptoms in my arms and fingers. Nearly every day I get a fresh fright which comes like a bolt from the blue, and I spare myself as much as possible between the concerts though it makes things very awkward to do so. Up to the present, though, I have been able to play whenever I wanted to, and I only had to cancel the first two concerts by telegram from Calais, for we had to wait there three days, as the sea was so rough that no ship could cross. Those were dreadful days ! Not a soul to speak to, not a book ! We had nothing with us—had to buy everything—no piano to be had and, above all, no money left. I have been punished enough for having said that the two hours at sea were no more than two on land. But such a thing occurs very seldom, though you may imagine that the crossing after that was not of the smoothest.

Stockhausen sang here once the other day and I am glad to say had a great success. But it was the only time he has sung in London. The day after he had to leave for Stuttgart *en route* for Russia. He will come back at Easter, but it was a pity that he could not go on singing. He had just made a five-weeks' tour in the provinces with two singers who were quite unworthy of him. He hoped to make himself known in London by this means, but nobody had heard of him here. It was the wrong way of setting to work. One does not make a favourable impression here by going about in such company and with such an impresario. But he always does things in the wrong way. He was hoping to become reconciled with Joachim but he did not succeed. Joachim merely replied—" You are a great singer."

I must tell you about a pleasure I have had. You know that Julie has been complaining bitterly about her bad upright piano in Turin and that I promised her and Marmorito that I would try to get a semi-grand piano for them at Broadwood's at trade price. When I spoke to Broadwood about it, however, he said at once that I must not talk about prices, and that he would be only too glad of the opportunity of showing me his gratitude and respect by making Julie a present of an instrument. Wasn't that splendid ! So then I asked a lady artist to paint me a piano being carried through the air by four Muses. This she did on a piece of notepaper and over it all she drew a charming little Cupid standing on tiptoe. Marie then wrote the sweetest little poem to it and I added the letter. She will receive this for her birthday, what a surprise it will be for her ! . . . Farewell, and think kindly of Your ever faithful CLARA.

. . . Write and tell me about the *Meistersinger* but not as if you were writing to an anti-Wagnerite.

BRAHMS *to* CLARA.

VIENNA, *March* 20.

I ought to have thanked you long ago for your kind letter. . . . We have everything wintery in its most luxuriant form here. I have never seen the snow so deep or the concerts so regular every day. . . . The *Meistersinger* had to be put on the programme five times and taken off again, and now the repetitions are causing just as much bother. This alone is enough to prevent the public from getting up any enthusiasm, for a certain amount of go is necessary for that. I think the public are much less sympathetic than I expected them to be. I am not enthusiastic either about this work, or about Wagner in general, but I listen as attentively as possible,—that is to say, as often as I can stand it. I confess that it provokes one to discussion. But I am delighted that it is not necessary

to say all that I feel about it plainly and aloud, etc., etc.   But
this I do know, that in everything else I attempt I step on
the heels of my predecessors who embarrass me.   But Wagner
would not hinder me at all from proceeding with the greatest
pleasure to the writing of an opera.   Incidentally, in the order
of precedence among my wishes, this opera would come before
the post of Musical Director.[1]

The other day I was in Klosterneuberg, which I shall often
visit again in spring.   It is one of the richest religious ecclesiastical foundations and I would very much like you to see
such an institution some time.   When they are at home the
ecclesiastical gentlemen have absolutely nothing to do.   I
think there are about sixty of them.   And yet if they like,
about twenty of them can take the richest livings in the
neighbourhood (Hietzing, for instance, is a living of about 5,000
to 6,000 florins), another twenty administer the huge estates
in Hungary, and the remainder stay at home engaged in the
occupation above mentioned.   A genuine monastery, such as
Einsiedeln in Switzerland, is certainly more interesting.   The
life of idleness and gluttony which they live here soon leads, as
the gentlemen themselves frankly and charmingly confess, to
their ceasing from thinking or doing anything.   Occasionally,
for a change, they go to Vienna, where they have a house,
and they are allowed to leave their ecclesiastical robes behind.
When they are tired they put them on again.

But for people like ourselves such a visit is a wonderful
change.   The institution is beautifully situated on the Danube
and the living-rooms, the wine one drinks, and the whole of
the hospitality is first class.   As soon as the spring is a little
further advanced I shall go there.   I know so little of Austria.
. . . Farewell for to-day.   I hope things will go well with you
and that the hand will be better soon.   Greet Marie and think
kindly of Your JOHANNES.

CLARA *to* BRAHMS.

BRUSSELS, *May* 5.

. . . We left London two days ago and found it hard to
part with our dear and excellent hosts [2] with whom we had

---

[1] At about this time he was eagerly striving to become Herbeck's
successor as Director of Concerts.   [2] The Burnands.

become so much at home that they thought we could not possibly leave them.   But my old German heart beats much too vigorously to allow me to remain long (longer than duty demands) in a foreign land.   Besides, Germany contains all that is dear to me.   But I must not be ungrateful to the English who once again have given me such a hearty welcome —I can really say the whole of the public.   Towards the end I gave a few nice concerts.   At two of them we (Frl. Zimmermann and I) played your Hungarian Dances, several of which were encored.   I then played them at a private matinée with Marie and at other places as occasion offered.   I think it very silly of publishers not to be more alive to their own advantage.   Before going to England I wrote to Simrock to say that I was going to play the Dances in London, and he ought surely to have sent over a number of copies at once.   But he could not have done so, as a lot of people wrote to me asking where they were to be had.   He ought to have had them advertised.

The story about Joachim was quite without foundation. I could not help laughing at the thought that you could have believed it for one moment.   From what I know of Joachim I do not think that he would take such a step even if he were unhappy, because of the children whom he loves so tenderly. People got the idea into their heads because, in the first place, she had been such a long time away from him and the children, and secondly because he had to be away too.   But they don't know anything more.   All the same I don't believe I am far wrong in thinking that Joachim is not happy, and I am frightfully sorry for him.   When one has been so happy oneself one is better able to judge of other people's happiness. . . .

Unfortunately I cannot tell you anything definite about my plans for they depend upon the weather.   I should rather like to go to Bad (Gastein) before my return to Baden, because when once I am back home I find it difficult to start off again. . . .   To-morrow I go to Düsseldorf and on the 9th Marie goes to Baden in order to have a few things done in the house ; and then, if I go to Gastein, we shall meet each other about the 15th or 16th.   But if I do not go there I shall join her at Baden about that time.   I cannot tell you how I long to be home.   And yet who knows what sorrows the summer holds in store for me ! Ludwig has been very ill, quite dangerously ill, for three or four weeks ; but he is better now. They kept it from me, which was a good thing, or I should not have known what to do. He was very well looked after by his hostess. How it came about (he brought it on himself) I will tell you by word of mouth. The strange thing is that he cannot be left alone at night, whereas during the day he goes for walks and eats with a good appetite. You can imagine how I feel. I have begged Hübner to consult one or two doctors and to act on my behalf, for this is a case only a man can deal with. In the end I shall have to send him to an asylum, because he cannot go on living alone in this way and he won't be amenable to anybody. It is really a hard fate to have two such experiences in one's lifetime, but I have made up my mind to bear it as calmly as a mother possibly can. I have such a strong conviction that I have to go on living for the others, and feel that the happiness that yet remains to me on earth does after all outweigh the pain. For I still have a number of good things left.

Eugenie is coming back to us next week. Everybody writes to me from Berlin that she has improved a great deal. Ferdinand is now a clerk and Felix is in the Sixth Form. Julie continues to write very happily about her life with her husband but also complains of homesickness a good deal. . . . And now at last I will do what I ought to have begun with and that is thank you for your dear letter, and add a request for more. . . . And now adieu, my dear Johannes, Affectionately yours, CLARA.

CLARA *to* BRAHMS.

BADEN, *June* 19.

Many thanks, dear Johannes, for your two letters. Just fancy, wasn't it funny, on the very morning after I had received your letter I wrote to Herbeck [1] refusing and told him quite openly that I could not celebrate any Beethoven Festival in association with Wagner who had assailed all that I hold

---

[1] Herbeck had written to Clara inviting her on behalf of the Beethoven Committee of Vienna to take part in the Beethoven Festival on October the 26th. But when she heard that Wagner and Liszt were conducting it, she refused.

highest and most sacred in Art and life, and who was pur-
suing a direction in Art which was quite unsympathetic
to me.

Owing to the fact that I had nobody to take it to the post,
the letter remained lying about until yours arrived. I then
wrote another letter in which I did not commit myself, but
only asked for details as to who was conducting, and what
sort of programme had been arranged, so that I might make
my decision. But you are quite wrong to suppose that Liszt
is the person to whom I object most, for personally he has
never done anything to me (neither to me nor to Robert),
whereas Wagner has not scrupled to speak in the most con-
temptuous manner about Robert, Mendelssohn and all of
you. And was I to sit down and play under his direction !
Even if in a weak moment, overcome by the wish to play
there, I had overlooked everything else and undertaken to
go, I am sure I should have cried off at the last moment, for
I should have been so much ashamed of myself. I am curious
to see what Herbeck will answer. If his reply is such as to
make it possible for me to accept, will you try to find out
what sort of fee they intend to pay ? They have asked me
how much I want, which puts me in a fix, as I don't want to
ask too much, nor would I like to ask less than they are giving
other artists. . . .

We have not had any news of Ludwig lately. You know
what little information such institutions give one. He himself does not answer any of our letters, but seems to go on
dreaming all the time. If only he is not suffering any
pain ! . . .

The family at present consists of Marie, Eugenie and myself,
and I am particularly pleased with Eugenie, who has developed
into a very nice girl. Next week Felix is coming ; I have
had a hard task to deal with his obstinacy.[1] It is so difficult
for a mother to be consistent towards her sons, particularly
when they are in many respects (this is quite between ourselves)
much cleverer than she is. Elise is coming for two or three

[1] Felix was causing her some anxiety at this time owing to his disagreement with his old and tried teacher, Dr. Planer. The latter
insisted on treating Felix as a boy still, and perhaps aggravated the
situation by pulling the reins a little bit too tight.—Tr.

days and then going on to Passerano and returning to us in
the autumn. And now farewell. Do not be silent too long.
Ever your most faithful CLARA.

CLARA *to* BRAHMS.

BADEN, *June* 28.

I should really like to begin by grumbling about this Viennese
business [1] for taking you away from me just at the wrong
time. But I am too fond of you not to put my own wishes
in the background. You see I have every desire to persuade
you to accept. You have been wanting a post like this for
such a long time and now one offers in which you will have
the finest material at your disposal in one of the biggest
cities in Germany (in a provincial town and harassed by
mediocre resources you would only have been annoyed and
you would not have stood it). With a good salary, without
too continuous a strain, and with your whole summer free
(which is not bad for Baden, for instance)—and you are thinking
of refusing ? Surely you have nothing to fear ? You have
shown often enough how brilliantly you can conduct and
no one can approach you in your capacity for grasping things
at a glance. In my opinion the only doubtful point is whether
you will be able to manage the schoolmaster side of the work,
the meticulous practising of pieces ; for this will be all the
harder for you seeing that for a true artist this sort of thing is
always very trying. Moreover, as a man, it is not your forte
to be able to communicate your ideas at a moment's notice,
or rather precisely when it is expected of you. But should
not a resolute will overcome such obstacles ? If only you
were to accept with the certainty of mastering the situation
it would really be fine. But let me remind you of one thing
which you may possibly have overlooked—do not let yourself
be overburdened with the business, secretarial and organizing
side of it, etc. To yield an inch here would mean that in the
end you would have the whole thing on your shoulders and
that you would be spending all your time in the dullest of
occupations. I can see this sort of thing going on now with
Joachim, who is at his wits' end to know how to rid himself

[1] Brahms had been offered Herbeck's post as Conductor of the
Gesellschaftsconcerte.

of all sorts of duties of a most prosaic nature. What are the
Committees there for ?   They should see to all that, and you
should undertake only the artistic part.   In the winter this
will give you quite enough to do, for there is a lot of work
connected with it which one can hardly foresee.   I am very
anxious to know what is going to happen—it would be magnificent if I could play at the Beethoven Festival under
your baton ! ! !   I can think of nothing I should like more.
Please do not leave me in suspense a moment longer than
necessary, you can imagine how concerned I am about it.

There is very little to tell you about ourselves.   You know
what trouble we are in.   This is only increased by the very
sad news which we have just had from Ferdinand who has
been to see Ludwig.   I won't attempt to describe his condition
to you, but it is so terrible that one can only pray heaven
to release the poor man from his suffering.   We have been
wondering very much whether one of us ought not to go
over there.   But it is such a terrifically long journey for the
brief pleasure that it might give Ludwig.   He cried for a
little while when he saw Ferdinand, but he soon returned to
his fantasies, occasionally crying out : " I am done for ! "   It
is appalling, and you can imagine how often I am overcome
with grief at night.   During the day, what with work and
the company of my children, I am able to forget it for a while.
If I thought I could be of the slightest use I should go to him.
But I know only too well what such invalids are like.   I am
expecting Felix in a fortnight.   His letters have lately shown
great maturity of mind and he has often stood comfortingly
and helpfully at my side.   When he leaves us (at the beginning
of August) we shall go to St. Moritz where I have already
taken rooms.   Do you know how wonderful the journey there
is from Vienna ?   I believe the line goes over the Brenner.
The Wittgensteins did it once.   Don't you think you would
like to come after all ?

I shall not go to Julie this year in any case.   It would
not be reasonable to select for my visit precisely a moment
when she requires the greatest peace and care and when
she will be confined to her room for weeks at a time.   My
visit would do her more harm than good.   Elise is going
there in a fortnight. . . .   And now farewell, dear Johannes.

Anxiously awaiting news of what is happening, Your faithful old CLARA.

CLARA *to* BRAHMS.

BADEN BADEN, *July* 28.

You can imagine how disappointed I was with the letter I have just received from you.[1] Ever since we got your letter of a week ago we have been expecting you daily. That is why I did not write to Munich. The route *via* Wildbad is often used for this journey and as you yourself wrote that you intended to take it I never doubted that you would come. I could not telegraph because telegrams are not accepted, and then I thought that you must be on the way. You surely must have known that if I had left Baden I should have written to you to say so. The letters you got were those I had written to you after I had received yours saying that you could not get away from Vienna. Everybody who has a house here (the Rosenhayns, the Viardots, the Guaitas) is advising me to stay quietly here, for if they can't get enough soldiers billeted on inhabited houses they will open closed ones and use them, and then everything will be ruined. So I am staying on though still feeling very anxious, as we have no man to protect us. That is why your promise to come, which would have been nice anyhow, was such a comfort, and I thought that if we had to leave in a hurry you might perhaps go with us to Switzerland. I have taken rooms at St. Moritz and a stay there would do me a great deal of good. But, as I say, I dare not leave. We discuss it all every day. If only one knew where the fighting would begin, but everything is so quiet and one hears nothing. As you may imagine we are very lonely here, for there is no intercourse between the families, and it would have been very dull for you, you would only have had us and perhaps the Viardots. One can, of course, work in such circumstances, but it requires a certain amount of self-discipline, particularly when one has such a weight on one's mind as this war.

Every day I force myself to work, and that after all is the

---

[1] Brahms had offered to come to Baden Baden in order to stand by her, but wrote to say he couldn't as railway communications had been stopped.

best thing to do although it only deadens the misery in my heart for the time being. It would be a good thing if I could get away so as at least to be revived by the fine mountain air. Ferdinand has been obliged to leave his business and join up, and he tells me that he will be sent out in a month. He had to go to barracks and is now being drilled. I ought to be ashamed of myself complaining about this fresh sorrow, but my mother's heart is not left untouched by it. . . .

Stockhausen wrote to me the other day directly after the declaration of war asking me to come to Cannstadt where things will certainly be quite quiet. It was really very nice of him but I shall not dream of going. Let me hear from you soon. Farewell, dear Johannes, and think sometimes of Your wretched CLARA.

1871

DÜSSELDORF, *Jan.* 10.

DEAR JOHANNES,

. . . I should not have been so long answering your last
dear letter if I had not been suffering for the last three weeks
from a most painful ailment. I seem to have caught cold in
my ears and have only been able to understand people speaking when they were close up to me. Every one of my own
words literally buzzed in my head, and the worst of it all was
that I heard all treble notes too high and all harmonies in the
bass entirely confused. This upset me so much that all my
energy seemed to be paralysed, and I could not write a letter
without exerting myself to the utmost. In this condition I
had to go to Hamburg, and I was a little bit better there ;
but the moment I returned to Berlin I was as bad as ever and
it is only a day or two ago that I recovered. Incidentally, in
connection with my illness, I discovered to my surprise through
the ear-specialist (and by means of a mirror) that, although
my ears are formed quite normally, the mucous membrane in
them protrudes and makes it difficult for me to hear.[1] The
doctor told me that as a child I could have had this removed,
but now all I can do is to be careful not to catch cold. But
now enough of this tale of woe. . . .

After having spent two months in Berlin I have once again
grown sick of it and no longer feel at home there. The people
seem to be too cold and censorious. I hardly saw Joachim

---

[1] The meaning here is not very clear. Clara says :—" *ich habe
erfahren, dass meine Ohren ganz normal beschaffen sind, und nur die
Schleimhäute es sind, die sich davor legen, und ich dadurch schwer höre.*"
From this it would appear that the mucous membrane of her ears
was in some way exposed so as to obstruct each orifice ; because she
says " *davor legen* " ; but as no other details are given, it is difficult
to make the nature of her ailment quite plain,—TR.

at all—three or four times.   She is always ill . . . so there
was no chance of any pleasant intercourse. . . .   The whole
atmosphere was one of deep depression in which I shared.
All this did not conduce to make things pleasant, and I should
have felt it much less in Vienna, for instance, where there
would always have been something to distract one.   We still
have very good news of Ferdinand who is now with Dr. Schap-
per [1] (a cellist whom you perhaps knew in Berlin) at Villiers
le Bel, and through the latter (who as a doctor naturally has
privileges and keeps a fatherly eye on him) he finds himself
very favourably situated.

It is true that outpost duties are hard and often dangerous,
but I could not help being pleased when he wrote to me the
other day to say that he had been invited for Christmas to
the Surgeon-General's, where they had a fine Christmas tree
and luxurious presents consisting of things to eat and drink.
If I had only known this before I should have been a little
bit more cheerful that night when, with my four children about
me (Elise had come over from Frankfort), I could not help
wondering all the time where he could be, and whether perhaps while we were standing round our Christmas tree drinking punch in a comfortable room, he was not doing outpost
duty with his teeth chattering with cold.   It was a hard
Christmas Eve.   The thought of poor Ludwig was bad enough.
How mixed my feelings were !   But I could not help being
grateful that after all I was allowed to have at least four of
my children with me, which had not happened for a long
time. . . .   And now with affectionate greetings and let me
hear from you (and about your work ! ! !), ever in the New
Year as in the Old, Your faithful CLARA.

Eugenie is going with me to England.   The Burnands have
kindly invited her.

CLARA *to* BRAHMS.
                    LONDON, *Feb.* 5, 14, HYDE PARK GATE.
DEAR JOHANNES,

Your greeting to England came later than I had hoped, but
I do not thank you for it any the less heartily. . . .   So here
we are in England again after a somewhat longer sea journey

[1] A regimental Doctor and friend of Franz von Mendelssohn.

than usual, which was not very pleasant as we had a heavy snow-storm and had some difficulty in landing at Dover. But we got to our dear friends at last and were received with the utmost kindness. We have no idea of such hospitality in Germany, and certainly we have not the money these people have either. This winter Miss Burnand asked Marie whether she had any wish to express about her bed in London, to which Marie replied that as Miss Burnand was kind enough to ask she would confess that she was in the habit of sleeping on a spring mattress . . . and lo ! when we arrived here we found two magnificent beds with spring mattresses, and now I sleep here as I have never before slept in England.

Imagine everything being done on this scale, and yet—I suppose I may venture to breathe it to my most trusted friends —hardly a moment goes by without my sending a secret sigh to Germany, which I hardly dare to confess to myself because it seems so ungrateful. But when I am here I feel as if every chord of my heart were bound to Germany. What makes it all the stronger this time is the anti-German feeling of the English who sympathize—and this in itself is quite nice of them—with the weaker side—that is to say, the French. I thought at first that this feeling arose from a certain envy of Germany because the Germans had shown themselves so power-ful. But the Germans over here assure me that this is not so, but that it is all due to pity. One has to listen to many things, however, which one finds it very difficult to swallow. But silence is best—and should at all events be the rule for women in politics.

The 10*th.*

A long involuntary pause, as you see ! And what a lot of things have happened in these five days, how many hours of anxiety ! God knows what I can do to overcome the nervous-ness which so often seizes me. And yet, as a rule, I play just as well as ever, though I frequently feel so nervous between one piece and another that I cannot attempt to describe it. What is more, I cannot make up my mind to play from the music, which always makes me feel as though my wings were tied. Nevertheless, I still feel full of soaring power, but more in regard to Art than in regard to life, which never ceases to impose fresh trials upon me. My hearing varies from day to

day, sometimes it is better, sometimes worse. Thank God
that our anxiety about Ferdinand is now somewhat allayed,
at least we know that he is out of any immediate danger.
All the young men have a really diabolical longing to go to
Paris where anything might happen to them. I hope they
won't get there!

I was so glad about your success at the Philharmonic Concert. And are you not producing your Requiem as a whole
soon? When? Are you going to Bremen again for Good
Friday? . . . We are longing with all our might for peace
and if it comes I expect to have Ferdinand with me from the
1st of July to the 1st of October. Then his year of military
service will be over and he will only go back to business in
October. My anxiety about it increases as I write. We are
expecting Joachim to-morrow. He plays on Monday for the
first time. I am very glad that he is coming, for I find it so
difficult to play with others. It all seems to me so insipid.
My reception here has again been most extraordinary. They
really greet me as though they loved me. How silly it is in
such circumstances not to be able to rid oneself of nervousness.
Madame Viardot made a very sad impression upon me here.
I saw her the other day in a most uncomfortable and dirty
lodging and she told me about the appalling pupils she has
here. What an indignity for such an artist, and how sad that
she should be forced to do it! . . . I don't think she will go
to Baden again. I imagine that she and Turgenieff who is
also here, and who is shortly going to Baden " to settle some
business," intend, as she says, to sell their houses. I pitied
her so terribly that when I was there the other day I had a
struggle to keep back my tears. It is a good thing she did
not suspect anything; she would certainly have laughed in
my face. But I must stop. Give me a sign of life soon, dear
Johannes. . . .

Marie and Eugenie send you heartiest greetings. Eugenie
is doing London thoroughly and the people here like her very
much. Marie is particularly pleased to have her, for with me
alone things are sometimes rather dull for her. Farewell.
With affectionate greetings, Your CLARA.

Julie is well and very happy with her baby. I am more
and more pleased with the way Felix is developing.

CLARA *to* BRAHMS.

LONDON, *April* 8.

You ought to have received my hearty greetings yesterday evening, but I have been so harassed lately that I have not even been able to write to my children. But I was with you in spirit yesterday evening [1] and recapitulated the wonderful evening of two years ago. I hope that yesterday too your joy over your magnificent creation was unalloyed. How glad I was to hear that you had been so successful in Vienna. I read various accounts about it. Were you satisfied with your Triumphmarsch or Lied ? Where and how was it performed ? You will be having a pleasant time now in Bremen and Oldenburg. How happily I shall follow you in thought ! What a blessing it is for the busy person that thoughts require neither time nor space.

I have once again finished here after having received the utmost consideration from everybody ; and, in spite of always feeling terribly nervous before the public, I have played on the whole very well. I have played things of yours on various occasions—ballads, waltzes, etc., and the Hungarian Dances will be on my programme again on the 20th at a matinée I am giving at this house. I shall also play the A major Quartet this time. It had been on our programme before, but had to be cancelled because Piatti fell ill and for weeks we were obliged to play things upon which we could venture without rehearsal. Then my over-strained muscles played me a trick and I could not attempt such a trying piece because I had to play three times a week and required all my strength. I exhausted myself on your Handel Variations, which I wanted at all costs to play at my recital, and finally was obliged to give them up because I had not the strength. I can't tell you how sorry I am that these Variations, which I am so enthusiastic about, are too much for me.

So far we have good news of Ferdinand, but the poor fellow has got to stay outside Paris for heaven knows how long. He has a strenuous life and suffers many privations, while for weeks he has only had a thin palliasse—how hard for him !

[1] In Bremen, where, on the 7th of April, the *Requiem* was produced in memory of those who had fallen in the war, and the first movement of the *Triumphlied* was played.

In these circumstances he can hardly get into Paris. We are now seriously thinking about going home. . . . Let me know soon what your plans are. You will probably go to Hamburg first. Have you seen my Felix in Berlin ? I heard that you were there at Tausig's ! ! ! To our great joy Felix is now in the Upper Sixth. He was very anxious to know whether he would be moved up. Things are just the same with Ludwig. We write to him occasionally but he never answers and we seldom hear from the Doctor.

You know where a letter will reach me. Let me have one soon so that I may know where to find you in thought. And now farewell, dear Johannes, and do not forget Your old CLARA.

CLARA *to* BRAHMS.

DÜSSELDORF, *May* 6.

Short though it is I feel that I must send you a greeting for to-morrow and it comes from the bottom of my heart. I must tell you that you have all my best wishes for your birthday. The past year has certainly brought you many artistic joys over which I have rejoiced. You have not celebrated your birthday in Hamburg for a long time. I hope it will be a happy one for you. But in view of your people's more or less unfortunate circumstances I fear it will not be as pleasant as many a previous one has been or as I could wish it to be.

We arrived here three days ago after taking a very sad farewell of the Burnands. Marie and Eugenie went to Baden yesterday to get the house ready and in response to the urgent invitation of Frl. Leser and the Bendemanns (which I was only too glad to accept) I am staying on here a few days. . . .

Things went very well with me in London, except that I had the misfortune of being robbed by burglars who must have come in by my window. I lost all my jewellery and over 100 thalers [£15] in money. But except for this and the loss of many a valuable memento which I cannot replace, I have made over 2,000 thalers [£300]. You must have read about it, for to my surprise I heard here that it had been in all the papers. I naturally felt it a good deal, particularly on account of the children to whom my mementos would have been doubly precious. But I immediately comforted myself with the thought that, after all, it was not the worst that could happen to one, and seeing what far more serious losses we were threatened with through the war, I should have been ashamed of my ingratitude towards the benevolent fate that allowed me to keep my son if I were to wail over my lost jewellery. But is it not extraordinary that this should happen precisely to me, who all my life have had such a childish dread of thieves ? The poor Burnands were exceedingly sympathetic, and I had to make such efforts to comfort them that I got over the first part of the shock much better than I should otherwise have done.

I expect to hear about your plans soon, whether and when you are coming. I shall be there from the 10th and not at number 12 (where you wrote last summer) but number 14. With an affectionate shake of the hand, dear Johannes, Your old CLARA.

1872

BÂLE, *Jan.* 1.

My first letter of the New Year bearing the first postmark
of the German Empire, is to you, dear Johannes. You ought
really to have had my greetings to-day (you know that I like
to keep to particular days), but the last days of the old year
were very anxious ones for me, and there were so many claims
on my attention, that I could not collect my thoughts.   It
was all about the business with the *Hochschule*,[1] which until
two days before the New Year, I thought was all over, as I
had made up my mind about it long ago.   Then I found that
I had to write to Joachim (he said I must send my reply by
New Year's Eve at the latest) and everybody round me, particularly Marie, pointed out to me that I ought not to refuse
a certainty like this without mature consideration, and that
I ought at least to state what I regarded as satisfactory conditions of acceptance in order that I might not have to reproach
myself later on.   The Bendemanns in particular were very
much in favour of the post, more especially on account of the
children, who would then have a home.   Ferdinand would be
able to live with us, Felix could always spend his holidays
with us, and there would be various other advantages.   So I
wrote to say that I did not want to refuse definitely, but felt
that I must make the following stipulations :—

1. A salary of 4,000 thalers [£600] for life, with five months'
holiday (February, March, July, August and September).

2. I should not be required to start work until the 1st of
October.

3. I should have the right to choose the pupils for my own
class.

4. Complete freedom to accept engagements elsewhere and

[1] See *Life*, Vol. II, p. 287.

also in Berlin itself, provided any lessons interfered with were made good.

5. I should have the right to take other pupils in addition to those from the Hochschule. Finally, I wrote to Joachim that I must stipulate that if at the end of the first six months I did not like my work I might resign without any objections being raised by the Governors. And I also told him (Joachim) that I should like him to consider whether it was possible without any risk to our friendly relations, for us to work together as equals, because at my age it was no longer possible to be an underling. Seldom in my life have I found anything as difficult as the sending of this letter. Everybody told me that they would never accept my conditions—I don't wish to be presumptuous, but I must confess that I hope they won't. If only I could have talked to you about it for a little while! I wonder whether, in view of the children, you think that I am justified in behaving as I have ?

Now I have eased my mind of a great load though I should have been much happier if I could have talked to you about something livelier. My mind is now full of the musical festival. If you are coming to Düsseldorf for it I must really see whether I cannot attend it too. But there is one thing I beg and implore of you—be consistent and don't undertake to produce any work of your own unless they invite you to conduct it yourself.[1] It is imperative that you should present your work in person, because besides the peculiar importance that would thus be attached to it, it would also be quite differently produced. If you are not there the piece will be disposed of with a few hasty rehearsals, which no one ought to dare to do in your case now. I am so afraid that Rubinstein [2] may succeed in having his way with you ; that is why I have said so much about it all. Please let me know at once whether anything is decided, as I am so frightfully anxious. . . .

My concerts in Heidelberg and Carlsruhe have fallen through —there is no longer any time for them ; besides, I must practise for at least a fortnight or three weeks before going to England. I came to Bâle to-day in order to fulfil my promise

[1] As Brahms was not thus invited, the proposal to produce the *Triumphlied* came to nothing.

[2] Rubinstein was directing the Düsseldorf Musical Festival.

about the orchestra concerto (it was a great sacrifice on my part, but I could not bring myself to leave them in the lurch), and on the 5th I am playing at the Museum in Frankfort at the concert which was cancelled a fortnight ago.   I also want to go for a day to Heidelberg to make inquiries about Felix who is going there at Easter.   Perhaps I shall be able to find a nice family where he can have a room—and on the 7th I am going back to the Bendemanns at Düsseldorf.

The tour with Frau Joachim is over.[1]   She is now going with her husband to Königsberg and Danzig, and then on to St. Petersburg, when she will return to Berlin.   She was a very pleasant colleague.   She sang beautifully, was always cheerful and easy to get on with, and as she left all the business side to me I had nothing to complain of. . . .

Have you invested your money well,—I hope not in Austrian securities ? . . .

But I have had one pleasant surprise—Herr Plaut has given Ferdinand a rise of 200 thalers [£30] although he has only been a clerk there for three months, so that now, with his Christmas gratuity of 100 thalers, his earnings for the year have been 1,000 thalers [£150].   You are certainly right in what you say about him in your letter.   But it is very difficult for a mother to stifle her own feelings and wishes and to act in accordance with what she thinks is right.   I must try to find a golden mean.   Marie sends her best wishes.   And now farewell, dear Johannes ; in the New Year as in the old, Yours ever, CLARA.

I ought not to thank you for your dear letter in a postscript, but it gave me such joy that I would not like to omit thanking you altogether.   I wish I could get another like it soon.

CLARA *to* BRAHMS.

LONDON, *Feb.* 21.

DEAR JOHANNES,

How very sad that you should now have to see the grave close on your father ! [2]   But at least you have the consolation of knowing that you were able to be with him at the end, and that he must have been happy to feel you at his side.   What

---

[1] Concerning Clara's concert tour with Frau Joachim, see the German edition of *Life*, Vol. III, p. 264.—TR.

[2] Jakob Brahms died on the 11th February.

you wrote about his wife pleased me very much—if only he could have enjoyed her companionship longer ! And how sad about the son.[1] You had not written to me about this. What is the matter with him ? Have you settled everything in Hamburg ? Have you taken your books, etc., back with you to Vienna ? Let me know more soon. I do not even know whether this letter will reach you in Vienna. I did not think that you would go back there first, as you intend to be in Carlsruhe on Palm Sunday.

Enclosed I send you a receipt from Novello, who has bought the Gavotte [2] for £20—I could not get more, because he said that other arrangements would come along which would spoil his sales, besides which the Gavotte by Senff is already selling in large numbers. The audience was delighted with it. Hallé [3] had already played it in Manchester, but not yet here. It would have been no joke for me if he had. Please sign the receipt by writing your name over the penny stamp, which you will find at the foot of it. I have made a cross where you must sign, because the receipt is only valid if it is done in this way. I am sending you the £20 by means of a bank-post-bill, which any banker will cash for you. I'm sorry I could not get more but—well, I'll tell you later about my conversation with Novello. . . .

As for myself, the news is good, for I have met with an enthusiastic reception. Everybody says I have never played so well, etc. But I am suffering terribly from rheumatism in the muscles of my arms and fingers—so much so that it is with genuine qualms that I look from one engagement to the next. Although I practise everything *pp.* I am quite exhausted at the end of an hour, and of course the rheumatism flies to the muscles which are most used.

Yesterday I was shocked by something Joachim said to the effect that I must be in Berlin from the 1st of October onwards, and must therefore make no plans for that period. (I had

[1] Fritz Schnack, Jakob Brahms' stepson, lay in bed seriously ill at the time.

[2] This was a Gavotte by Gluck, which Brahms had arranged for the piano, and which Clara was pleased for Brahms' sake to dispose of to Novello. She had played it with great success at the Popular Concert.

[3] Charles Hallé of Hagen, Westphalia. a concert organizer, who became famous on the Continent, in Paris and in London.

just been doing so, for, as he had not yet mentioned the matter to me, I thought it was all at an end.)   I did not sleep the whole night.   If I accept I believe I shall be utterly miserable.   All night long I deliberated whether I should write to him and beg him not to mention the matter again, as I felt I could not undertake it.   But I do not wish to make the mistake of being over-hasty.

Although I have much to say, I must now close, as I really ought not to write at all.

I should like to know your address.   I don't like the idea of addressing your letters to music publishers, because letters so often go astray if sent to third parties.

My heartiest greetings to you, my dear Johannes, and remember Your faithful old friend, CLARA.

. . . Have you heard Rubinstein's Don Quixote music (Humoresque) ?   Surely it is the end of everything !   But it is a pity, for the man certainly has imagination.

Joachim is delighted with Russia.   He could have earned a good deal more if only he had not had to come back.   I warned him that it would be most unsatisfactory to have to leave in the middle of it all. . . .   One more shake of the hand. Addio !

CLARA *to* BRAHMS.

LONDON, *Feb.* 27.

DEAR JOHANNES,

Although I do not know where you are, I cannot wait for your answer, as I should like to be the first to tell you that we played your A major quartet at the Popular Concert yesterday.   This in itself is not much, but the reception was most gratifying.   You know that until now I have never been able to arrange for a performance of it ; but this time I made it a condition, and so I am doubly pleased that, in spite of Davison,[1] it had such a cordial reception.   Every movement was loudly applauded.   After the adagio the clapping seemed as if it would never end, and after the finale we were recalled.   I need hardly tell you with what love I played it.   I enclose the programme.

[1] The musical critic of *The Times*, regarded by English people as the greatest authority on musical matters.

I have just begged Simrock to send me your Hungarian dances. Shall I be able to master some of them ?

The Berlin business is off my mind now. It is true that Joachim says he does not think the matter at an end, and perhaps I may reconcile myself to it in a year's time, etc. But I stuck to it that I felt I could not undertake it. How greatly relieved I was when I had spoken out !

I am longing to have news of you, dear Johannes !

Let me have a word soon. Your devoted CLARA.

BRAHMS *to* CLARA.

VIENNA, *Easter Monday, April.*

MY BELOVED CLARA,

I always enjoy festivals in solitude, quite alone, with perhaps just a few dear ones in my room, and very quietly—for are not all my people either dead or far away ? But what a joy it is to me then to remember how big with love is a certain human breast. For, after all, I am dependent upon the outside world—the hurly-burly in which we live. I do not add my laughter to its medley of voices, nor do I join its chorus of lies,—but it is as if the best in man could shut itself up, and only half of him sallied forth dreaming.

How fortunate you are, or, I should say, how beautiful, how good, how right ! I mean that you bear your heart as a conscious possession, securely ; whereas we are obliged every minute to conceal ours. You see everything so warmly, with such beautiful serenity, just like a reflection of yourself ; and then with the same serenity you give unto each his due. All this sounds so stupid, and I cannot say what I think ; although it would be even more stupid to speak of lilies and angels, and then to come back to you and your sweet nature.

. . . The whole winter I have been studying counterpoint most assiduously. What for ? To be able the better to run down my beautiful things ?—I did not need counterpoint for that. To become a Professor at the Academy ?—no not that either. To be able to write MS. music better ?—I do not even aspire to that ! But there certainly is an element of tragedy about becoming in the end too clever for one's needs.

You have no notion, and, as it would seem to me, no comprehension of how chaotic things are over here. I don't believe you are even interested in the matter.   (I am neither referring to nor thinking of Wagner.)

I was extremely glad to hear that Felix had done so well.[1] . . . I hope we shall enjoy the burgeoning and budding of the trees together in Baden.   But I have not yet heard whether you and Joachim have agreed to go to Carlsruhe.

With heartiest greetings and remembrances to Marie, Joachim and your friendly host, Yours, JOHANNES.

CLARA *to* BRAHMS.

LONDON, *April* 6.

I am replying to yours at once ; and, first of all, heartiest thanks for your dear letter.   But I should like to know what all this is about Carlsruhe.[2]   You ask me to tell you whether Joachim and I have agreed to go ; but I do not even know what we should agree to go for !   Can it be that Levi has put off the Triumphlied so long that we may now possibly hear it there ?   That would be splendid !   Why was it not performed on Palm Sunday as they arranged ?   You even wrote to me yourself about it, asking whether I could be in Carlsruhe to hear it.   That was why I sent you a line of greeting there.

After your last letter I wrote to Levi to find out what was happening, and begged him to answer at once, as the affair at Carlsruhe might possibly clash with my future arrangements. But I received no reply.   I cannot write to him again, so will you please tell me what you propose to do ?

In any case I shall stay here until the 23rd, and then I intend going to see the Kufferaths and the Bendemanns for a few days.   I hope to be back in my dear little home early in May, when perhaps I may also see my friend ? !

I should like to know what you mean about the chaos in your part of the world.   Do you mean that I should show some interest in the Rubinstein humbug ?   I feel nothing but aversion for the present trend of art.   I really cannot understand

---

[1] He had passed his leaving examination of German college students.

[2] This refers to the first complete performance of Brahms' *Triumphlied* on the 5th of June at Levi's farewell concert, before he went to Munich as Musical Conductor to the Court.   Clara and Stockhausen performed at this concert, at which the *Triumphlied* was received with wild enthusiasm.   *Life*, Vol. II, pp. 290–291.

it.   Thank goodness that a man like you is still among us !
Only that which is genuine turns out to be right in the end,
and this the future will show.   Indeed the present shows it
already, but not on a universal scale.   That which is great
and lofty is not for everybody.   In order to grasp it some
depth is necessary and, above all, senses which have not been
debauched.

I suppose you will have a good deal to tell me.   I sometimes glance at the *Signal*,[1] and then think myself lucky to
be so far away.

You wrote to me the other day about Julie.   It's not as
bad as all that. . . .   The doctor had qualms and therefore
sent her to the seaside, where she stayed for six weeks.   She is
better now, but, unfortunately the great expense of her trip
has made her visit to us rather doubtful, so that I sincerely
hope to see her in Baden.   Thus we have to learn resignation
ever more and more in life, and should be thankful if anything
at all remains to us.

All here thank you for your kind messages and reciprocate
them.   Farewell, my dear Johannes.   With most affectionate
greetings from Your CLARA.

CLARA *to* BRAHMS.

DÜSSELDORF, *May* 5.

After all I am obliged to wish you many happy returns of
the day by letter ;   and yet I had felt so certain of being able
this year to celebrate your birthday with you once more.
This was, however, prevented owing to an invitation from the
Queen, which forced me to remain a week longer in London.
Here then I send you my heartiest good wishes.   May the
coming year bring you much happiness and other good things,
particularly in connection with your new artistic activities.
You will almost certainly celebrate the day with Levi.   If
you do, give a thought to me now and then, and remember
that my heart is with you as affectionately as ever.

Thanks for your note from Baden.   I was particularly glad
to see that it came from there.   Unfortunately I cannot come
back yet, however much I may long for home, because Marie
must first get things straight for me, and we have not even a

[1] A musical periodical.

servant in view. Much as I liked to be with the dear Bende-manns and Rosalie, and much as I longed for them in England, I feel now as if I would give anything to be home after seven months' absence. I shall therefore remain a week here, then spend the day with Felix [1] and go on a visit to Baden. I shall not go to Carlsruhe, but it would please me very much to go to you in Oos. I shall write more precisely in a day or two, but in any case you will also hear all about it from Marie who will be in Baden on Tuesday. Eugenie ought to get there to-day I should think.

Now what about the concert in Carlsruhe? Is the Phil-harmonic Society giving it or is Levi? I asked him about it, but he did not answer.

There is much excitement here owing to the Music Festival. I am supposed to stay, but of course I shan't dream of doing so. All news when we meet, and with a hearty handshake, Your old friend CLARA.

BRAHMS *to* CLARA.

VIENNA, *Dec.* 24.

I feel I must write to send you my heartiest good wishes for Christmas and the New Year. May many New Years go by without robbing you of so many precious things as the last one did.[2] But it is obvious that we who go on living must see many things vanish with the years—things with which it is more difficult to part than with years of life.

What I feel about New Years is that I wish for nothing more than that you should always believe that my attitude to you remains the same. Nothing will alter or diminish the regard and admiration with which you have always inspired me.

Often, by way of making a miserable joke, I have said you look upon me as the police look upon one who has undergone three terms of imprisonment. I can only hope that this un-favourable opinion of me has frequently proved unjustified,

[1] Who was studying in Heidelberg.
[2] In the spring Clara's mother, Frau Bargiel, died. On the 10th of November Julie, who was seriously ill, and who with her husband and child had been in Baden-Baden in August and September, was released from her suffering. *Life*, Vol. II, p. 292.

just as I fear your more favourable opinions of my artistic work have been. I no longer contest either point of view, but neither of them need rob you of the feeling and belief that no one can be more attached and devoted to you than I am.

I might have written a good deal more, but I am being constantly interrupted. I will therefore bring this hurriedly to a close by reiterating my best wishes to you. Hiller arrived yesterday. I have not yet seen Fraulein Marie again. . . . Please remember me to the Joachims, Fraulein Eugenie, etc. Your heartily devoted JOHS. BR.

1873

CLARA *to* BRAHMS.

LONDON,[1] *March* 6.

DEAR JOHANNES,

Long as it is since I heard from you I cannot remain silent any longer, or would very much prefer not to, as I am sure it would please you to hear from one who with both eyes and ears can testify to the fact that your Sextet in B Flat was again performed with very great success the day before yesterday. The Scherzo was played a second time, and, after the finale, all the performers were given a call. But owing to their hesitation, because all six did not wish to come forward together, it took some time, and yet the public did not stop their applause for a moment. The Serenade in D sharp was also performed at the Crystal Palace quite recently, and Joachim assured me that it was very well received. Unfortunately I had to play at the Popular that day. The audience at the Palace is very mixed, but at the Popular it is the best in London. This month I am thinking of giving the Quartet in A major again. The other day I played it at Liverpool with great success. I should be so glad now if I could play the Handel Variations, but I can hardly practise at all, and shall be glad when I have got through the concerts successfully, for the pains in my hands and arms have grown so bad that I am often beside myself with anxiety.

. . . I really ought not to write, so with most affectionate remembrances, Yours, CLARA.

The Burnands have asked me (I must therefore discharge the duty faithfully) to tell you that they were delighted with the sextet.

---

[1] Clara had come to London on February 9. *Life*, Vol. II, p. 294.

CLARA *to* BRAHMS.

LONDON, *April* 12.

DEAR JOHANNES,

Our last letters must have crossed. I wanted to write to you the moment I received yours, but all this time I have been suffering, as I have never suffered before, from rheumatism in the arms, hands and shoulders. Only by means of the utmost care have I been able to fulfil all my engagements,—that is to say, by practising with only half my usual strength and by doing no writing at all. By these means I have been able to carry on, and with great success, but the last time, which was on Monday a week ago, I could only move my fingers, and could not lift my arms at all, so had to spend the whole week applying fomentations. Now I have started with homeopathy which has excellent remedies for my kind of trouble. I wanted to go direct to Teplitz, but this was impossible, chiefly because, as I am due to play at the Music Festival at Aix-la-Chapelle, I should be forced to exert myself instead of taking the complete rest which is necessary after drinking the waters. I therefore gave up the idea, and shall remain here until April 29th, giving one or two lessons and a farewell matinée on the 26th.

I want to hear Bruch's Odysseus on May 4th at Düsseldorf, and then go on to Baden—perhaps for the last time. What are your plans for the summer ? Will you go to your cottage in Lichtenthal again ?

Many thanks for your news of the musical world ! How glad I was to hear that the last concerts were so successful.[1] The idea that you might again give up your post in Vienna, or think of doing so, never occurred to me, and I should have thought it a great mistake. Nowhere else would you find such splendid forces at your disposal and such high appreciation for your achievements both with orchestra and choir.

As to Bonn,[2] I could tell you a few things. Joachim and I are conspiring to get your Requiem on the programme. But they won't hear of it, and have availed themselves of an interview with me in order to interpret one of my remarks in such

[1] See *Kalbeck*, Vol. II, p. 416.
[2] This refers to the Schumann Festival at Bonn and the preparations for it. See *Life*, Vol. II, p. 294.

a way as to make it appear that I said I did not want the Requiem. Dr. Heimsöth spoke to me about it, before I went to Vienna, and asked whether I did not think that it would be best if you composed something specially for the occasion, to which I certainly agreed. . . . Joachim has just gone to Bonn, and I have written a letter in which I say that it is my wish as well as his that your Requiem should be performed, and give many reasons for this view. I am now curious to see what they will decide to do. Joachim hinted that he would resign if they did not agree. But this would surely be a great pity! Who would then conduct the orchestra? In that case I would not go either. Please do not mention the matter to anyone. Misunderstandings so easily occur. But I think it is such a fine opportunity for the Requiem, and eminently fitting into the bargain.

Mr. Behrens, a rich Manchester man, with whom Joachim always stays, is the same person who for a long while was an intimate friend of Woldemar. Ought you not to write him a few lines of thanks? I think it would be the proper thing. His address is . . . Would you do me the favour of sending me the best small photograph of yourself which you happen to have at the moment? The Burnands are so anxious to have it in their book. If you have no time to write, just send it to me with a greeting. Please sign the photograph.

In other respects we are all quite well. The Burnands are very charming and my reception at the hands of the public has been more enthusiastic than ever. Nevertheless, I am longing to be back in Germany, and am literally counting the hours that yet remain before my departure. It is with reluctance that I have to acknowledge this, because it seems to me almost like ingratitude. In feeling, however, I am so German to the core, that I cannot adapt myself anywhere else. By the bye, since the affair of the fund [1] has become known, I pass here for a rich woman, as I probably do to some extent in Germany. . . . People hear large sums mentioned, and do not trouble to think any further.

The children wish to be remembered to you. Eugenie is

[1] In December a group of Clara's friends had, through the agency of Windelstadt of Cologne, presented her with a gift of Rhenish 5 per cent. Railway Stock to the value of 30,000 thalers [or £4,500].

studying diligently.   Were you serious when you thought that we were looking for people with big names as teachers for them ?   At present I am the only one who gives them lessons. And apart from you, you know there is no one in whose hands I would willingly leave them.   My heartiest greetings to you, dear Johannes, and think occasionally of Your old friend CLARA.

P.S. Your Sextet was performed again just lately, and aroused the same enthusiasm as before.   The Scherzo was encored.   Was your idea of the latter that it should be played extremely fast ?   I like it fast but severe.   The Requiem was performed recently.   Suffice it to say that it was in the hands of an amateur, and badly translated into the bargain.   Let us remember to discuss it one of these days.

CLARA *to* BRAHMS.

LONDON, *April* 22.

We have succeeded in getting the *Requiem* on the programme at Bonn.   Joachim had suggested that only this should be played on the first day, but for various reasons I did not agree with the idea.   I suggested that it should be followed by the 2nd Symphony, and hope that this will be arranged.

Your innuendoes anent the Schumann Fund have greatly annoyed me.   It would have been better to tell me clearly all about it, than to leave me to surmise all kinds of unpleasant things.   Unfortunately, what I discovered the day after your letter came far surpassed all that I had suspected.

I am beside myself with fury over this disgusting advertisement in the Graz Gazette.[1]   I, who, thanks to the strength that has been vouchsafed me, have been able honourably to keep myself and my children from want all these years, who throughout the whole of last winter was still working with the utmost energy and success, and who, owing to the gift from the Schumann Fund, was able to look a little less anxiously into the future—I am now to allow other artists to give concerts for me, and to this end to suffer the publication of such mendacious advertisements for the collection of more money ! It is an indignity.   I am so thoroughly infuriated, I do not know what to do for the best, and have just written to Bende-

[1] A concert in aid of the Schumann Fund had been announced in Graz.

mann and begged him to do what he can in the matter.   I must
be vindicated.   The fact must be stated in the leading Vienna
newspapers and in the principal organ of Graz, that the whole
thing is a lie, and that I knew nothing about the concerts, and
could not therefore have consented to them.   Then steps must
be taken to prevent so much as a farthing of the receipts from
coming to me—they can be given to some charitable institution
or to a poor musician.   Or ought I to write to Hanslick and
Gehring ? [1]   How I hate such things !   In my opinion it is
my friends in Vienna who should take the matter up, for it is
through them (one or other of them, it does not signify) that
I have had this dreadful experience.   They owe it to my honour
to vindicate me.

Farewell !   I can think of nothing else than this fatal business.   I have not slept for two nights.   Oh, why could I not
have been spared this ordeal !   As always, Your CLARA.

The Burnands thank you for the photograph.   I wish you
had sent another.   I know better ones of you.

CLARA *to* BRAHMS.

BADEN, *Sept.* 17.

Your dear letter was the first written greeting I found awaiting me on the morning of my birthday.   And it pleased me
more than I can say.   The *Regenlieder* followed yesterday—
thank you for everything.

So you are now back in Vienna.   Still at the address in
Ausstellungsgebäude I suppose ?   We are now seriously thinking about packing, but with horror ; for think of all that one
requires to make one's self passably comfortable within one's
four walls !   You are probably right in thinking that Felix
would work better in Berlin.   If only he could get well again !
Four days before my birthday he got pleurisy, which, as the
doctor said, had been coming on for some time.   The danger
is now over, but he is still in bed, and will not be able to leave
his room for a week.   The doctor says the greatest care will
be necessary to prevent his lungs from becoming affected.
You can imagine what an anxiety this will be for me.   My
poor heart seems always to be subjected to fresh trials.   How
glad I am now that we decided to have Felix with us, and all

[1] Franz Gehring, musical critic of the *Deutsche Zeitung*.

I regret is that I cannot undo the eighteen months he has spent at Heidelberg. For my birthday Felix had written a little play which they were going to perform, but now of course they cannot do so. I will send you his poems with the copies of the songs before the end of the month, and I should be very glad if you would read them through and mark anything that pleases you. Some of them are really quite good ; he often shows profundity and humour. We are terribly busy just now, and that is why I am sending the lot instead of copying out the best ones for you. Tell me frankly what you think of them, and do not imagine that, like a weak mother, I fancy him a genius—on the contrary, I am so fearful of overestimating *his* [Robert's] children's gifts, that I dare say I often exact too much from them.

I am delighted that you are getting such a good fee for the quartet. I never cease to marvel at the way fees have increased during recent years. How much more easily my poor Robert could have taken it, if it had been the same some years ago. Now be careful how you invest your money ; it is better to get a low rate of interest and to have it safe. Will you soon be arranging the quartets for four hands ? And are we to have the Variations ? [1]

I played here a little while ago (as there are no gambling tables here I did not like to say " no ") and was presented with vast quantities of flowers. But this was rather clumsily done, and I was made to look an awful fool, thanks to a gigantic basket of flowers which it required two lackeys to bring on to the platform. If only they had sent it to my address it would have been much more pleasant for me—because the laurel wreaths and beautiful bouquets which they threw on to the platform might surely have sufficed ! It is an extraordinary thing how easily tactlessness creeps into such demonstrations. But now good-bye ! Let me hear from you soon, my dear Johannes, and remember Your old friend CLARA.

CLARA *to* BRAHMS.

HAMBURG, *Nov.* 24.

For a long time now I have been meaning to write to you and to give you belated thanks for all your trouble over my

---

[1] This refers to Op. 56, *Variations on a theme by Haydn.*

songs. But we have been through a most exhausting time owing to our move,[1] and in addition I have been suffering a good deal from pains in the joints of my arms and hands, so that I am obliged to dictate almost everything. But you have known for ever so long how reluctantly I dictate my letters, particularly to you. To-day, however, I must send you a greeting from your native town which, especially from your point of view, is, both inside and out, beginning to look quite different. Surely our native town should always remain just as we loved it; but everything, everything is becoming different! Indeed things have altered so much that in many quarters even you will not know where you are. I saw your sister. She seemed *quite happy* with her husband, who struck me as a very decent fellow, and who, so she says, waits on her hand and foot. She looks very well, but is about to go through a hard time. I hope she will get over it all right. She is longing for you, and wishes you could see her in her bliss.

I had a delightful time in Munich and enjoyed it immensely. I shall live upon it all through the winter, for everything is commonplace in Berlin, except what Joachim gives us. I even heard good quartet playing in Munich—your two quartets. You can imagine with what interest I listened to them and *enjoyed* them. Manfred [2] was also quite wonderful. But I was not at all moved by the actor Possart, though he is un-doubtedly a great master, because both his acting and enuncia-tion seemed to be merely the outcome of great care and industry. Neither his voice nor his attitudes seemed to be inspired by deep feeling, and therefore failed to touch a single heart-chord. The music and scenery were wonderful, but to my sorrow I was unable to hear a bar of the address to Astarte, which I was looking forward to with so much pleasure, because it was played so softly that I only caught the sound of the violins here and there. Altogether I failed to hear a good deal of the music, which made me feel very wretched. But of course I did not let Levi notice anything because he had put his heart and soul into the production.

I was not able to wait for the performance of *Genoveva*,

[1] To Berlin.

[2] A performance of *Manfred*, given under Levi's direction.

because Marie wanted me in Berlin. I cannot tell you what this meant to me, and the children have no inkling of what a sacrifice it was to my love for them. Only a thorough artist can understand the delight which people like ourselves take in a great artistic production.

I am living quite comfortably here with Friedchen, and am pleasantly impressed by the sight of the contented circle over which she presides. Surely nothing is more stimulating than the sight of happy people ! I wonder whether you have sold the grand piano.[1] It is very foolish to make anybody such an inconvenient present. One often cherishes illusions which vanish with the years, but good Dame Nature allows us to keep a few all the same. I often find myself guilty of one illusion or another, and would gladly keep them as long as possible.

Farewell, my dear Johannes ! Eugenie, who is with me, wishes to be remembered to you. Don't be long answering and give joy to Your old friend CLARA.

CLARA *to* BRAHMS.

BERLIN, *Dec.* 12.

Let me answer at once about the grand piano, so that you may know what to do about it. I am sorry you should have so much bother about it. I would prefer not to sell it ; but would you present it to the *Gesellschaft der Musik-freunde* ?[2] It is really your property, and I should not mind this at all. If the Society do not want it, ask Fabers whether they can dispose of it. Joachim said he would gladly take charge of it, but the carriage here would be too costly, and would only add to the price.

Oh to think that I was unable to be present at a concert like that ! How it would have uplifted me, and how pleased I should have been to see you at the conductor's desk, looking so happy ! Apart from Joachim's quartet we hear *nothing* here. The theatre is mediocre, the *Singakademie* old-fashioned, and the symphony concerts incredibly dull, etc. But I have enjoyed happy—I might say blissful—hours, thanks to your

[1] Robert Schumann's grand piano.
[2] A Society composed of lovers of music. This Society accepted the grand piano from Brahms.

concerto.[1]   It is too beautiful and it went very well when I
played it in Leipsic.   The orchestra was good, though not
quite at its ease ; but what could one expect with a work
that was so strange to them and so difficult ?   Reinecke [2]
had taken great pains, I couldn't complain of him.   The public
listened respectfully and called for me.   But the musicians
and connoisseurs who were present in great numbers, all
came and thanked me for producing the magnificent work,
and I was overjoyed.   I ought to play it three or four times
every year, and then the public would begin to be familiar
with it.   But who knows whether I shall ever be able to play
it again, for the pains in my arm are very bad.   At present
I cannot play at all, and ought not to be writing.   But I
have so much to tell you, and I do so hate dictating !   I
can only hope for Teplitz in May, but I don't know what will
happen about London.   I have already cut down my engagements to two performances a week for five weeks ; but if my
pains don't go, I shall have to give up playing altogether.

I was in Dresden for a couple of days before I went to
Leipsic—they were unspeakably sad days for me.[3]   I found
mother [4] all alone in another house (the old one is already half
pulled down, and a new one is being built there).   Oh how
cruel death is when it cuts so deeply.   I felt how strong my
love for my father had been (of course I love my mother in
him) and how gratefully I think of him.   If only I could have
seen him once more and kissed him again !   Fancy, he who
lived so simply himself, and whose wants were so few, who
up to the very end was always working for others, has left
quite a nice fortune—nearly 60,000 thalers [£9,000], and has
remembered me more kindly than I ever expected.   Can you
understand how this very fact makes my grief the deeper ?
I do not know what it is, but I cannot think of it without
bursting into tears.   I could not bear having to open his

[1] The D minor.

[2] Carl Heinrich C. Reinecke, pianist and composer, born 1824.   He
was first a pianist at the Court of Denmark ; then he became a professor at the Cologne Conservatoire, and successively musical director
at Barmen and at the University of Breslau.   After that he settled
in Leipsic.—Tr.

[3] Friedrick Wieck, Clara's father, had died on October 6, 1873.

[4] Really her stepmother, Clementine Wieck.

strong box with all its papers, and to touch the shares which he had collected for us. I take no pleasure in all the pretty things I have. I cannot help recalling his simplicity, and it seems unjust that I and my children should be enjoying many things which he never dreamt of having. Forgive me for saying so much about it. But I feel I am speaking to the truest of friends and must unburden my heart.[1]

Felix is much better, but he still coughs a good deal! He studies diligently, and seems to be happy with us, which is particularly gratifying to me, because it is on his account that we are here. We often see Joachim, but he always looks so harassed that I often feel anxious about him.

Now with fondest remembrances, my dear Johannes, Your ever affectionate CLARA.

CLARA *to* BRAHMS.

BERLIN, *Dec.* 17.

I answer your dear letter at once so as to tell you that in case you accept the proposal from Leipsic,[2] choose your Requiem and conduct it yourself. It has already been greatly appreciated,[3] but there was considerable dispute about the tempo, and it would be a good thing if the people could hear it performed as it should be.

My reason for suggesting the Requiem is that it has been practised and is known. I should not like you to make your appearance in Leipsic unless it were with a work about the success of which you are certain—I mean precisely in Leipsic. You don't depend upon Leipsic, but if you go there, you may as well for your own sake make a success of it. If I am wrong, at least you know that I mean well by you. I know it won't affect your fame. Or are you invited only to provide one item in a mixed concert programme ? In that case, I should choose the Variations.[4] But you must conduct. When is the concert to be ? You'll try not to forget, if you come, that I am near at hand ? I don't know yet whether my arm will allow me to go to England. It is still very bad.

[1] In the margin : " My people were very kind and friendly."
[2] An invitation from the Governors of the *Orchester-Pensionsfonds*.
[3] On November 13 at a concert at the *Gewandhaus*.
[4] Op. 56.

But if I can I must try to do it and keep my word. I shall remain here until the 12th of January and shall be back here again from the 19th to the 30th. God willing, I shall return from England on April 3rd or 4th in order to spend Easter here with the children. Possibly as Easter is early this year your concert in Leipsic might take place during Easter week. Please think of me in settling it. . . .

Thank you for the article. Oh how my heart bleeds when I think of all the musical treats I could have in Vienna, particularly through you ! Adieu, my dear Johannes, Your CLARA.

1874

BERLIN, *Jan.* 10.

DEAR JOHANNES,

I am eagerly waiting for an answer and for news of all kinds. But I must not forget to thank you for the telegram received yesterday, although it only doubles my longing for a detailed report. For I only believe good reports when I hear them from you.

Oh, how wretched I feel to have to be so far away when I could enjoy so many musical treats! What a miserable existence I am now leading—you have no idea! Not only am I reduced to artistic inactivity myself, *but I also hear nothing* that gives me the smallest pleasure. I do not even see anyone with whom I can talk music. I have had to cancel a certain number of my engagements, because my arm is always the same, although the doctor assures me that it will soon be quite well. What is more, the present cold weather is bad for such troubles. I cannot tell you how this depresses me—more than the hardest misfortunes I have suffered, because my Art helped me to endure these, but now I have nothing.

The fact that you have not answered my letter inquiring about Leipsic in which I told you that if you went there I should like to be there too, and have not even told me whether your visit has been fixed, has made me very miserable. I heard about it from many quarters, but not from you! Wouldn't you like me to come? And could you not come here at least for a day or two, either before or after the event? Simrock said to me the other day that you had no time. Is that really so?

There's one other matter—the children wished me to write to you some time ago, and Felix begged to be allowed to write for all of them. And now they fear that he did not thank you heartily enough for the delightful surprise you gave

278

them.[1]   So let me thank you again now.   Felix has struggled with the song until he has at last mastered it.   It was not easy for his amateur fingers.

Do not let me wait too long, dear Johannes, otherwise I shall really begin to think you don't want me !   Cordially yours, CLARA.

Joachim is still away travelling for a month.

CLARA *to* BRAHMS.

BERLIN, *March* 2.

DEAREST JOHANNES,

You would certainly have had a letter from me before I got one from you, had it not been that I find it so hard to write nowadays and that I hate dictating.[2]   My heart was so full that I should have been glad to be able to tell you once again how greatly I enjoyed the days in Leipsic—how eagerly I drank in your wonderful creations, like the most exquisite nectar of flowers, and how they revived me at a time when I was more depressed than you can imagine.   For the time being I was taken completely out of myself, and that refreshed and restored my spirit.   In the midst of all your glorious preoccupations I did not wish to speak to you about it, but now I can hardly hold my peace, and I must confess that I feel more desolate than I ever have before in my life. In all my trials hitherto I have had my Art as a faithful help-meet at my side.   But now that has gone, and with it I feel as if I had lost the mainstay of my life.   I cannot get away from my troubles, first it is Felix and then it is myself— not that I care about my life, but about that which is my life's light and breath.   What makes me most miserable is

[1] Brahms had selected one of the poems by Felix sent him in the letter dated September 17 and had set it to music.   It was the receipt of this music that had constituted the surprise referred to.   In a letter dated January 1 Clara tells Brahms how delighted Felix was when the song was played to him and he saw that the words were his own.—TR.

[2] In a previous letter, written on January 20, Clara had said : " As to my arm, it is bad.   I am cancelling all my engagements, one after the other.   But that would be the least of my trials.   What really is hard is that my piano has been closed for weeks.   At such times one needs all one's courage to carry on.   I hope that the time in Leipsic will give me the necessary strength."—TR.

that with all this depression I cannot be a source of good cheer to my children. For, try as I may day and night to be brighter, how is it possible, with this fresh terrible anxiety about Felix ? [1] He is not to go south in the height of the summer, but to Davos. There he will remain throughout the winter, and there is a splendid doctor on the spot with whom patients live.

After moving here on his account, we shall now have to stay here all next winter without him ; and his sisters had been making such wonderful plans for the winter season ! I was never a very brave builder of castles in the air ; all I did was to collect the materials. But youth is always building right up into the breasts of the clouds. He would not be able to travel now, even to the south, as, owing to a slight temperature, he is obliged to remain indoors. Can you imagine what a mother feels, when one son is buried alive, [2] the other, who is so highly gifted, in failing health and possibly never to be seen well and sound again, and another dear child, also exceptionally gifted, stricken down in the midst of a happy life and already buried ! [3] And how many more troubles have I had ! If you could put yourself in my place you would not think less of me for occasionally allowing my heart to unburden it- self in the hearing of a sympathetic friend. I may say that Felix is working diligently—how else could he kill time all day ?

As to my arm, for the last fortnight I have been trying massage under a woman who has effected wonderful cures.[4] . . . She declares that she will cure me, but I must have patience, as the trouble is of long standing and therefore stubborn. Well, I do not lack patience.

3.3.74. People are all talking here about Stockhausen's appointment. If ever I was grateful for not having a post at the *Hochschule*, it is now. But fancy, Joachim has been

---

[1] On Clara's return from Leipsic, the doctor had declared that one lung was already affected.

[2] This refers to Ludwig, who had to be sent to an asylum owing to his mind having become unhinged.

[3] This refers to Julie, Clara's third daughter, who died November 10, 1872.

[4] The diagnosis pointed not to rheumatism but to excessive irritation of the muscles.

1874] AND JOHANNES BRAHMS 281

imprudent enough (I cannot call it anything else) to forbid his wife from singing at Stockhausen's next concert on the 11th, although she had promised to do so. He writes that to help his enemies in their undertakings is both noble and foolish. . . . On that very day we happened to be at a large party at Radecke's house, and Frau Joachim exhibited such passion (or fanaticism I ought to say) that I was quite angry. Meanwhile, of course, the so-called " good friends " of whom Simrock was one, egged her on by telling her she was quite right. I went to her the following day and implored her to be calm, to think of her husband, and to show a little more pride in the matter. Just imagine how Joachim's enemies—the Langhans clique and Stockhausen's (the *Stern*) [1] party rejoiced that she could make Joachim look such a fool. Joachim and Schulze now say that henceforward Frau Joachim, Henschel and he will only sing and play for the Hochschule. . . . It is possible that the new glamour of the Stern Choral Society will draw over many who would otherwise have belonged to the choral society of the Hochschule, which intends to double its performances next autumn. But is not Berlin large enough for two such societies, however big they may be ? And if this is so, artists of their stamp ought surely to show themselves above such petty trifles.

If only Munich were not so far away,[2] and I were not undergoing a cure which must not be interrupted ! But send me your programme, so that I can follow your movements from day to day. This will take no time, as you'll have no leisure for writing when you are there. Writing is such an effort to me that I have taken three days to write this letter.

Enjoy yourself, my dear Johannes, and occasionally give a thought to Your faithful old friend CLARA.

[1] This probably refers to the *Stern* Choral Society, or to the friends of Julius Stern.—TR.

[2] On March 13 at the Odeon, Brahms played his Piano Concerto and conducted the Haydn Variations and the Hungarian Dances. Vogl sang some Brahms songs. The Walterquartet played the A major Quartet (with Brahms) on a Chamber Music evening, and the G major sextet.

BRAHMS *to* CLARA.

VIENNA, *March* 19.

I find it extremely difficult to convey to you even in a few words how deeply and anxiously I feel for you. Ever since I last saw Felix you cannot think how sad I have been at the thought of you. I feel your pain and anxiety all much too deeply to be able to express it to you in words. For I am so thoroughly accustomed to endure even my own suffering in secret and without making a sign.

But I feel much more deeply, much more heartily about your troubles. Not a thought flies to you, but it embraces both you and all your woe. I can only wait in silence to see how far you are able to bear this new trial. God grant that you may be spared any further care, for you have surely had enough for one human life.

I cannot attempt to try to comfort you. In your efforts to bear up you will long ago have thought of all I could say. May you succeed in this as you have succeeded before, no matter what has befallen you. I cannot tell you how many people sent kind messages to you ! Let this deep love of mine be a comfort to you ; for I love you more than myself, and more than anybody or anything on earth. But after all one can only suffer with you, one cannot relieve you of one iota of your own suffering !

I need hardly tell you about Munich. Everything went off just as you would have liked it to, while you followed us in the spirit. The production was very good, the public very friendly ; and we, apart from the performing musicians, especially Heyse and Bernays, spent many happy hours together. Wüllner and Lachner were also present the whole time.

It is particularly fortunate that neither you nor I am in the Hochschule. The things one hears about it are certainly not edifying, and as all these things have their serious reasons, the prospect is not enlivening. . . . We are unfortunately having an enormous amount of music in Holy Week. In addition to the *Singakademie* and the Men's Choral Society, they are giving the Messiah at the Opera and a concert besides, and I, Salomo. I can never bear the thought of " too much music." . . .

With my heartiest remembrances to all yours, and begging

you to let me have news of you as soon as possible, with deepest sympathy, Yours, JOHANNES.

CLARA *to* BRAHMS.

BERLIN, *Easter Sunday, April* 5.

Two dear letters already lie before me unanswered, and yet my heart was so full after the first that I should have loved to write at once to tell you how much your kind words had comforted me.   Often enough have I thought of it since, and now that I am able to thank you, my thanks seem so dry and cold.   A touch of my hand and a look of love would have told you my thanks so much better.   I have been through a great deal since I last wrote, and am still full of trouble.   The doctors advised us to send Felix away as soon as possible, so we availed ourselves of the mild days, wrapped him up in a fur coat, and he went off to Montreux, where he has now been for ten days, and whence he has written enthusiastic letters about the magnificent scenery.   While he was here he was hardly allowed to leave his room.   But there he is almost always in the open, across the fields covered with the most lovely flowers.   This is certainly a relief, but even if things go favourably with him, he must not return north for at least two years.   How hard such a parting is !

To suit him we have modified our plans for the summer to the extent of going to Engelberg in July.   He is to spend the summer there and we shall stay with him a month.   (My second object in going there will be more or less to complete the cure which I shall take at Teplitz in May.)   Then I should like to see the Bavarian Hochgebirge, with the view of finding a place where we can stay in the future.   I can hardly sell my house now, for this is not a favourable time of year, but I will let it from July onwards, although I should like to spend June in it.   Whether economic considerations will make this possible, I do not know, but I hope so.   Would you not perhaps think of staying there until July ?   The wooded solitude would certainly do you good after all the turmoil you have been through.   I have been thinking that I must attend one of the musical festivals,[1] perhaps in July in Zürich **or** Bâle ?

[1] In Cologne, May 24 ; in Bâle, June 9 ; in Zürich, July 12.

And when ?   It cannot be Cologne as I shall not be back from
Teplitz as early as I at first thought. . . .

I heard Salomo [1] the other day, but found it so tiresome
that I had to leave at the end of the first part.   I must confess
that I always have difficulty in sitting through such an Oratorio,
particularly when the choirs are uninspiring as these were to
me—for they are as a rule the greatest feature in Handel's
music.   But the singing was certainly monotonous under
Blumner (Grell cannot conduct any longer).   I felt the same
at the performance of Christ [2] yesterday.   I heard little (for
three weeks I have had trouble with my ears, which prevents
me from hearing plainly), but what I did hear left me so
utterly cold that again I left at the end of the first part.   The
Reichshallen moreover became so hot and full of an odour of
food and beer, that it was insufferable.   Naturally Frau
Joachim and Stockhausen sang beautifully, but the rest was
very poor.   Altogether it struck me that the performance
did not bring out the vocal quality of the music, besides which
the choir seemed to me to lack strength entirely.   But on these
matters I am not an adequate judge, as I heard little and that
little badly.   Nevertheless I am prepared to swear that this
music is dull.   But how seldom do I enjoy a musical treat from
these new things !   I only seem to enjoy them when they are
yours. . . .

Write to me soon about Berlin, and also what you seriously
think about Baden Baden.   And now, my dear friend, with
most affectionate remembrances, Ever your loving CLARA.

CLARA *to* BRAHMS.

BERLIN, *April* 11.

The day before yesterday they elected you an honorary
member of the Academy of Arts and Science [3] here.   I don't
know whether you are pleased about it, but be this as it may, I
wished to be the first to tell you, before it is announced officially.
Recognition of this sort is always pleasing, and, as Joachim
says, it is not really so easy to obtain.   I certainly incline to
the view that committees of this sort chiefly honour themselves
when they elect important people as fellow-members.

---

[1] By Handel.   [2] By Kiel.
[3] The Academy of Arts.

You must certainly have received my last letter by now, and I shall soon hear from you. Kiel's Christ will be performed again next week, for the Bach Monument Fund, for which Joachim has brought 3,000 thalers [£450] from England. I only wish they had chosen another work. . . .

Farewell, dearest Johannes. Remember your CLARA.

I should like to know whether you too, like Joachim, are all ablaze about this monument for Bach. I should have thought it would be far better to found an institution with the money. But maybe I am wrong ?

CLARA *to* BRAHMS.[1]

TEPLITZ, *June* 2.

DEAREST JOHANNES,

. . . Have you, in your part of the world, heard about the proposal for a new tombstone ?[2] My one fear is that they will produce something in bad taste. What I should like above all is something quite simple. You know my views about monuments, which, in my opinion, are best erected by notable people in their own works. . . . Joachim must have told you about *Faust* in Berlin. At times the choral parts were quite beautiful. Musicians, however, cannot help every minute recognizing the amateur in Stockhausen. It is extraordinary how it creeps out, and, when a man has not made a thorough study of music in his earliest youth (I refer to the actual craft of music, if I may so express it), the fact remains stamped upon him for the rest of his life. . . .

[Written with her own hand] Your comforting remarks on unwarranted cares about money did me good. I find it so necessary to have these dissipated from time to time. I had become so accustomed to work and an active life, which brought me an income, that now, when I can do nothing and yet have heavy expenses, I often have the unhappy feeling of having done nothing after all.

June 4th. Just received your letter, so I can thank you for it at once. The joy it has given me may well compensate you for the pains it cost you to write. What I like more particu-

---

[1] Dictated.

[2] This was to be erected over Robert Schumann's grave to replace the simpler one already put there by Clara. See *Life*, pp. 306–307.

larly is that you frankly acknowledge the pleasure which such recognition must give you. It cannot be otherwise ; an artist's heart must feel warmer for it. And I must say that to witness your growing fame constitutes the happiest experience that the latter years of my life could bring.

Now please sacrifice a little more time and send me a few words after the festival. Think of the lonely friend who is concentrating all her mind upon you now, and to whom every stroke of good fortune that reaches you is an added joy. Your old CLARA.

1875

CLARA *to* BRAHMS.

BERLIN, *Oct.* 23, 11 ZELTEN N.W.

DEAR JOHANNES,

. . . The plan about the Hochschule has come to nothing, though I did not hear about it until the end of last month.[1] At heart I am very glad and now I am back here I feel it all the more, for, as you say, a post of that sort brings many unpleasantnesses in its train. Joachim writes to say, however, that in spite of this they have not given up all thought of me.

I had an idea that you would come to Munich too. Manfred[2] was beautiful, but I was a little disturbed by the scenic arrangements, and Possart, despite all his art and mastery, leaves me cold. Unfortunately the pleasure I had that evening was somewhat marred by the evening that followed, for, being in Munich, I had to see Tristan. The Vogel couple are certainly magnificent singers, but I cannot remember ever having heard or seen anything more odious than this opera. Anyone who can listen to it or see it with pleasure must surely lack all moral feeling. That they should dare to offer such a piece to a cultured public, or to a public desiring to be cultured, is a terribly sad proof of the demoralization of the age. But even to think about it makes me boil with indignation, so let us say no more about it. . . .

I hope you are investing your money safely. These are dangerous times with all these swindling concerns about. What about your Author's Rights in Paris ? Do not fail to see to this. All you need do is to write a friendly word or two to Durand et Schoenwerk (you can write in German but use Latin script).

Give me the pleasure of news from you soon, dear Johannes, and with affectionate remembrances, I remain Ever yours, CLARA.

[1] This refers to her proposed appointment at the Berlin Hochschule.
[2] In order to please her children Clara had gone to Munich to hear *Manfred* at the beginning of August.

1876

14, HYDE PARK GATE, LONDON, *April* 4.

DEAREST JOHANNES,

I have not written to you for a long time—I could not on account of my arm. But I cannot rest to-day before having told you what a pleasure I had yesterday. We played your F minor Quintet and had a tremendous success with it. The enthusiasm rose after each movement, and at the end we were recalled amid loud cheers. As you can well imagine, we played with no little enthusiasm ourselves. Although I know you do not care to hear other people play your things, I could not help thinking that you would have been rather pleased all the same. I was again completely carried away by the profundity, thoughtfulness and passionate feeling of this piece. It is a wonderfully stirring work!

I have engagements for another week, and then I shall have finished. I shall have played in all only nine times. Everything has gone very well; but I had to be extremely careful. I lived very quietly and dictated everything, and that is why you never heard from me, for you know how reluctant I am to dictate letters to you. But I do not regret having come here, for never before in my life have I been more warmly received than I have been here this year. And as I always played little at a time, and at long intervals, I have hardly ever felt so fresh and inspired.

I shall write to you again when I have left. I shall probably go in ten or twelve days, and shall stop two days in Brussels and two in Düsseldorf, and hope to be back in Berlin during the third week in April. I should be so glad to hear from you. How long it is since I last heard from you! Certainly it was my fault, for not writing; but, as I say, I was not allowed to, and ought not to have written even to-day, but I had to.

Best love from Your ever faithful old CLARA.

CLARA *to* BRAHMS.

BERLIN, *May* 5, 11 IN DEN ZELTEN.

DEAREST JOHANNES,

Here I am once more at home and my first letter is to send you my best wishes for the 7th of May—how often now have I been obliged to convey my birthday wishes to you on paper, which seems so cold compared with a hearty shake of the hand! I have ceased to count all the good things I wish you, but what I wish you for our own sakes is that you may be given ever fresh strength for your creations. How glad I should be to know what you are working on now! I have an idea that the next thing you will give us will be a Symphony!

Many thanks for your last letter! We are not yet quite agreed about our plans for the summer, but I think we shall go to Klosters again—I was so pleased with Florin's where it was not so full; the hotel proprietors were nice and the walks beautiful, with lovely woods full of green trees among the pines, where one could sit all day long without being disturbed. In short, I feel drawn to the place once more, particularly as the air is magnificent. But first I shall go to Kiel for three weeks to try the cure there to build up my strength,[1] and then go for a week to Büdesheim to Elise who will soon be back from Italy. Thus will the summer slip away, and what pleases me is that I have at least earned a portion of my holiday expenses, and so shall spend money more light-heartedly than if I had to draw upon my savings.

In London I had another Recital; they would not let me off, and it was very successful. It was more crowded than ever, and Chappell cleared £70 after covering all expenses, including my fee. I played your Variations for two pianos with Miss Zimmermann, and once more revelled in it.

Just fancy, on the return journey I heard Liszt again for the first time for many years, and was carried away by some of Schubert's things which he played wonderfully, but certainly not by his own works—a Duet for two Pianos on B.A.C.H. was odious, but it became diverting when he flew from one end of the piano to the other. It is true that he is unique in his mastery of the instrument—what a pity it is that one derives so little calm enjoyment from it, one always feels as if some

[1] See *Life*, Vol. II. p. 308.

devilish force were sweeping one along. I observed him closely and saw all his petty coquetries, his noble urbanity, etc. The women were, of course, mad about him—it was revolting.

Oh, how my heart yearns for Baden once more! Marie was there for a few days in order to get the house ready for another tenant—we have now let it till the middle of June. It is always rather a blow to me.

This evening we go to the Hochschule; we are to have the *Jahreszeiten*. I am looking forward to it very much.

. . . What about the Doctor's degree? I suppose you will have to go there and take your degree in cap and gown. Joachim was saying only a little while ago that he was going there for that purpose, so it looks as if you would have to as well. It is easier to bear Honours than to go and receive them.

I was very glad to find Eugenie here looking much better than when I left her; we also have better news from Felix. Unfortunately Ludwig is causing me great anxiety. He wants to leave the asylum and declares he can look after himself again, which is, of course, out of the question. This is a terrible worry to me; he expects us to be constantly visiting him, and this is such a torture for me that I am ill for weeks after it. It looks as though I were doomed to have no peace in life. The thought of Ludwig casts a black shadow over every joy I have. If only I could know that he was happy!

But everything seems to pass away except my cordial wishes for your welfare and my friendship which remains as true as ever. Your CLARA.

BRAHMS *to* CLARA AND HER DAUGHTERS.

SASSNITZ IN RÜGEN, *June*.

DEAR CLARA, MARIE AND EUGENIE,

I cannot write three letters at once and do not trust myself to write three one after the other, so I hope this greeting may go *via* Berlin to Kiel.

We are not organized for letter writing here! The post is calling at Sassnitz to-day! The general provider will have some ink in a few days! At the *table d'hôte*, which is laid for nearly a hundred people, I sit—all alone.

As a matter of fact, I have a great deal to tell all three of you and thank you for, but I hope you realized how happy I was with you, and how the whole town delighted me, probably because everything at your place was so pleasant and comfortable.[1]

But Rügen is really very, very beautiful, apart from the dear old Low German, in which I am at last able to indulge again. There is the most beautiful forest coming right down to the sea ; you would be enchanted if you could take a walk in it. I am certainly not getting any better acquainted with the sea here. As for the murmuring roll of the waves, I believe the Baltic has to be in a particularly vicious mood for that. However, I shall wait and see.

Living is expensive here. The people have only two months in which to make their money and to pay themselves for all they provide. My room is beautifully situated, my window looks out on to the sea, the village straggles up the hill to my left, and cornfields in front of me are for the present providing the murmuring roll of the waves. As it is still early in the season I am for the time being paying only $5\frac{1}{2}$ thalers [16/6] a week for two rooms with balconies, but as a rule they demand more for this accommodation.

It is a pity that the papers mention nothing of the dispute between the teachers of harmony and professors of counterpoint ! But in case Bargiel suspects me of anything not above board in this matter I hope I shall be told of it. Joachim and Schulze among others have known my views on this matter for a long time. . . . I hope Frau Joachim is quite well.

I shall write to you again soon (this is how one comforts oneself when one has written nothing and wanted to write a lot). With my most affectionate remembrances and reiterated thanks for the delightful time in Berlin. Ever yours, J. BRAHMS.

CLARA *to* BRAHMS.

KLOSTERS, GRAUBÜNDEN, *Aug*. 14.
. . . A little while ago I played Herzogenberg's Variations for four hands on a theme by you, which astonished me by their deep thoughtfulness.[2] Do you know them ? Your

[1] On his way to Rügen Brahms had spent a few days with Clara in Berlin in the middle of July.
[2] Op. 23.

influence is very noticeable in them, but that does not matter, provided it falls on fruitful soil. I certainly found a great deal to criticize in the Variations, for instance, that the first should immediately introduce the theme, which is none too easy, into the bass, before it has really been properly grasped. I often speak about you to Volkland. He is an enthusiastic admirer of your works, and of course knows them all !—He always wants to know from me what you happen to be composing at the moment. But alas, I do not even know myself, and I have not heard from you for ages ! Please let me know as soon as you can how you are getting on and what you are doing, and where you are. Can you really stand it in Sassnitz ? And how much longer do you expect to stay ? . . .

If we go [to Hertenstein] we shall have the pleasure of being with Felix for a few weeks longer. He is much better, but I will not alter my decision not to take him with us to Berlin, because he is not cured yet and is still coughing. At the end of·September we shall spend a week or a fortnight with Frau Kann in Baden Baden, and then the children at least will go to Berlin. Then I should like to keep my promise to go to Mannheim to play for the orchestra, and I also have an engagement in Barmen, etc., etc. . . .

With fondest remembrances from us all and especially from me, Yours ever, CLARA.

CLARA *to* BRAHMS.
HERTENSTEIN, *Sept.* 10.

I am sending you the enclosed letter just received from Steinmetz,[1] and remind you once more to be sure to keep the whole of your summer free—better this and only 1,500 thalers [£225] than 2,000 [£300] and to be tied in the summer ! —That you were not disinclined to accept, did not surprise me ; I thought it would be worth your while to think about it seriously !—Conditions there are sure to change a little if the Government takes the matter in hand—I think they will improve. I think it ought to be possible to do something with the means at your disposal in that quarter (Choir and

---

[1] This refers to the proposed appointment of Brahms as Musical Director in Düsseldorf. Steinmetz was at that time *Regierungsrat* in Düsseldorf, i.e. an official in the District Governor's department.

Orchestra), but it will certainly be necessary to have a thick skin and to exercise great authority, which in your case, of course, goes, without saying !

But would you not find 1,500 thalers much too little ? If you are coming *via* Baden let me know beforehand. . . . I expect to be there on the 16th or 17th. . . .

I was delighted with your letter—the news about your people filled me with joy. With affectionate remembrances, Your CLARA.

P.S. Do not forget to write to Schönewerk about the Author's Rights. Do it at once, before the winter begins. You can write in German and ask them to send you a form which you can fill up and return. . . .

BRAHMS *to* MARIE SCHUMANN.

BADEN BADEN, *Oct.* 13.

DEAR FRÄULEIN MARIE,

Herewith the recipe [1] for your cookery book and my heartiest greetings to you both. Since your departure [2] the sky is grey, and there is not enough blue to be seen to make a waistcoat out of.

So that all we can do is to look back to the lovely happy days—and also write no letters.

Give my kindest greetings to everybody, but keep the best for yourselves, Your wholly devoted J. BRAHMS.

CLARA *to* BRAHMS.

DÜSSELDORF, 26*th of October*.

I have been bursting to say something to you about the post here, but have not been able to do so because I have been so frightfully busy that I have had to spare myself too much writing, and should not care to dictate to anybody here. As a matter of fact, I hear that Bitter [3] has approached you to try and persuade you to allow the terms of your appointment to be altered, by adding the fee paid for the Musical Festival to your salary. My view of this is that it would be better to

---

[1] This was a recipe for making ink in Jean Paul's handwriting.

[2] Concerning their life together at Baden Baden, see *Life*, pp. 319–320.

[3] At that time Governor of the District of Düsseldorf.

be content with 1,800 thalers [£270] with 500 thalers [£75] extra for the Festival (which is the standard fee paid to well-known conductors) than to have it included in the salary. I told Steinmetz a little while ago that I did not think you would change your mind about the salary. What did you tell Bitter ? There is great excitement here about all this ; naturally all right-minded people hope it will be settled, but there will be the usual intrigues, against which you will easily be able to hold your own. It is said that Tausch wants to keep the Choral Society to himself and give concerts on his own account. You need not worry any more about Bruch, for he told me himself that he did not intend to accept the post, because, being a Rhinelander he feels that he could not face the conditions here without prejudice. I told him a little while ago that you had felt scruples about the matter because of him.

. . . Everybody is very much excited about the Symphony.[1] Oh, if only I could hear it ! It seems to me an eternity since I heard from you ; please, dear Johannes, do not forget me entirely. You can well understand how my thoughts are doubly with you now, at a time when you are deliberating a step, which, after all, is an important one in your life.

My children are now in Berlin. I have been through unhappy times, and find separations harder than ever !—But from the artistic standpoint I have done very well. Unfortunately, Manfred was only pleasing in parts ; Pott [2] got the time wrong from the start, so that almost the whole effect was lost. In any case the piece is a difficult one to enjoy because it is dreadfully monotonous, and can only make a good effect on the stage if supported by music. The production was excellent.

. . . With fondest love, Your CLARA.

CLARA *to* BRAHMS.

DÜSSELDORF, *Oct.* 29.

Our letters have crossed. Many thanks, dearest Johannes, for yours, about which I should like to say a word to you at once.

---

[1] Op. 68. C minor.
[2] A violinist of Oldenburg who was probably taking Dietrich's place as conductor.

Bitter has written to say that he is quite agreeable, so the terms are 1,800 thalers but with a benefit concert thrown in. That is just what you didn't want ! I am glad that you will be paid extra for the Musical Festival ; but get it in writing —500 thalers is the traditional fee.

I am very much excited by the whole affair ! You have given Marie great pleasure—many thanks.

Let me have news at once about the Symphony. My heart is full of thoughts and good wishes for you. Your faithful CLARA.

Same evening.

I had already closed my letter when Steinmetz sent me Bitter's message saying that everything had been settled with you. But there is one paragraph which is very odd, and Bendemann thinks it must be a misunderstanding. It is as follows :—

4. " Brahms wishes it to be understood that all decisions regarding programmes for concerts and musical festivals as well as the choice of solo singers and artists are to be left to him to suggest, and that his opinion shall be asked on all musical matters."

Now Bendemann and advocate Euler say that to ask your opinion is the very minimum ; what it should be is that, on the contrary, you should ask the opinion of the Committee and as far as possible conform to their wishes regarding programmes, but that you should have the last word. Euler says that the paragraph is framed in the most extraordinary way and might make things very unpleasant for you. Regarding the selection of artists, it would be all right if you were consulted, but you could not have the responsibility of engaging them ; that ought surely to be the concern of the business manager.—Euler says that in all institutions, high schools and technical schools, etc., after consulting the managing committee the final decision lies with the Director.

Paragraph 5 is also curious : " the question to be raised whether in the event of the governing body of the *Allgemeiner Musik-Verein* wishing to allow him to give a concert, such concert would not be held for the benefit of the *Verein*, but that they would make him (Brahms) some small (?) allowance for it." Please do not mention B. and E. I am only writing all this in order that you may judge and think over the conditions.

You surely cannot agree to the first-mentioned clause. You must have sole responsibility as regards choice of programme. I remember what unpleasant experiences Robert had with the Committee, as for instance on one occasion with regard to Rossini, whom he did not want to have on the programme, and which led to endless annoyance.

I am terribly pressed for time, as I have got to go to a party and the carriage is waiting. But as I am going away to-morrow I did not want to postpone writing you all this.

Once more, much love, Your CLARA.

I am very anxious; write to me soon about everything.

CLARA *to* BRAHMS.

HAMBURG, *Nov.* 4.

All my thoughts are with you to-day.[1] I hope that you will be quite satisfied; for that, after all, is the principal thing!

Thank you for your prompt reply, which has relieved my mind somewhat. Regarding your benefit concerts, what I disliked was the expression " small allowance," besides which the honorarium ought to be fixed. What would you do if they gave you 50 thalers [£7.10.0]? Don't be angry with me for bothering you about these things, but they made me feel anxious; I know these people so well.

But to return to the Symphony. Please do not let it be performed at the concert in Leipzic at which I am playing, because it makes me so excited, and I cannot bear any disturbing influence. So please leave it for a concert in January— as I would prefer to come specially from Berlin when I could enjoy it in peace. I could easily manage this between Christmas and the New Year. It has just occurred to me that if the Symphony is played at the concert of the 7th December, then I could wait there to hear it, as I am playing in quartets on the 2nd or 3rd, so there would be only four days to wait. Send me word soon, above all about to-day! To-morrow I am going to Bremen, and will have another talk there with

[1] This refers to the first performance of the C minor Symphony under Dessoff in Carlsruhe.

Reinthaler,[1] after which I will write to you and tell you what his objections are to your Düsseldorf appointment.

Things went very well with me here yesterday, but Bargheer's quartet had to be postponed. While we were rehearsing it a telegram arrived to say that Bargheer's wife was hopelessly ill ; he did not want to give up the quartet, because I was playing in it and thought this would help his work considerably. But my view was that he ought to go to his wife, so I promised to come back on the 22nd when the second quartet was to be performed. This was a great sacrifice for me, but I thought it was the right thing to do. But the whole incident proved very clearly how very much more importance he attaches to his post here than to his wife.

Now, good-bye for to-day.

May everything succeed with you, Your old friend CLARA.

CLARA *to* BRAHMS.

BRESLAU, *Dec.* 11, C/o Frau Geheimrätin Storch,
                                    3 Teichstrasse III Stock.

Here I am writing to you again, and you will end up by being angry with me as a pest, but I cannot get the matter out of my head, and a conversation I had with Scholz yesterday evening upset me again so much, that I must write again to-day. If only we could have a talk, writing is so tedious. Scholz is also of opinion that it would be ridiculous for you to accept a post under such conditions. As long as Tausch remains on the spot, you will only have vulgarity to deal with (they are already writing libellous things about you). Scholz cannot see why you should let yourself in for cleaning out the Augean stable of this corrupt musical gang. In any case you could not bear it for long, and then what a fatal thing it would be for you to leave at the end of a year. And were you ultimately to found a School of Music, which must after all be the object in view, for otherwise the Ministry would grant no subsidy, you would have to deal with two sets of

---

[1] Carl Martin Reinthaler, composer (1822–1896). He was a professor at the Cologne Conservatoire in 1853. In 1858 he became musical director of the city of Bremen, where he also filled other posts both at the Cathedral and the Academy.

malcontents, H. and J., your task would be colossal, and what thanks would you get ?

I would naturally rather have you in Düsseldorf, but not as things are. In Vienna you lead a different life, and have other powers at your command, if you want them, and, above all, friendly sympathy. No, indeed, if you accept a post it must be a very different one, and in the first place you must be unanimously welcome.

For weeks I have been full of fears, with this on my mind, and worrying as to whether I should dissuade you from it definitely ; but I have now spoken to many unprejudiced parties, even in Leipsic, and have found them all of one opinion, that you are too good for the post and can do better than go there to wage a perpetual battle with vulgarity, which is always in the majority in Düsseldorf, where right-minded people are few and far between.

To-morrow the A major Serenade,—how I rejoice at the thought of it ! Scholz says they play it very well.

Good-bye, dear friend. Do not be angry with Your CLARA.

CLARA *to* BRAHMS.

BERLIN, *Dec.* 22.

So here is Christmas with us once more, and we were half hoping that you might have come to us, although as you have only just got back to Vienna, you would not feel very much inclined to stir, particularly as there are not many attractions here ! So I must let my thoughts wend their way to you, which seems to be a fairly frequent occurrence nowadays. I have not yet heard anything from you about the Symphony on the 17th,[1] and to-day have heard definitely from Düsseldorf that Tausch has not been elected Musical Director, etc.—I am sending you one of the letters (I have received two), but it does not contain the news that your appointment has been confirmed, which is in the other one. I am now very uneasy again, but am sending you on the friendly note—perhaps, after all, we have attached too much importance to Tausch's party. In regard to this matter (if you ultimately accept, be sure to have everything down in black and white—forgive this womanly

[1] Performed in Vienna.

fretfulness) I had almost forgotten the principal point which was to send you the heartiest good wishes for Christmas.

I expect you will spend the evening with the Billroths, at least I think so, or else at home with a few bottles of champagne. We shall be very quiet, there are so few of us, and in any case it is not a joyful festival for me ; I miss those who are absent too much, and though I try to bear up outwardly, I am sad at heart. I am longing for news from you.

As regards Breslau, I must tell you that I enjoyed the A Sharp Serenade very much, [1] I had never heard it done so well before, and enjoyed every bar of it, and as I listened many heartfelt thanks went speeding to the giver of such wonderful joys.

With heartiest wishes for Christmas and the New Year— what does it hold in store for you ? Only good fortune, I trust. With fondest love, Your CLARA.

[1] Performed under Stolz.

END OF VOLUME I